Bernard Shaw and His Contemporaries

Series Editors
Nelson O'Ceallaigh Ritschel
Massachusetts Maritime Academy
Pocasset, MA, USA

Peter Gahan
Independent Scholar
Los Angeles, CA, USA

The series *Bernard Shaw and His Contemporaries* presents the best and most up-to-date research on Shaw and his contemporaries in a diverse range of cultural contexts. Volumes in the series will further the academic understanding of Bernard Shaw and those who worked with him, or in reaction against him, during his long career from the 1880s to 1950 as a leading writer in Britain and Ireland, and with a wide European and American following.

Shaw defined the modern literary theatre in the wake of Ibsen as a vehicle for social change, while authoring a dramatic canon to rival Shakespeare's. His careers as critic, essayist, playwright, journalist, lecturer, socialist, feminist, and pamphleteer, both helped to shape the modern world as well as pointed the way towards modernism. No one engaged with his contemporaries more than Shaw, whether as controversialist, or in his support of other, often younger writers. In many respects, therefore, the series as it develops will offer a survey of the rise of the modern at the beginning of the twentieth century and the subsequent varied cultural movements covered by the term modernism that arose in the wake of World War 1.

More information about this series at
http://www.palgrave.com/gp/series/14785

Eglantina Remport

Lady Gregory and Irish National Theatre

Art, Drama, Politics

Eglantina Remport
Eötvös Loránd University
Budapest, Hungary

Bernard Shaw and His Contemporaries
ISBN 978-3-030-09534-5   ISBN 978-3-319-76611-9   (eBook)
https://doi.org/10.1007/978-3-319-76611-9

© The Editor(s) (if applicable) and The Author(s) 2018
Softcover re-print of the Hardcover 1st edition 2018
This work is subject to copyright. All rights are solely and exclusively licensed by the Publisher, whether the whole or part of the material is concerned, specifically the rights of translation, reprinting, reuse of illustrations, recitation, broadcasting, reproduction on microfilms or in any other physical way, and transmission or information storage and retrieval, electronic adaptation, computer software, or by similar or dissimilar methodology now known or hereafter developed.
The use of general descriptive names, registered names, trademarks, service marks, etc. in this publication does not imply, even in the absence of a specific statement, that such names are exempt from the relevant protective laws and regulations and therefore free for general use.
The publisher, the authors and the editors are safe to assume that the advice and information in this book are believed to be true and accurate at the date of publication. Neither the publisher nor the authors or the editors give a warranty, express or implied, with respect to the material contained herein or for any errors or omissions that may have been made. The publisher remains neutral with regard to jurisdictional claims in published maps and institutional affiliations.

Cover illustration: Granger Historical Picture Archive/Alamy Stock Photo

Printed on acid-free paper

This Palgrave Macmillan imprint is published by the registered company Springer International Publishing AG part of Springer Nature
The registered company address is: Gewerbestrasse 11, 6330 Cham, Switzerland

*For my mother and father, in gratitude
for our Grand Tours*

Acknowledgements

My first words of acknowledgement are to Queen's University Belfast and the Department of Education and Learning of the Government of Northern Ireland for their generous financial support of my research on Lady Augusta Gregory. I am especially thankful to the School of English at Queen's and its former Head, John Thompson, for supporting my research visits to the Special Collections and Archives Division of the Robert W. Woodruff Library at Emory University, Atlanta, GA, and the Albert A. and Henry W. Berg Collection at New York Public Library. I am thankful also for the experience of the vibrant research community both at the School of English and at the Institute of Irish Studies at Queen's between 2004 and 2008. The late Siobhán Kilfeather and Caroline Sumpter have commented on earlier drafts of this work, and generously shared their views on the social and political contexts for nineteenth-century Irish and English history and literature.

The staff members of various libraries have offered kind assistance in the realisation of the present research project. I would like to thank Kathy Shoemaker at the Robert W. Woodruff Library, Emory University, Isaac Gewirtz at the Albert A. and Henry W. Berg Collection, New York Public Library, Honora Faul at the National Library of Ireland, as well as the staff of the Special Collections in the main library of Queen's University Belfast, the Old Library of Trinity College Dublin, and the Newspaper Library of the British Library. Nóra Szegedi and Pál Tömöry at the Library of the Hungarian Academy of Arts and Sciences (MTAK) have been most accommodating, and likewise the staff of the National Széchényi Library in Budapest.

This book would not have been realised without the enthusiasm of my editors Tomas René and Vicky Bates, as well as that of Nelson O'Ceallaigh Ritschel and Peter Gahan, editors of the *Bernard Shaw and His Contemporaries* series at Palgrave Macmillan. Emilie Pine has been supportive in granting permission to publish parts of an earlier article of mine on Lady Gregory and the visual arts that had appeared in the *Irish University Review* in 2011.

Within the Irish Studies scholarly community, I thank: Giovanna Tallone for drawing my attention to Lady Gregory's travel sketchbooks several years ago when information was less readily available; Carla De Petris for those first conversations on Lady Gregory and Italy; Dawn Duncan for encouraging my interest in pursuing research on Lady Gregory and the visual arts; Eamonn Hughes for his advice on the political *tableau vivant* tradition in Ireland; and Lionel Pilkington for his comments on Irish history and social politics. I am very thankful for Deirdre Madden's enthusiasm in the later stages of my writing on the most significant woman dramatist and theatre director of Ireland.

On a personal note, I am very thankful for the support of the following friends and family members: Ágnes Pázmány, Márta Gyapay, Gábor Gyapay, Zoltán Szirmai; Györgyi and Mihály Kocsis; the Hárshegyi family; Yi-ling Yang and Keerty Nakray; Owen O'Neill and Ann-Marie Connolly; and Andrea Velich, Natália Pikli, Judit Friedrich, Ferenc Takács, Győző Ferencz, and János Kenyeres at Eötvös Loránd University, Budapest. I appreciate the support of my brother Ádám and his family Éva and Laura. I thank my husband Michael for the many years of enriching conversation that helped the research project to blossom, for his unfailing belief in my ability to bring it to completion, and for all the nice times on this long and winding road. I would also like to thank Michael's late mother and his father, as well as his brothers and sisters, for warmly welcoming me to their family. Finally, my mother and father have been incredible in guiding me through life and research; I lovingly dedicated this book to them.

Contents

Introduction	1
'My Education': Sir William Gregory, the *Grand Tours*, and the Visual Arts	17
'The "whorl" of Troy': Celtic Mythology, Victorian Hellenism, and the Irish Literary Revival	51
'Ní neart go cur le chéile': Education, Social Reform, and the Abbey Theatre	85
'See a play as a picture': The Pre-Raphaelite Brotherhood, the Sister Arts, and the Irish Plays	121
The Light of the World: Christianity, Cultural Politics, and Constitutional Reform	157
Conclusion	205
Bibliography	215
Index	229

Introduction

George Bernard Shaw described his friend Lady Augusta Gregory as 'the greatest living Irishwoman'.[1] Shaw praised her in remarkable terms during a speech delivered in London on 3 February 1910:

> If ever there was a person doomed from the cradle to write for the stage, to break through every social obstacle to get to the stage, to refuse to do anything but write for the stage, nay, to invent and create a theatre if no theatre existed, that person is the author of *Hyacinth Halvey*, of *The Workhouse Ward*, and of *The Rising of the Moon*. There are authors who have achieved considerable reputation and success as writers for the theatre, who have not had a tenth of her natural faculty for the work.[2]

Lady Isabella Augusta Gregory, née Persse, was a prodigious and influential dramatist, an amateur painter, and a dedicated social reformer who worked during the period of the Irish Literary Revival. She was co-founder and co-director of the Abbey Theatre in Dublin, known at the time as the Irish National Theatre, and was friends with fellow playwrights Shaw, John Millington Synge, William Butler Yeats, and Sean O'Casey. She was a prominent figure of the Home Industries Movement and the Co-operative Movement in Ireland, both of which aimed at improving the living standards and working conditions of Irish farmers and tenants. Through her husband Sir William Henry Gregory of Coole Park in County Galway she was a woman of high social standing, someone who fostered friendships with Sir Henry Layard of the British Arundel Society, Sir Frederic Burton of the National Gallery in London, and Sir John Everett Millais of the Royal Academy of Arts. Sir William had been born into a family in which politics played a hugely significant role, his grandfather having been Under Secretary for Ireland. Sir William had been educated at Harrow School, London, and at Christ Church College, Oxford, and had served as Queen Victoria's Governor of Ceylon. He was known for his commitment to establishing and maintaining the social prestige of the fine arts in Victorian society, being on the Board of Trustees of the National Gallery in London and a Member of Parliament in Westminster.

Shaw's admiration for Lady Gregory arose, in part, out of this rich cultural heritage and the social ideals that she brought to her work for the Irish Revival at the beginning of the twentieth century. One of the most significant influences in this regard was John Ruskin. When the defrocked Irish priest Peter Keegan delivers his famous condemnation of the ethos of 'commercial efficiency' at the end of Shaw's *John Bull's Other Island* (1904), the English businessman Thomas Broadbent replies that Keegan's persuasiveness reminds him of the 'great man' Ruskin.[3] Ruskin, the 'Victorian Sage,' was a profoundly influential social and art critic during the Victorian period, holding the prestigious Slade Professorship of Fine Art at Oxford University between 1870 and 1878, and again between 1883 and 1885. Ruskin had made a name for himself by promoting the social importance of the arts, arguing fervently for the existence of a correlation between their social standing and the condition of society in general. Through his numerous books, pamphlets, and open letters, Ruskin developed a programme that aimed at increasing the social awareness and prestige of the arts in Britain. Through this work, he created a special framework within which artists, workers, and politicians functioned during the late nineteenth century.

Ruskin's theories influenced many diverse social, political, and artistic movements, including the Christian Socialist Movement, the Home Industries Movement, the Co-operative Movement, and the Arts and Crafts Movement. He was convinced that there was a connection between a nation's appreciation of its home-grown artistic talents and the general state of that nation. For this reason, he fervently promoted the work of British artists such as William Turner, John Everett Millais, William Holman Hunt, Dante Gabriel Rossetti, George Frederic Watts, William Morris, Edward Burne-Jones, and Frederic Leighton. Ruskin was aware, of course, that these artists had read his works and had appreciated the aesthetic and social ideals that he had formulated in the many volumes of *Modern Painters*, *The Stones of Venice*, *The Seven Lamps of Architecture*, *Unto This Last*, and *Fors Clavigera*. Ruskin had engrained in these artists a deep love of the visual arts and instilled in them the idea that an artist carried a moral responsibility to the society in which s/he lived and for which s/he worked. In the later nineteenth century, this sense of responsibility became manifest in a number of ways, particularly through the involvement of some of these artists in the Working Men's Colleges of Britain.

Sir William Gregory, John Ruskin, and Sir Henry Layard were diligent in raising public awareness of the fine arts, as shown by their dedicated work for the Arundel Society. Sir Henry Layard's palace on the Grand Canal in Venice—located not far from the one the Brownings would purchase—was visited by many Victorian *art connoisseurs*. Lady Gregory wrote in her memoirs that Sir Henry 'was treated with ceremonious honour by those who recognised the value of his service to archaeology and art' and that '[t]here was no one of distinction among his countrymen there whose gondola was not often at his door'.[4] Ruskin was one of the countrymen who visited him, a man who, in Lady Gregory's words, always 'seemed to be [the British] Ambassador in Venice'.[5] She cited one of his letters on Ruskin's visit in her memoirs: 'Ruskin is here, and in very gentle humour, but in very low spirits'; this was due to Ruskin's old age and his slowly deteriorating physical and mental condition.[6] Ruskin was known for his writings on Venice and Venetian architecture; on this occasion he came to inspect the restoration of the Ducal Palace and St. Mark's Cathedral. Ruskin was satisfied with the restoration work carried out on the famous buildings. Sir Henry wrote that Ruskin thought 'the restorations of St. Mark's [Cathedral] have been carefully and lovingly done' and that 'the new capitals of the columns supporting the Ducal Palace [were] so admirably executed that you would not tell them from the old'.[7]

Lady Gregory understood the significance of Ruskin's remarks. She had read *The Stones of Venice* and during her married years she had undertaken many long walks around the town, searching for buildings or art works that Sir William, Sir Henry, or Ruskin had considered worthy of visiting or viewing. Lady Gregory's friend, the novelist Henry James, wrote that it was customary at the time to walk around the streets and canals holding a copy of Ruskin's *The Stones of Venice*, which James thought to be every visitor's perfect guide to the artistic richness of the

Mediterranean city.[8] Lady Gregory herself was well aware of the aesthetic and emotional significance that Venice held for the Victorian critic, and she appreciated his approval of the work of those artists and workmen who had been involved in the restoration project.[9] Both Venice and the Layard's Ca' Capello, where Enid Layard was instructed in drawing by Ruskin himself, became an important place for Lady Gregory as well.[10] Later in her life, when times were troubled in Ireland, the Venetian palace was where she found solace, a place to which she returned time after time.

Lady Gregory often found herself engaged in conversation about Ruskin's aesthetic and social principles with Sir William's *art connoisseur* friends. In fact, her views on the social function of the arts and the social responsibility of the artist were shaped, in large measure, by Ruskin's social and political thought. *Lady Gregory and Irish National Theatre: Art, Drama, Politics* analyses the many different ways in which Ruskin's teachings shaped Lady Gregory's own aesthetic, social, and political views that subsequently influenced the literary and cultural revival in Ireland. As an integral part of this, I argue that Lady Gregory's way of thinking was fundamentally Ruskinian in character. One of the consequences of this was that her ideals were markedly different to those of her closest friend, William Butler Yeats, with whom she founded the Abbey Theatre in 1904. The book illustrates how Lady Gregory's determination to realise a Ruskinian social and educational programme in Ireland helped the cultural and literary revival to develop and flourish in the ways that it did at the beginning of the twentieth century. This is not to claim that she worked alone in this respect, or that she was the sole driving force behind the cultural developments in Ireland. It is to assert, however, that Lady Gregory had a clear, independent vision, one that was markedly different from that of Yeats, J. M. Synge, Maud Gonne, Annie Horniman, and other figures of the Irish Literary Revival period, including Alice Milligan, Patrick Pearse, and Thomas MacDonagh.[11] She envisaged the possibility of a programme similar in kind to that which Ruskin had envisaged for the British Isles being achieved specifically in Ireland. She was convinced that the implementation of Ruskin's social programme would benefit Irish people immensely, particularly the large swathes of rural people living in various levels of poverty during the late Victorian period.

Of course, Lady Gregory could not realise any such programme in Ireland without the support and assistance of others. Fortunately for her, at the time there was a consensus among a number of literary, cultural and political figures in Ireland that Ruskin's social and cultural educational proposals should be enacted in Ireland as far as possible. Sir Horace Plunkett, George Russell, Standish O'Grady, and William Butler Yeats were all disciples of Ruskin to varying degrees; they were avid readers of Ruskin's works and were figures who appreciated the significance of his social programme. This was so despite the fact that each of these writers and thinkers had derived a different set of perspectives from Ruskin's vast body of writing, resulting in important differences of opinion among them as regards how best the ideas might be implemented in Ireland. Yet all of these writers accepted Ruskin's notion that the arts should play a central role in any educational programme that aimed at elevating public taste in Ireland, and by doing so, enriching the quality of life for the majority of the Irish population. Spokesperson of the the Irish Co-operative Movement George Russell wrote in *Co-operation and Nationality* (1912) that, in an ideal Irish community, work and art should complement one another, granting Irishmen 'a more intellectual and enjoyable social life' as well as a certain degree of 'political power and economic prosperity'.[12] Later, in *The National Being* (1916), Russell envisaged co-operative communities throughout Ireland with libraries, choirs, bands, and halls for dances and concerts that would become central components of Irish village life.[13] Russell proposed that Irish schools should be decorated with reproductions of well-known pictures, that picture galleries should be established in the larger Irish towns, and that Irish roadsides should be beautified.[14] Russell's ideas call immediately to mind Ruskin's famous Victorian road-building project in Ferry Hinksey near Oxford, one of Ruskin's first attempts to put his social theories into practical usage. Russell's ideas on the decoration of schools and picture galleries recall Ruskin's lines from his open letters to the workmen of Great Britain, published as *Fors Clavigera*. Ruskin wrote that more pictures, sculptures, books, and other 'objects of art and natural history' should be used as decorations in British and Irish schools.[15] Ruskin wished this to enrich the artistic sensibilities of both the school children and their middle-class or working-class parents coming from rural or urban backgrounds.

Ruskin was well familiar with social conditions in Ireland. Following an invitation by John and Maria La Touche of Harristown in County Kildare, Ruskin visited Ireland in 1861. While his first comments on the state of the Irish countryside were far from complimentary, his first impressions of Irish men and women induced in him a great sense of sympathy. Later, during the Home Rule debate, Ruskin wrote an open letter to the *Pall Mall Gazette* (1886) in which he stated that Irish people were 'artistic', 'indefatigable', 'witty', and 'affectionate', and that these characteristics should be taken into account in any programme that the British government would seek to enact in addressing the social and political problems of the country.[16] Ruskin added that, in seeking to understand the 'Irish character', educated Englishmen would be well advised to consult the writings of Maria Edgeworth. Of Edgeworth's *Ormond*, *Ennui* and *The Absentee* Ruskin asserted that they 'contain[ed] more essential truths about Ireland than can be learned from any other sources whatsoever'.[17] When assessing the impact of Ruskin's thought on Lady Gregory's social ideals, it is important to keep in mind this impact that Edgeworth had on Ruskin, recognising the precedent of the early nineteenth-century Anglo-Irish female novelist for the late nineteenth-century Anglo-Irish female dramatist and mythographer. Ruskin was a devoted reader of Edgeworth's novels, keeping them at his bedside, along with works by William Shakespeare, Lord Byron, Walter Scott, and Thomas Carlyle. Indeed, he would read from Edgeworth's novels to his guests who stayed at his home in Brantwood.[18] Ruskin admired the general sentiment of her novels as well as her use of the Hiberno-English dialect. Furthermore, Ruskin knew of the close friendship between her and his favourite author, Walter Scott. Ruskin was always keen to observe the thematic and stylistic similarities and differences between the fictional works of two of his favourite writers.

Although significant, these connections between Scott and Edgeworth would not have deepened Ruskin's love of her novels had it not been for what Ruskin perceived as Richard Lovell Edgeworth's dedicated work to alleviate poverty on his Irish estate in County Longford. Ruskin considered the work of Maria's father to be one of the finest examples of benign landlordship throughout the British Isles: on the Edgeworth estate there were, in Walter Scott's words, 'but snug cottages and smiling faces all about'.[19] Written by an avid admirer rather than by a stern critic of Richard Edgeworth's social experiments, Scott's comments were, of course, sentimentalist. Nevertheless, Scott genuinely intended to convey how differently the Edgeworth family approached social and educational issues in Ireland to their landowning contemporaries in the country, many of whom were absentee landlords indifferent to the welfare of their tenants. As admirers of Jean-Jacques Rousseau's theories, the Edgeworth family proposed a programme for educating Irish children (both Catholic and Protestant), which was regarded by other reformers of the period as decidedly unconventional, if not radical. Seeing the circumstances of those who lived in abject poverty, the Edgeworth family sought to combine the education of children in theoretical and devotional aspects with the acquisition of practical skills. Their intention was to enable children to acquire practical skills while developing them intellectually and to influence their parents' behaviour at home and at work. As Helen O'Connell observes, the Edgeworth *père* was even engaged in parliamentary debates on the suitable forms and means of educating Irish children. Some of the principles of his *Practical Education* (1798)—a book he had co-written with his daughter Maria— were later used in the proposal that the Board of Education submitted to the British government in 1812.[20] The Edgeworth proposal inaugurated a long period of debate, during which Chief Secretary Robert Peel proposed that government funds should be channelled into voluntary, non-denominational educational organisations.[21]

Established by John David La Touche, Arthur Guinness, and Samuel Bewley, the Kildare Place Society was one such organisation, receiving large amounts of funding from the British government. O'Connell writes that although the Kildare Place Society was accused of proselytisation, especially during the Second Reformation of the 1820s, it was known that Repeal campaigner Daniel O'Connell had served on its first Board of Commissioners.[22] By this time, however, debates had been ongoing regarding the state of schooling in Britain and Ireland, especially in relation to the introduction of a National School System. This debate developed many social, political, dogmatic as well as religious aspects during the first half of the nineteenth century, partly because the issue of creating a new school system in Ireland became entangled in discussions over the political future of the country. Astutely, Maria Edgeworth had hinted at this problem in her 1809 novel *Ennui*, a novel that she wrote as a political allegory of the Act of Union between Britain and Ireland. *Rousseauisme* at its foundation, *Ennui* is a novel in which the characters of McLeod, Hardcastle and Lord Y—offer various alternative perspectives on the improvement of circumstances for Irish men, women, and children through learning.

Ruskin wrote the volumes of *Modern Painters* and *The Stones of Venice* in the context of these nineteenth-century debates on education. What Ruskin added to the debates was his persistent insistence upon the importance of the fine arts in education and social formation. While Ruskin accepted the necessity of combining theoretical learning with practical instruction in schools and 'other educational establishments', he felt that too much emphasis was being laid on practical skills in the Industrial Revolution era, with too little emphasis on the aesthetic cultivation of children's tastes and stimulating their interest in literature, drama, painting, and design. Through her readings of Rousseau, Edgeworth, Scott, and Ruskin, Lady Gregory had become familiar with all the major issues involved in this debate on social formation. While of course she belonged to a socially privileged, Protestant land-owning class in Ireland, like her literary forerunner Maria Edgeworth, she was keen to explore new possibilities for improving the conditions of the tenants who rented the land on the Big House estates. She knew that selling Coole Park was never an option she could contemplate, as her personal circumstances and those of her country were changing during her lifetime. She was, however, concerned to improve the quality of life and working conditions for tenants on the Gregory estate and indeed for those tenants on other Big House estates during and after the period of the Land Agitation. She found that Ruskin's social and cultural ideas offered a way to achieve this goal at both local and national levels. In this study I explore the ways in which she went about realising the multifaceted social and educational programme that Ruskin had hoped to see implemented in the British Isles as a whole. In so doing, I adopt an interdisciplinary approach in drawing attention to the variety of Lady Gregory's life experience that resulted in her involvement in the worlds of art, archaeology, antiquarianism, theatre, local industry, co-operative enterprise, and constitutional politics.

As for the content of the book, the chapter "'My Education': Sir William Gregory, the *Grand Tours*, and the Visual Arts" reconstructs Lady Gregory's own education in the fine arts during the years of her marriage to Sir William. Sir William organised a number of *Grand Tours* of European museums and art galleries for his young wife; this occurred for a number of reasons. For one thing, he derived great pleasure from seeing beautiful artefacts displayed in stunningly designed buildings. For another, he felt compelled to widen his wife's horizons on matters relating to the visual arts, ranging from their history to their possible social functions. This was so because conversations in the upper echelons of Victorian society often revolved around the arts, influenced to a great extent by Dr. Heinrich Schliemann and Sir Henry Layard's new excavations in Greece and the Middle East. Drawing on previously unpublished material from her holograph diaries, travel notes, and travel sketches, the chapter "'My Education': Sir William Gregory, the *Grand Tours*, and the Visual Arts" examines the ways in which Lady Gregory broadened her knowledge of the latest developments in the fields of art and archaeology, and the ways in which this knowledge was beginning to shape her thinking about art as well as about colonial politics. Significant in this regard is her status within late Victorian society: knowledge of the fine arts and ability to draw were generally considered as indicators of a woman's social status. As wife to a Trustee of the National Gallery in London and a Member of Parliament in Westminster, Lady Gregory was expected to be knowledgeable about the state of the arts both in Britain and in Continental Europe. The chapter "'My Education': Sir William Gregory, the *Grand Tours*, and the Visual Arts" ends with an analysis of the multifaceted social and theoretical debates concerning painting, sculpture, and architecture in Victorian England. As part of this, the infamous Whistler-Ruskin trial of 1878 is considered in some detail because theorists and historians considered this event as the epitome of the debate on the true function and value of the arts. This trial will receive more attention in later chapters of the book, when the focus turns towards Lady Gregory's friendship with the young aspiring poet William Butler Yeats and their joint efforts to establish a National Theatre in Ireland.

The chapter "'The "whorl" of Troy': Celtic Mythology, Victorian Hellenism, and the Irish Literary Revival" considers the principle of *noblesse oblige* as a guide to evaluating a new phase in Lady Gregory's life following the death of her husband in 1892. As Sir William's widow, she began editing the biography of her husband and the letters of his grandfather, who had acted as Under Secretary for Ireland at the beginning of the nineteenth century. However accurately or not, she portrayed both men as politicians who cared for the welfare of the people of Ireland, in what she presented as deeply challenging times for both the Anglo-Irish political *élite* and the British administration in Ireland. Lady Gregory positioned Sir William's family at the heart of a social reform movement that, in her interpretation, the socially concerned politicians of the era had hoped to realise in Ireland. Partly because of these biographical works, Lady Gregory was successful in establishing herself as a distinguished member of the Gregory family of County Galway. By the end of the 1890s, she was not only a prominent member within late Victorian English society but also one of the leaders of the literary and cultural revival that was underway in Ireland. She compiled materials for two further books, *Cuchulain of Muirthemne* of 1902 and *Gods and Fighting Men* of 1904. Through these works, she hoped to educate the reading public in Irish mythology and promote *noblesse oblige* as a principle to be adopted by leaders from all sections within Irish society and by British political leaders dealing with the pressing issues of land reform and Home Rule. Lady Gregory's attitude to the compilation and dissemination of ancient legends is compared with the intentions of authors of earlier collections, with those of Eugene O'Curry in *Lectures on the Manuscript Material of Ancient Irish History* (1861) and Standish O'Grady in his multi-volume work, *History of Ireland* (1878–80). Furthermore, my chapter "'The "whorl" of Troy': Celtic Mythology, Victorian Hellenism, and the Irish Literary Revival" considers her mythical compilations within the context of the Victorian art world when the theatre was regarded as an important dimension of the educational role of the arts. This dimension was evident in Frank Benson's production of Aeschylus' *Agamemnon* in Oxford in 1880, a performance that exerted a significant influence on the theatre reform movement in England as well as on the dramatic movement in Ireland that would culminate in the foundation of the Abbey Theatre in 1904. Katherine Newey, Jeffrey Richards, and Anselm Heinrich have investigated Ruskin's multifaceted influence both on the Baliol Hall production in Oxford and the wider theatre reform movement in Britain in the last decades of the nineteenth century.[23] The invaluable and ground-breaking study of theirs, however, calls for further investigations, particularly with regard to the theatre scene in Ireland before the outbreak of the First World War in 1914.

The chapter "'Ní neart go cur le chéile': Education, Social Reform, and the Abbey Theatre" addresses the connections between Lady Gregory's engagement in the Irish Home Industries and Irish Co-operative Movements along with her efforts to build a suitable repertoire for the Abbey Theatre. Ruskin had argued that the fine arts and the theatre were capable of (re-)forming people's characters to the end of a general improvement of the quality of life throughout society. Lady Gregory drew on this perspective when creating the repertoire of the Irish National Theatre. Some of her own plays of rural Ireland focus directly on the theme of character formation, a question that was central to the Co-operative Movement from the 1890s. Plunkett's and Russell's objectives for the Irish Co-operative Movement were indebted to Ruskin's ideals formulated in the aims of his St. George's Guild that dated back to the late 1860s and early 1870s. Indeed, Plunkett and Russell followed more closely in Ruskin's footsteps than did the leaders of the Co-operative Movement in England. Of course, social problems in Ireland, where the majority of the population worked in the agricultural sector, were profoundly different to social problems in Britain, where most of the working population belonged to the industrial sector. Nonetheless, Ruskin's ideas on social (re-)formation resonated with critics and reformers on both sides of the Irish Sea. William Morris's lecture 'Factory Work' from 1884 advocated the idea that factories should become 'palaces of industry' where workers could cultivate their 'love of art' and 'sense of beauty and interest in life' and where children could learn the 'pleasure' and 'honor' for working for one's community. These sentiments were in many respects akin to those of George Russell, formulated in his seminal work on the aims of the Irish Co-operative Movement, *Co-operation and Nationality*.[24] In their own ways, Ruskin, Morris, and Russell envisaged an alternative social system in which the arts contribute to the improvement of the working conditions and the living standards of men and women, be they farmers in Ireland or manual labourers in British factories. Lady Gregory, for her part, shared the view that the arts should be used as instruments of social reform. Furthermore, under Ruskin's influence, she was of the view that the theatre itself should be utilised as a vehicle for fostering progressive social change. In this aspect, her views differed significantly from those of her co-directors at the Abbey Theatre. She aimed to establish an institution that could realise in an Irish setting the ideals of some of her contemporaries who believed, along Ruskinian lines, that both theatre as an institution and plays themselves could bring about a general change of character within Irish society. William Archer and Henry Granville-Barker, for instance, were two of her contemporaries who intended to establish a theatre with character-forming effects. As the Chapter "'Ní neart go cur le chéile': Education, Social Reform, and the Abbey Theatre" argues, the imprint of Ruskin's outlook was evident in their 1904 proposal to found a National Theatre in London, featuring a wide selection of plays from William Shakespeare to Henrik Ibsen.

Continuing the examination of Lady Gregory's plays from my chapter "'Ní neart go cur le chéile': Education, Social Reform, and the Abbey Theatre," the chapter "'See a play as a picture': The Pre-Raphaelite Brotherhood, the Sister Arts, and the Irish Plays" investigates the influence of Ruskin's aesthetic philosophy (intricately entwined as it was with his social thought) on Lady Gregory's own work as playwright and theatre director. More precisely, the chapter looks at the staging of Lady Gregory's, Yeats's, and Synge's plays at the Abbey in the decade preceding the First World War. This is examined within the context of Victorian debates on the relationship between the Sister Arts. Ruskin enjoyed narrative *tableaux*, artworks that were didactic in nature; he was particularly taken with stage performances that employed the kind of *tableaux* that he had encountered in the paintings of Leighton, Watts, Alma-Tadema, and Burne-Jones. Back in the 1880s and 1890s, their works were seen as contributing to a wider theatre reform of the nineteenth century, particularly in their use of historical realism, a new trend in theatre that was inspired in large measure by the archaeological findings of Schliemann and Layard. Ruskin was greatly impressed by another kind of the narrative *tableau*, that painted by artists of the Pre-Raphaelite Brotherhood. Given her knowledge of art and aesthetics acquired during those Grand Tours of Continental Europe, Lady Gregory understood that the generation of Pre-Raphaelite artists aimed at renewing a long-standing narrative tradition, one that dated back to the masterpieces of Jan van Eyck, Diego Velázquez, Peter Paul Rubens, and William Hogarth. She herself made use of this narrative tradition in painting when composing her plays or when planning stage designs for performances. The chapter "'See a play as a picture': The Pre-Raphaelite Brotherhood, the Sister Arts, and the Irish Plays" contrasts her idea of theatre and staging with that of Yeats and of Synge, setting their different approaches against the latest developments in British theatre against the late nineteenth and early twentieth-century period. This allows a comparison to be drawn between the work of the Abbey directors and that of their contemporaries Frank Benson, Henry Irving, Herbert Beerbohm Tree, and Edward Gordon Craig.

Finally, the chapter "*The Light of the World*: Christianity, Cultural Politics, and Constitutional Reform" examines the politics of her plays during the ten years prior to the rebellion in Dublin of Easter 1916. Only a small number of her many dramatic works have been taken by Irish critics as illustrating her political attitudes, the consequence of which is that her commitment to Irish nationalism has been mostly overstated as has been the influence of advanced nationalist politics in Ireland on her vision for Ireland's future in terms of Irish-British relations. Lady Gregory's political views have even been set alongside those of the radical and militant Irish Republican Patrick Pearse, leader of the Easter Rising, Head of the Provisional Government, and signatory of the

Proclamation of the Irish Republic, read out in front of the General Post Office on Dublin's Sackville Street (now O'Connell Street) on Monday, 24 April 1916. Lady Gregory and Pearse did indeed share certain views. Both regarded the prominence of the fine arts in Irish society as crucial to character formation and social development, and art and drama as fundamental to the education of Irish children. Pearse included these ideas in the educational programme of the schools of St. Enda's and St. Ita's, where teaching of devotional matters was combined with the teaching of art, literature, and science in both the Irish and the English languages. Playing fields, gardens, a handball-court, an open-air gymnasium, an art room, a museum, a library, a science laboratory, an infirmary, a playroom, and a school chapel also served the cultivation of young Irish minds, and corridors were beautified with artworks by Jack B. Yeats, George Russell, and Sarah Purser.[25] No doubt, St. Enda's school was Pearse's unique and remarkable achievement; however, it may well be regarded as a particular realisation of all the educational reform plans that had been the subject of so much debate through the course of the nineteenth century in both Britain and Ireland. Over time, however, Pearse's politics turned revolutionary, while Lady Gregory's remained reconciliatory, indicating strikingly different approaches to the idea of a brighter future for Ireland. My study takes serious account of Ruskin's, Pearse's, and Lady Gregory's Christian faith when evaluating their political thought, drawing attention to the writings of Ernest Renan, Rev. John Wesley, Cardinal John Henry Newman, as well as the ideas of the La Touche and Cowper-Temple families in Ireland (close friends of Ruskin). At the end of the chapter "*The Light of the World*: Christianity, Cultural Politics, and Constitutional Reform," Lady Gregory's politics of reconciliation are considered in detail in relation to aspects of the Home Rule policies of the Irish Parliamentary Party leader Charles Stewart Parnell as well as those of British Prime Ministers William Gladstone and Herbert H. Asquith from the 1880s to the 1910s.

As regards the time frame of the book, Katherine Newey and Jeffrey Richards have drawn attention to the impact of the First World War on the reception of Ruskin's aesthetic ideals in Britain.[26] Tim Hilton, Sarah Atwood, and Stuart Eagles have made similar observations with respect to the reception of Ruskin's educational ideals in Britain, although none of them consider the case of Ireland.[27] With the outbreak of the European war, a new chapter in Britain's imperial history began, one that would include the stories of independence movements taking hold in various parts of the Empire. Lady Gregory herself had to end a chapter in her own life-story during the Great War: her son Robert died on the Italian front fighting against the armed forces of the Austro-Hungarian Monarchy in 1918. Losing her son in the war marked for her the beginning of the drawn-out affair in which she eventually lost her home at Coole Park. Robert's widow, Margaret Gregory, inherited the residence and its lands after his death but had no interest in keeping the estate within the Gregory family. Within the literary scene in Ireland, as the country was about to enter upon a new chapter in its history, disagreements between actors, directors, and managers turned into bitter rivalries over the running and the financing of the Abbey Theatre as it tried to establish for itself the position of Ireland's National Theatre.[28] Furthermore, Lady Gregory was slowly losing her closest friends and allies, those upon whom she had come to rely in past times in realising the artistic and social programme that Ruskin had envisaged for the British Isles.

For years, she had campaigned with her nephew, the art collector Hugh Lane, for public funding to establish a Gallery of Modern Art in Dublin; an endeavour which testified to the deep imprint that her years spent visiting Continental museums and galleries had left on her and the strength of her commitment to Ruskinian ideals concerning art that had expounded in the nineteenth century. Tragically, Hugh Lane died on board the *Lusitania* when it was hit by a German torpedo off the southern Irish coast as it was crossing the Atlantic Ocean in May 1915 on a journey from New York to England. Following the end of the Great War in 1918, the Irish Co-operative Movement was damaged severely as the country entered into a violent struggle to attain independence from British rule. Plunkett and Russell could not prevent the destruction of co-operative creameries, meat factories, and linen halls during the Anglo-Irish War of 1919–1921 and during the bitter civil war that followed the signing of the Anglo-Irish Treaty in December 1921. Despite the enormous changes that Ireland underwent during this era, Lady Gregory never ceased to believe that realising some aspects at least of her artistic and socio-economic ideals in Ireland remained possible. In a truly Ruskinian fashion, she stuck to her conviction that the arts and the theatre should work towards the betterment of society and should facilitate progressive social reform, enriching the quality of human life in creative and co-operative ways. This book is an evaluation of her far-ranging achievements as a playwright, a theatre director, and a social reformer during the turn-of-the-century period.

Notes

1. Dan H. Laurence and Nicholas Grene, eds. *Shaw, Lady Gregory and the Abbey* (Gerrards Cross: Colin Smythe, 1993), 66.
2. Laurence and Grene, *Shaw, Lady Gregory and the Abbey*, 63. My italics.
3. George Bernard Shaw, *John Bull's Other Island* (London: Penguin, 1984), 160.
4. Lady Augusta Gregory, *Seventy Years* (Gerrards Cross: Colin Smythe, 1974), 172.
5. Gregory, *Seventy Years*, 171.
6. Gregory, *Seventy Years*, 172.
7. Gregory, *Seventy Years*, 171.
8. Henry James, *Italian Hours* (London: Penguin, 1995), 8.
9. Ruskin was often critical of the quality of restorations carried out on famous buildings; Lady Gregory was glad to hear that, this time around, the art critic was pleased with the workmen's efforts.
10. Lady Layard and Lady Gregory referred to 'Ca' Cappello' as 'Ca' Capello'; the book retains the spelling they used.
11. R. F. Foster examines the varied nature of the drama scene in Ireland at the beginning of the twentieth century, pointing out the significance of smaller and provincial companies and playhouses in the building of a revolutionary atmosphere in Ireland. Foster's study offers no indication that Lady Gregory could be regarded as a member of these revolutionary 'generation-units', to use his term. R. F. Foster, *Vivid Faces: The Revolutionary Generation in Ireland, 1890–1923* (New York: Norton and Company, 2015), 8, 24, and 75–113.
12. George Russell, *Co-operation and Nationality* (Dublin: Irish Academic Press, 1982), 41. The idea was stated earlier by Plunkett in *Noblesse Oblige*. See Horace Plunkett, *Noblesse Oblige, An Irish Rendering* (Dublin: Maunsel, 1908), 12.
13. George Russell, *The National Being* (Dublin: Maunsel, 1916), 48.
14. For the schools, see Russell, *The National Being*, 49; for the picture gallery, see *The National Being*, 146; for the beautification of the roadside, see *The National Being*, 49 and 149, and *Co-operation and Nationality*, 44. For Ruskin's ideas on school reform, see J. A. Hobson, *John Ruskin, Social Reformer* (London: Nisbet, 1899), 252 and 255.
15. E. T. Cook and Alexander Wedderburn, eds. *The Works of John Ruskin*, vol. 30 (London: George Allen, 1903–1912), 5. Hereafter, Ruskin, *Title of the individual work* volume number of collected works.page number. Example using the source for footnote: Ruskin, *The Guild and Museum of St. George*, 30.5.
16. Ruskin, "The Irish Question," 34.582.

17. Ruskin, "The Irish Question," 34.582.
18. Ruskin, *Elements of Drawing*, 15.227 and Ruskiniana, 34.700.
19. Ruskin, *Fors Clavigera*, 27.520.
20. Helen O'Connell, *Ireland and the Fiction of Improvement* (Oxford: Oxford University Press, 2006), 66. Differing markedly from previous ones, the new proposal of the Board of Education included the idea of establishing a state-supervised educational system, one that would provide children with both theoretical and practical learning, and one that would be set up along strictly non-denominational lines. Whatever the practicality of this proposal, it was immediately conceived of by many in Ireland as reducing the influence of religious education and secularising the educational system in a seemingly irreversible way. For these reasons, the proposal was fervently opposed by the Roman Catholic Church, fearing the loss of its social influence established through the network of local schools, hedge schools, and Christian Brothers schools.
21. O'Connell, *Ireland and the Fiction of Improvement*, 66.
22. O'Connell, *Ireland and the Fiction of Improvement*, 67.
23. Katherine Newey and Jeffrey Richards, *John Ruskin and the Victorian Theatre* (Basingstoke: Palgrave Macmillan, 2010); Anselm Heinrich, Katherine Newey, and Jeffrey Richards, eds., *Ruskin, the Theatre and Victorian Visual Culture* (Basingstoke: Palgrave Macmillan, 2009).
24. William Morris, *Factory Work, As It Is and Might Be* (New York: New York Labor News Co., 1922), 21 and 26–27.
25. Joost Augusteijn, *Patrick Pearse: The Making of a Revolutionary* (Basingstoke: Palgrave Macmillan, 2010), 159.
26. Newey and Richards, *John Ruskin and the Victorian Theatre*, 208.
27. Tim Hilton, *John Ruskin: The Later Years* (New Haven: Yale University Press, 2000), 594; Sarah Atwood, *Ruskin's Educational Ideals* (Farnham: Ashgate, 2011), 164; and Stuart Eagles, *After Ruskin: The Social and Political Legacies of a Victorian Prophet, 1870–1920* (Oxford: Oxford University Press, 2011), 245.
28. See for this Lauren Arrington, *W. B. Yeats, the Abbey Theatre, Censorship, and the Irish State* (Oxford: Oxford University Press, 2010).

'My Education': Sir William Gregory, the *Grand Tours*, and the Visual Arts

MARRIAGE AND MUSEUMS

Isabella Augusta Persse married Sir William Henry Gregory of Coole Park in a quiet ceremony on 4 March 1880 in St. Matthias Church, Dublin. The rather low-key occasion was nonetheless of momentous cultural significance as Sir William's bride was about to enter the esteemed art circles of Victorian England. Lady Gregory had enjoyed a privileged upbringing on the Persse estate in Roxborough, Co. Galway, but the family was large and there were many children desiring the attention and financial support of the parents. Longing for intellectual stimulation, she found companionship in books and passed much of her time reading poems and novels. As she recalled later in her autobiography *Seventy Years*, by the age of 15 she had become familiar with the works of Thomas Malory, Lord Tennyson, Walter Scott, Robert Burns, John Keats, Robert Browning, and Matthew Arnold, while also holding long conversations on the stylistic and romantic beauty of William Shakespeare's sonnets with Trinity College students from Dublin.[1] She expanded her knowledge of English literature through the reading of Chambers's *Encyclopaedia of English Literature*, from which she made lists of authors and works for further consultation. As Judith Hill writes, she was a young lady for whom 'books soon became indispensable; her love of poetry, novels, essays, words, images, the rhythm of sentences a badge of identity. She had become

© The Author(s) 2018
E. Remport, *Lady Gregory and Irish National Theatre*,
Bernard Shaw and His Contemporaries,
https://doi.org/10.1007/978-3-319-76611-9_2

a bookworm and an object of curiosity and ridicule for a family that never quite rid itself of the belief that her interest was a pretence'.[2]

She reaped rewards for this love of literature when she became the wife of Sir William Gregory, former Governor of Ceylon and owner of the estate that neighboured Roxborough. Sir William was captivated by her knowledge of literature and described her to his friend Sir Henry Layard as a woman whose mind was 'original' and 'well cultivated'.[3] The young woman was pleased to find in Sir William a man who appreciated her passion for literature. Almost 35 years her senior, Sir William found in her a companion who appreciated his own lifelong devotion to the fine arts. Whereas the wide age gap between them recalls that between Casaubon and Dorothea in George Eliot's *Middlemarch* of 1871–1872, Dorothea's impatience with the artworks of Rome marks a distinct contrast to the young Lady Gregory's passion for art.[4] Augusta had a genuine interest in the visual arts; the physical demands that a traveller had to endure during the *Grand Tours* of art history on the European Continent were as yet unknown to her. Sir William was pleased to undertake the task of deepening his wife's knowledge of art, and during their marriage he took her on many art tours around the world. In her unpublished memoir, *Seventy Years*, she liked to refer to her married years as the time when her real education in matters of art began, evidence of the importance that she attributed to the formative years of her marriage.[5] Brian Jenkins writes that Sir William, who typified the Victorian aristocracy's passionate interest in the arts, exerted a decisive influence on the developing interests of his young wife.[6]

Soon after the wedding, she began to make the acquaintance of the most prominent figures of the London art world and to familiarise herself with debates on the nature of art and its function in society. As a devoted Trustee of the National Gallery in London, and the staunchest supporter of the museum in parliamentary debates at Westminster, Sir William was a well-known figure in Victorian art circles. He often enjoyed the company of: Sir Frederic Leighton, President of the Royal Academy of Arts; Sir Charles Robinson, Keeper of the Queen's Pictures; and Sir Frederic Burton, Director of the National Gallery in London. He and his wife were friends with Sir Coutts Lindsay of the trend-setting Grosvenor Gallery, Sidney Colvin of the Fitzwilliam Museum, Alan Summerly Cole of the South Kensington Museum, Claude Phillips of the Wallace Collection, and J. W. Comyns Carr of the fashionable New Gallery. In fact, Lady Gregory counted Sir Frederic Burton among her closest friends, one with whom she shared her passion for watercolours.

Sir Frederic bequeathed the watercolours he had painted of Connemara and of County Clare in 1869 to Lady Gregory so that she could keep 'the sketches of that happy time'.[7]

Interest in the fine arts had been customary in Sir William's family. Due to his various obligations as a landlord at Coole Park, a Member of Parliament at Westminster, and the Governor of Ceylon, Sir William was obliged to spend a considerable amount of time away from the National Gallery. In spite of this, he always made the point of following the trustees' work rigorously and he kept records of all financial transactions relating to the museum. His devotion to the visual arts stemmed from his forefathers, who had decorated the rooms of the house at Coole with beautiful works of art.[8] The formidable family collection was originally founded by Sir William's great-grandfather, who was once the Chair of the Board of the East India Company. Sir William's grandfather, who acted as Under Secretary for Ireland in the early nineteenth century, continued the tradition of collecting and enlarged the already considerable collection with art works bought during his numerous trips on the European Continent. Sir William's uncle, Richard Gregory, further enlarged the art collection. Jenkins argues that the aesthetic influence on the young William (heir to the estate) of the surroundings at Coole Park was only deepened during his undergraduate years at Oxford University. When he was at Oxford, the Guise Collection of fine works of Italian and Dutch masters was housed in the library of Christ Church College, the institution the young heir attended.[9]

Lady Augusta Gregory was Sir William's second wife, arriving at Coole Park in 1880. She immediately felt drawn to these men of artistic cultivation, in particular to Richard Gregory.[10] She recognised the value of the work of Sir William's forefathers who had turned the house into a visual album of paintings worthy of being exhibited in any palace of art. She supported her husband's efforts to enrich further the already impressive collection with new acquisitions, and added her own artistic touch to the building after the death of Sir William in 1892. By the 1900s, traditional and modern art works were housed side by side at Coole, signalling the continuing interest in art from the founders of the collection down to the generation of Lady Gregory's son, the painter Robert Gregory. Colin Smythe's *A Guide to Coole Park* emphasises the uniqueness of this Irish country house, describing it as a home where art ranged from the Classicism of Canova and Canaletto to the Modernism of Jack B. Yeats.[11]

Lady Gregory dedicated her last book *Coole* (1931) entirely to Coole Park. This publication was her last, emotional appeal to her readership and to the people of Ireland, for whom she felt she had done so much in terms of cultural promotion, to draw attention to the importance of her home in order to save it from destruction. She painted a vivid picture of herself walking the squeaky rooms of the old house, browsing the contents of the old bookshelves. Books on Ireland and on the visual arts appeared side by side in her narrative, emphasising both the historical and the artistic legacy of her home. Her account of the library opened up the depth of artistic culture surrounding her: among many other works, the shelves kept the volumes of *Il Vaticano*, written and illustrated by Erasmo Pistolesi; the *Specimens of Ancient Sculpture, Ægyptian, Etruscan, Greek, and Roman*, Charles Rogers's *A Collection of Prints in Imitation of Drawings*, published by the Society of Dilettanti; the 'sumptuous volumes' of Horace Walpole and George Vertue's *Anecdotes of Painting in England; with Some Account of the Principle Artists and Incidental Notes on Other Arts*; and books dedicated to individual artists such as George Augustus Sala's *William Hogarth: Painter, Engraver, and Philosopher*.[12] Coole was her final farewell not only to the old house but also to those Continental trips during which she had absorbed the rich traditions of European art.

Some members of her own family were strongly committed to art collection, most notably her nephew Hugh Lane. Lane had amassed a fabulous collection of French Impressionist paintings, which he intended to bequeath to Ireland if a suitable building was erected for storage and display. The idea was to found a new Gallery of Modern Art which would house his famous collection. Lady Gregory hoped that, aside from the gallery functioning as a storehouse of paintings, it could also contribute to the artistic cultivation of both students of art in Ireland and of the wider public in general. The Abbey Theatre's first tour of the USA in 1911 was evidence that she attributed great significance to this project. She used the tour to raise money for the Citizens' Fund to clear off part of the gallery guarantee; she met US millionaires to talk business; and she ordered the Abbey touring company to put on additional performances in New York and Boston in order to help raise the several thousand pounds required for the project.[13]

The museum as an instrument for the artistic education of the general public was an idea that John Ruskin had been propagating for some time in his writings, and was something that Sir William took very seriously. Sir William vehemently opposed the relocation of the National Gallery in London from the city centre to the more inaccessible suburb of

Kensington. Sir Charles Eastlake, the Director of the Gallery, approached Sir William about the possibility of relocating some of the collection to Kensington. Sir William agreed that the Gallery's present building on Trafalgar Square, which it shared with the Royal Academy, was 'unfitted in every respect for the reception of a national collection of pictures'.[14] However, he objected to the selection of the Kensington site. Using his political influence, Sir William submitted a proposal to Westminster about the acquisition of a suitable property and the idea of removing the treasures of the Gallery. His concern was that a move to the fashionable Kensington district would place the collection outside the reach of the general population of London, leaving it accessible only to upper-class residents of South Kensington or to those who had the financial means to drive out to this fashionable district.[15] Many years later, during the battle to secure a site for Hugh Lane's art collection, Lady Gregory believed that a new art gallery in Dublin would fulfil an important educational purpose for the people of Dublin, just as the National Gallery had done for the people of London.[16]

Ruskin himself intended to set up a system of museums, with a central museum functioning as a storehouse for researchers, and a network of local museums for those whom he regarded (quite simplistically) as 'simple persons'.[17] After an extensive campaign, St. George's Museum opened its doors in Walkley, near Sheffield, in 1882. Ruskin thought that he would invite distinguished speakers who would give lectures on the relationship of work and economics to the arts. Ruskin hoped that by providing venues for the education of people from all walks of life—be they researchers or labourers—the museums would restore the status of the arts in a society which he described in *Time and Tide* as increasingly driven by industrial and profit imperatives.[18] Ruskin argued that museums ought to be a means to serve and to educate the general public for the purpose of general social enhancement, drawing art away from the monopoly and the elitism of the private collections.[19]

Sir William managed to engage Ruskin directly in his project to make the finest examples of the visual arts available to the public. Ruskin became a member of the Arundel Society, an organisation which, as Sir William explained in a pamphlet, intended 'to make generally known the purest and worthiest remains of the arts of former times'.[20] The idea was that the Society would raise funds to reproduce and popularise both lesser and more well-known masterpieces of Italian, Flemish, and German art from the Middle Ages to the period of the Italian Renaissance.

A devotee of the work of Italian *trecento* artists, Ruskin was undoubtedly a profound influence in this regard, having already taken considerable steps to promote the appreciation of Italian art in the volumes of *Modern Painters* and of *The Stones of Venice*. These books were also the first in which Ruskin expounded the view that the state of the visual arts in a society was indicative of the state of society as a whole. For this reason, he launched thundering denunciations of the general state of England in the nineteenth century, vigorously promoting the view that the arts should be granted a leading role in the transformation of British society. Many prominent figures of the Victorian art world shared this view and joined the Arundel Society. These included Sir Coutts Lindsay, Sir Frederic Burton, Sir Edward Poynter, George Frederic Watts, and Tom Taylor.

While the Arundel Society did its utmost to promote the visual arts, Sir William Gregory was adamant that more was required of a true *art connoisseur*: '[e]asel pictures can be studied and compared in galleries with comfort, but to obtain a thorough knowledge of Italian fresco, many a long mile has to be travelled, and many a rough night to be endured'.[21] Marrying Sir William, Augusta became a prominent member of the political and artistic *élite* in England, where conversations revolved as much around the arts as they did around politics. She testified to this in *Seventy Years* when she recalled a comment by Sir Joseph Edgar Boehm, a sculptor and a member of the Royal Academy, that travelling in those days was 'an education, a training, because artist or architect had to make his drawings of what he would keep in memory'.[22] As Sir William noted, this was true also of art enthusiasts. By way of cultivating her appreciation of the visual arts, Lady Gregory undertook many art trips and museum visits before her involvement in the Irish Literary Revival. By way of sustaining her memories of the many marvellous paintings, buildings and sculptures that she viewed and visited during her travels, she kept many written and painted records of the *Grand Tours*.

THE GRAND TOURS

Lady Gregory's first art tour commenced immediately after her wedding. She had visited Continental Europe before but her honeymoon was her first extended tour of European art galleries and museums. Her diaries are real testimony to the breadth and depth of the artistic knowledge that she acquired during the trip. Her notes of the pictures, galleries, and museums show that she visited some of the collections most favoured by Ruskin, and she saw works that exerted a profound influence on Victorian painters in England. Just two days after the wedding she described her visit to the collection of the Old Masters held at the Royal Academy in London. Her diary entries of her honeymoon that followed the visit to London contain an extraordinary list of places and art galleries, highlighting the knowledge of fresco, secco, and oil painting that she was in the process of acquiring. After leaving Paris, Sir William and Lady Gregory arrived in Turin to view the works of Botticelli, Memling, and Veronese. Further visits followed to galleries and churches in Genova, Pisa, Siena, Cortona, Perugia, and Assisi.[23] Among the dozens of places that she and her husband visited and the hundreds of frescos and paintings that they viewed on the journey down to Rome were the architectural complex of the Duomo, the Battisterio, and the Camposanto in Pisa. She saw Gozzoli's cycle of frescos of the Old Testament (1460s–1480s) decorating the Camposanti (destroyed during the Second World War), which inspired the early work of the Pre-Raphaelite Brotherhood. Ruskin regarded these frescos as the ultimate pictorial representation of his aesthetic theories.[24] In the San Domenico of Siena, Lady Gregory admired Pinturicchio's Renaissance masterpieces. In the San Severo of Perugia, she saw frescoes by Raphael and Perugino. Works by Ruskin's favourite painter Fra Angelico were also on their list; Sir William and Lady Gregory went to see his *Madonna* from the 1430s.

As the highlight of her Northern Italian trip, Lady Gregory visited the Basilica di San Francesco in Assisi.[25] Giotto and Cimabue's famous frescos there were amongst Ruskin's favourite art works. Ruskin considered Giotto 'one of the greatest men who ever lived'.[26] When he was at Oxford, Ruskin had dedicated a whole series of lectures to his work; he delivered 'The Aesthetic and Mathematical Schools of Art in Florence' in the Michaelmas term of 1874. The second lecture in the series was dedicated entirely to the work of Cimabue; here Ruskin provided an elaborate description of the San Francesco of Assisi. Ruskin referred to Giotto's frescos in the Lower Church as the painter's 'four great moral poems': 'Standing on the steps which descend from the upper cloisters into the north transept of the Lower Church, we have, on the wall beside me, an exquisite fresco by Giotto in front, his four great moral poems'.[27] These 'poems' were Giotto's allegorical paintings of 'Poverty', 'Chastity', 'Obedience', and 'The Glorification of St. Francis'.[28] Ruskin's knowledge of the frescos in Assisi stemmed from Sir William's closest friend Sir Henry

Layard. Sometime later, Sir Henry and the Arundel Society financially supported the publication of one of Ruskin's longer essay on Italian art that came out under the title *Giotto and his Works in Padua*.[29]

During their three-week stay in Rome, Lady Gregory and her husband went to see numerous galleries and villas that held extraordinary collections of art works.[30] They visited the Borghese Gallery, the Villa Doria, the Palazzo Colonna, the Palazzo Barberini, the Villa Volkowski, the Villa Ludovisi, and the Villa Albani. Lady Gregory went to see many of the landmark churches decorated with the finest of Italian paintings and sculptures. Destinations included the San Pietro in Montorio, the Sta Maria Maggiore, the Sta Maria del Popolo, the San Paolo fuori le mura, the San Giovanni in Laterano, and the San Pietro in Vincoli. Lady Gregory noted that they visited San Giovanni in Laterano to see a Giotto fresco and the San Pietro in Vincoli to view Michelangelo's famous *Moses* (c. 1513–1515). She and her husband saw the exceptional collection of art works in the Lateran Museum and in the Museum of the Vatican. In the latter, she viewed those sculptures of which Pistolesi had made sketches; sketches that were published in his famous *Il Vaticano*, a book that the Gregorys held in their private library in Coole Park. Lady Gregory visited the Sistine Chapel several times in order to view Michelangelo's breathtaking frescos covering the walls and ceiling. Unsurprisingly, given the circles in which she was now moving, on one of the visits to the Vatican, she and her husband accompanied Kaiser Wilhelm II and his daughter to marvel at the work of another Renaissance master, Raphael.[31]

Leaving behind Rome at the end of April, the Gregorys continued their honeymoon southward on the Apennine Peninsula.[32] The couple walked the ruins of the ancient town of Pompeii. Since the 1860s, grand-scale excavations had been carried out on the Pompeii site to discover the events of the day upon which Mount Vesuvius erupted in the first century, covering the small town entirely in volcanic ash, pumice, and lava. Everyday objects such as clothing items and kitchen accessories, as well as the dead bodies of the inhabitants cast in plaster, had already been excavated and were stored in the National Museum in Naples. Sir William and Lady Gregory went to see this exhibition as a follow-up to their tour of the excavation site. As a result of the dedicated work of tireless archaeologists, the original historical catastrophe seemed to unfold before her eyes and she came to understand the historical influence of archaeologists' underground work at the National Museum in Naples.

This introduction to the world of archaeology was significant as Augusta was about to meet two of the greatest archaeologists of the nineteenth century: Dr. Heinrich Schliemann and Sir Henry Layard. She met Schliemann in Greece. When she and her husband arrived there she was greatly impressed by the undulant hills of the coastline, and the ways in which they were coloured by the rays of the setting sun. A wide variety of programmes awaited her in Athens. She was taken around the ancient site of the Acropolis and was lectured on ancient Greek art and politics; she visited the National Museum to study the symmetry and proportions of Greek statues; and she walked around 'Dr Schliemann's Museum of things found at the tomb of Agamemnon', which stored Golden death masks, cups, and pottery.[33] Her friendship with the German archaeologist deepened when the Gregorys visited his home: 'Dr Schliemann entertained us at his house, and gave me a "whorl" from the ruins of Troy'.[34] Taking an archaeological find like this in her hand, Lady Gregory was deeply conscious that she was holding a precious piece of ancient history. This was so because Schliemann's excavations in Mycenae lent historical credibility to Homer's famous epic narration of the Trojan War.[35]

Rounding up their trip to Greece, the Gregorys drove out to a small town of immense significance for Greek civilisation and for European cultural history: Marathon. The name of the place and the memory of the battle that had taken place in 490 BC had been kept alive in the writings of Greek historians Plutarch and Herodotus. The story of the heroic battle between Miltiades's Athenian army and Darius's Persian forces, and the sacrifice of the messenger who died after delivering the news of the victory to the Athenians, were topics in classical learning during the era in which the Gregorys' visit took place. Furthermore, it had been taught as part of the curriculum at Oxford University, where the young Sir William had been educated. Phidias, who had sculpted and supervised the execution of the marble ornaments on the temples of the Acropolis, was also commissioned to sculpt a statue in honour of Miltiades and his victory, a piece that was placed at what was believed to be the site of the battle. Ruskin himself wrote in admiration of the Greek sculptor that he was the 'noblest son' of Greece.[36] This followed comments in *Modern Painters*, in which Ruskin placed Phidias, Michelangelo, and Dante above even Homer and Shakespeare because of the spiritual quality that he observed in their work.[37]

Lady Gregory became sharply aware of her new social position and its privileges during this part of the European journey. As Michael R. Booth explains, many English aristocrats could read the scholarly literature relating to these excavations, could see the pictorial views of the archaeological discoveries disseminated in newspapers and lithographs, or could visit exhibitions in London displaying archaeological finds from the various excavation sites. Most notable among these were the Great Exhibition of 1851 and the Crystal Palace Exhibition of 1854. Only the privileged few, however, had the opportunity to meet and converse with the archaeologists who made the outstanding discoveries.[38] Furthermore, although the discoveries at Nimrud dated back to the 1840s, those at Niniveh to the 1850s, and those at Pompeii to the 1860s, Schliemann's discoveries at Troy and Mycenae were relatively recent. The site only came to light only in the mid-1870s, not long before the Gregorys set out on their trip to Greece in 1880. Because she had seen those treasures so close at hand, Lady Gregory subsequently acquired a rather elevated status among the *art connoisseurs* of English society.

After encountering the archaeological treasures of ancient Greece, Sir William and Lady Gregory travelled on to the final destination of their honeymoon: Constantinople. In the capital of the Ottoman Empire, the newly-weds spent a few days as guests of Sir Henry Layard and his wife, Lady Enid Layard. Sir Henry had been appointed as British Ambassador in 1877 and taken up residence at the summer house of the British Embassy in Therapia. The beautiful spacious villa that lay on the European shore of the Bosphorus was situated halfway between Constantinople and the Black Sea and had stunning views overlooking the waterway. In *Seventy Years*, Lady Gregory remembered with much affection her days there:

> They were wonderful days there, where we went for rides in the forest, or to rummage in the Constantinople bazaars, or took our kettle across the Bosphorus and made our tea beside the 'sweet waters of Asia'.[39]

As G. R. Berrige explains, the Sultan and the Ottomans treated all ambassadors with great respect because they regarded embassies as 'flattering, valuable sources of information and alluring gifts, important props to commerce and useful mediators'.[40] For a while, Sir Henry and the British Embassy were no exceptions. There was talk of the Gregorys visiting the Sultan, but Sir William objected on political grounds relating to imperial rivalries between Britain and the Ottomans. The couple went to see the Sultan's Treasury instead. Lady Gregory thought that the Treasury was 'a wonderful vision of precious stones cut and uncut, heaped in gold and silver basins, where our eyes were soon dazzled. It was the very cave of Aladdin'.[41] Graciously, to show his affection, the Sultan even made a gift of studded chine cups to the wife of the British Ambassador.

During her sojourn with Sir Henry and Lady Layard, Lady Gregory took trips to study the intricate nature of oriental ornamentation. Sampling the beautiful architecture of Constantinople, she and her husband went to see the Blue Mosque, the Hagia Sophia, as well as some of the most impressive minarets of the Muslim world towering over the city landscape. The Gregorys also decided to drive out to take a walk on the shores of the Black Sea.[42] After her European experiences, the Ottoman part of her honeymoon opened a new field in her knowledge of art. She learned about intricate, non-figurative, Islamic decorative art and about the significance attributed to the fine arts in the Muslim world.

On their way back from Constantinople to London, the couple stopped at Marseilles, Lyon, Rouen, and Paris before returning to England at the end of May in 1880. They took another walk around the Louvre to study the French School and visited the Salon in Paris. On their last evening in the French capital the couple attended an amusing performance of Jacques Offenbach's light-hearted operetta *La Vie Parisienne* at the Théâtre des Variétés.[43] After the short stopover in Paris, the couple travelled on to London. Lady Gregory continued to visit places that she had seen recently in order to further reflect on the experiences accrued during her honeymoon. In the few weeks following the extended art journey, she visited the British Museum to marvel at the Elgin Marbles, taken from the Acropolis in Athens by a former ambassador to Constantinople, Thomas Bruce, the 7th Earl of Elgin, at the beginning of the nineteenth century (when Greece was part of the Ottoman Empire).[44] These treasures of marble friezes, *metopes*, and pediments of the Parthenon and of the Temple of Nike had been sculpted by or under the supervision of Phidias, whose works were deeply admired by both Lady Gregory and Ruskin. She also drove to the South Kensington Museum to view the collection of Schliemann's archaeological finds; paid a number of visits to the National Gallery to discuss art with Sir Frederic Burton; called on Sir William's Arundel friends; and visited the Grosvenor Gallery to attend a social occasion held in honour of the Prince of Wales.

Finally, she met up with Sir Henry and Lady Layard, recently joining the London season, to hear the latest political and art news.[45]

Lady Gregory's next art tour granted her the opportunity to study Northern European art and to distinguish the works of Flemish, Dutch, and German masters from those of their Italian contemporaries.[46] During this trip with her husband, who was anxious to return to Continental Europe as soon as possible after the birth of their son William Robert, she travelled through the Low Countries and Germany in July and August of 1881. Sir William's itinerary included art collections in Brussels, Rotterdam, Leyden, Delft, Amsterdam, Cologne, Cassel, Hannover, Hildesheim, Braunschweig, Berlin, Dresden, Leipzig, and Weimar. She took precise and detailed descriptions of the many paintings. These ranged from Lucas Cranach's famous medieval altarpieces and his portrait of the Protestant reformer Philipp Melanchthon to various landscapes, seascapes, and interiors painted by such celebrated artists as Peter de Haag, Jan van der Meer, and Jacob von Ruysdael. There were also descriptions of famous Flemish genre paintings and portraits by Jan Steen, Frans Hals, and Rembrandt. She also took the opportunity to examine Rubens's various allegorical masterpieces and analyse the works of Anthonis van Dyck and Jan van Eyck, whose works were well known in Victorian Britain. Jan van Eyck, in particular, was known to have influenced the painters of the Pre-Raphaelite Brotherhood.[47]

The second tour of 1881 took her to Venice, the city she knew so well from the pages of Ruskin's *The Stones of Venice*.[48] Leaving her new-born baby in nursing care for the second time that year, she set out with her husband in mid-October to travel from Coole Park to Egypt via Italy. Following further visits to picture galleries in Brussels, Frankfurt, and Munich, the couple stopped at Verona on the way to Venice. There, they viewed the Renaissance works of Raphael and Correggio. The Venice, that Ruskin so adored, left a lasting impression on Lady Gregory. On her arrival, Sir Henry greeted her in his gondola and welcomed her and her husband to his impressive palace on the Grand Canal. Lady Gregory confessed in *Seventy Years* that the visits to the Venetian palace on the Grand Canal:

> stand out in memory with their days of delight, the sight of the passing boats, the rafts from the mountain forests, the sound of the water plashing against the wall at night, the cry of 'Stali' as a gondolier turned the sharp corner from the narrow to the great canal.[49]

As Carla De Petris has noted, Lady Gregory would come to think of the palace as her 'second home'; and she would make little drawings of it in her sketchbook.[50] Ca' Capello was the base from where Sir William and Sir Henry's many art tours started. The Layards and the Gregorys went on many tours in search of masterpieces by Mantegna, Bellini, Carpaccio, Giorgione, Veronese, and Tintoretto. During the tours, Lady Gregory familiarised herself with the beautiful art works that decorated the Basilica San Marco, the churches of San Sebastiano, San Zaccaria, San Salvatore, Il Redentore, San Giorgio degli Schiavoni, and the Basilica dei Santi Giovanni e Paolo, as well as the Palazzo Ducale on St. Mark's Square. Her records from this period are no longer mere catalogues of paintings viewed but develop into critical evaluations of styles and comparisons between schools of paintings. Some art works she liked, some less so. She thought what she entitled the *Madonna with Saint* (in fact, *Madonna Enthroned with Child and Saints* or *Sacra Conversazione*) in San Zaccaria was 'a very fine Bellini', and she found Carpaccio's paintings of St. George and St. Jerome in the Scuola di San Giorgio degli Schiavoni to be 'fine compositions'.[51] However, she disliked Giorgione's painting of the pursued Daphne in the Seminario della Salute, and considered the church of Il Redentore artistically disappointing and 'not worth seeing'.[52]

Lady Gregory remembered that when she and her husband arrived in Cairo to complete their art tour, they 'tumbled into a revolution'.[53] The political situation was certainly very tense in Egypt: the country was a colony of the Ottoman Empire but the authority of the Sultan had been weakening. During the 'revolt of the Colonels', leaders of the Turkish army rebelled against the Khedive, Tewfik Pasha, and the Prime Minister, Sherif Pasha. Meanwhile, Britain was trying to assert its political and economic power in the region by extending its military control over the Suez Canal. The Khedive tried to assassinate Ahmed Arabi Bey, one of the leaders of the military revolt, but the attempt failed and it only spilled more oil (anticipating twentieth-century upheavals in the region) over the already smouldering situation. Against the backdrop of this political turmoil, Lady Gregory's artistic education continued in Egypt.[54] After attending various society events at the Ezbekiya Palace, given by the Khedive, the Sherif Pasha, and Princess Nazli Khaman, Lady Gregory and Sir William travelled out to Heliopolis to visit Wilfrid Scawen Blunt and Lady Anne Noel, granddaughter of Lord Byron. Blunt became a close—at times more than close—friend of Lady Gregory in the years that followed; his strong identification with the nationalist cause both in Egypt and in Ireland has been brought into connection with Lady Gregory's political attitudes in Ireland.[55] Records of unfolding political events blend with detailed descriptions of visits to archaeological sites and museums in her diary entries of this period. In Cairo, she saw the impressive architectural complex of the Mosque and Madassa of Sultan Hassan, the al-Azhar Mosque, and the Coptic Church of Cairo. She also went several times to the recently established Boulak Museum on the Nile to discover the cultural heritage of Ancient Egypt and to see a museum which was designed with the aim of reawakening the national sentiments of Egyptians by displaying ancient artefacts manufactured many thousand years before Egypt was colonised by the Turks. Further up the Nile, she and her husband visited the temple complexes of the Ramesseum, the Medinet Habu, Luxor, and the 'magnificent ruins' of Karnak. They then travelled on to see the other wonder of the Upper Nile region, the Valley of the Kings. What she called the 'Tombs of the Kings' was the royal burial ground for generations of Egyptian Pharaohs, including some of the most powerful and well-known, such as Tutankhamun and the Ramesseses.

She saw the extraordinary royal burial ground in the Valley of the Kings and visited some of the oldest pyramids in the world in Sakkara, the necropolis of the ancient city of Memphis. This necropolis, or burial ground, had been used by generations of Egyptian Pharaohs. Here she saw the unique step pyramid of Djoser of the third dynasty of the Old Kingdom, from the 2600s BC. The journey to these sites was tiring and she did not find the modes of travel the most comfortable, but she assiduously walked the burial grounds. In Sakkara, she was allowed to enter the secret passages hidden inside one of the pyramids to walk to the death chamber of the ruler, where his mummified body lay in an immense granite sarcophagus decorated with inscriptions. Having familiarised herself with the system of Egyptian hieroglyphs, she noted in her diary the elaborate ornamentation on the inside walls of the passages and chambers of another pyramid that she visited in Sakkara.[56] Her knowledge of Ancient Egyptian art was further deepened by the conversations that she had with Emil Brugsch, the Assistant Curator of the Boulak Museum.[57] He accompanied her on one of her visits to the Boulak in order to show her archaeological finds from the Sakkara and Theba excavation sites, where he had been given permission to take the first photographic records of Ramesses II's mummified body.

Returning from Egypt to England via France, Lady Gregory and Sir William sailed to Catania in Sicily to spend a month on the Mediterranean island.[58] In the shadow of Mount Etna, she admired the Greek and Roman amphitheatre of Taormina from the third century BC and marvelled at the Byzantine-style golden mosaics of the Cathedral in Messina and at the beauty of the small Sicilian coastal resort of Acireale. She visited the Benedictine Monastery in Catania, the most elegant and prestigious cultural centre on the island since the eighteenth century. In Agrigento (Lady Gregory refers to the place by its Sicilian name 'Girgenti') on the Southern coast, she saw an exhibition holding Egyptian antiquities, Greek coins and Etruscan vases. In Monreale, on the Northern coast, she went to see the most remarkable ecclesiastical compound of the Cathedral and the Monastery, elaborately decorated with glistening Byzantine and Venetian mosaics. In Palermo, Lady Gregory and Sir William discovered the beauty of the Saracen-style church of San Giovanni degli Eremiti, famous for its underground Christian catacombs; the Palazzo Reale, praised by art historians for the sparkling, golden Byzantine mosaics of the Cappella Palatina; and the church of Santa Caterina, prime example of the Palermitan Baroque from the seventeenth and eighteenth centuries. Walking the old streets of Syracuse and Nicosia was also on her itinerary. Besides taking notes of the major works by the Sicilian artist Antonello da Messina, she took Italian lessons to ease her communication with the islanders and to build an appropriate vocabulary for the discussion of art works. During the Sicilian tour she became intensely aware of the intertwined nature of art historical styles and periods which influenced the artists and craftsmen of the island so profoundly. Almost all of the sites that she visited in Sicily bore the marks of the successive art historical periods of the Greek, Etruscan, Roman, Muslim, Norman, Byzantine, and Venetian eras. On their way back to England, the couple stopped once again in Marseilles and in Montpellier to visit collections holding works by Ruysdael, Rubens, Willem van de Velde, and Jan Steen. While in France, the couple also attended the Parisian Salon to view the latest art works from the American Continent, including those of James McNeill Whistler, and called into the Egyptian Museum to reminisce on their stay in the North African country.

Augusta well understood what Sir William had meant when he said that an *art connoisseur* has to travel many long miles and has to endure many rough nights when she and her husband returned to Italy for another extended tour of galleries in 1884. After another short visit to the Louvre in Paris, the couple travelled on to Northern Italy, where they stopped at Como, Milan, Venice, Parma, Florence, Bologna, and Ancona. Once again, she walked the picture galleries diligently, spending her days amongst wonderful masterpieces of Italian medieval and Renaissance art and architecture.[59] She was enchanted by the 'large, solemn & impressive' Como Cathedral and by the sombre early medieval facades of San Fedele and of Sant'Abbondio, with a silk manufacturing house nearby. The paintings in the Brera Gallery, the Poldi Museum in Milan, the Pitti Gallery, the Palazzo Strozzi, and the Uffizi Museum in Florence, were by now her old friends. Her evaluations of pictures from this period are more informed, displaying the influence of her art tours of previous years. She wrote more extensively in her diaries of the works of Bellini, Bonifazio, Guido Reni, Carracci, Correggio, Parmigianino. She confessed that her favourites were the frescos of Bernardino Luini, exhibited at the Brera Gallery (especially *St. Catherine Carried to the Tomb by Angels*, c. 1520), and the oil canvases of Carpaccio (in particular, *The Presentation of the Virgin*, 1502–1505), also at the Brera Gallery.[60] Her diary entries from this period reveal her keen interest in delicately painted religious artworks.

It is in the written records of this art tour that she repeatedly refers to Ruskin. In her remarks of early Renaissance religious art she wrote very favourably of Fra Angelico, Cimabue and Giotto, painters who were held in high esteem by Ruskin. She wrote that during her visit to the Accademia in Florence, she had been taken by the reverent beauty of Cimabue's *Madonna and Child Enthroned with Angels and Prophets* (after 1285), Giotto's *Enthroned Madonna with Saints* (c. 1305–1310), and Fra Angelico's *Last Judgement* (after 1425).[61] The golden background and the style of painting reveal the Byzantine sources of the two *Madonna*s, especially in the case of Cimabue's painted wooden panel.[62] She continued to evoke Ruskin's writings in her comments on Galileo's tomb in the Santa Croce of Florence, and on the paintings in the Santa Maria Novella of Florence. She wrote about the Santa Maria Novella that 'in spite of Ruskin' the allegorical, more elaborate painterly decoration of the church and its many chapels was generally more admired than Giotto's work, but she confessed that she preferred Giotto's 'more natural and simple' style.[63] Sir Henry Layard and Sir Frederic Burton were travelling companions of the Gregorys during this tour of the arts. Lady Gregory wrote in her diary that Ruskin's rather emotional depictions of art works were much closer to her heart than Sir Henry's learned and technical observations of styles and techniques.[64]

Due to pressing art matters in London, the worsening political situation around land agitation in Ireland, and his own slowly deteriorating health, Sir William could not travel to Europe in his later years as frequently as he would have liked, but he took his wife to sample the best of Spanish art in 1887, before bidding farewell to European museums and art galleries with an extended visits to Italy the following year. So after her trip to Portugal in 1883, Lady Gregory travelled back to the Iberian Peninsula once again in 1887. While visiting Toledo, near Madrid, and the towns of Seville and Granada, in Andalusia, she remarked on the staggering beauty of the Moorish influence on Spanish architecture.[65] She was also taken with the grandiose Baroque style of the Spanish royal palace, the Escorial, near the Spanish capital. In the Prado, she studied paintings by Dürer, van Eyck, van der Weyden, Murillo, and Velázquez. Velázquez was one of Sir William's favourites: he had purchased Velázquez's *The Kitchen Scene with Marta and Mary* (1618) in a deceased sale in 1881. Sir Charles Robinson, Keeper of the Queen's Pictures and authority on Spanish art (who had authored the essay 'Bodegones and the Early Work of Velazquez' for the *Burlington Magazine for Connoisseurs*) said once to Sir William that 'all Spain boiled down to a pint pot'.[66] Sir William and Lady Gregory experienced this when they were travelling around the country with Sir Clare Ford. Sir Clare, the newly appointed British Ambassador to Spain whom Lady Gregory called simply 'an artist' for he 'was out sketching' often, was greatly bothered by the ceremonies of politics.[67]

Lady Gregory's and her husband's farewell tour of museums and art galleries of 1888 took them to the usual places, including Bergamo, Milan, Ferrara, Florence, Orvieto, Rome, the Vatican, Pompeii, and Palermo.[68] By this time, Lady Gregory was no longer a novice in art matters but a *connoisseur* of the major schools, art historical periods, and scholarly trends. In addition to the Continental tours, her development as *connoisseur* continued in Victorian England. Lady Gregory's weekly routine consisted of visits to the Royal Academy, the National Gallery, the British Museum, the South Kensington Museum, the Arundel Society, the Natural History Museum, and Christie's. She was invited to various private viewings held at public museums and private art collections. When not accompanying her husband to a museum or gallery, she took to accompanying groups of children to exhibitions.[69] Completing her artistic education, Lady Gregory took up classes in Heatherley's studio in Newman Street, London, in 1890. Heatherley's was a prestigious art institute where she studied the application of colours, the use of light and shade, and the methods of perspective.[70] Heatherley's was one of the most sought-after drawing studios, where some of the greatest Victorian artists learned to perfect their art, including Dante Gabriel Rossetti, John Everett Millais, Edward Burne-Jones, and Edward Poynter. The studio was not simply the location at which Lady Gregory studied the principles of artistic expression but was a place where she widened her social circle. John B. Yeats did so when he enrolled in it after moving to London in the late 1880s, writes art critic Karen E. Brown.[71]

During the Continental art trips, Lady Gregory was keen to take time to sketch some of the buildings and sites that she visited. She found it a useful practice as it helped her remember the places, and painting allowed her to find an artistic expression for the variety of aesthetic impressions that she was gathering during the trips. There can be little doubt, however, that the practice of sitting down and sketching also alleviated the burden of endless walking around various sites and museums. Melita Cataldi has argued that these sketches should be regarded as the first artistic examples of Lady Gregory's reflection on European art.[72] The sketchbooks that she kept provide a pictorial record of the journeys, depicting scenes from Italy, England, and Ireland. The sketchbooks suggest that she was closely following the principle of 'live painting', a practice that Ruskin recommended in his manual *The Elements of Drawing* (1857).[73] Mary Gartside's *An Essay on Light and Shade on Colours and on Composition in General* (first published in 1805), T. H. Fielding's *Manual of Colours used in the Different Branches of Watercolour Painting* (1844), Samuel Prout's *The Rudiments of Landscape, in Progressive Studies, Drawn and Etched in Imitation of Chalk* (1813), Aaron Penley's *The English School of Painting in Water-colours* (1861), and Ruskin's *The Elements of Drawing*, were some of the most influential art manuals teaching techniques of landscape painting and still life. These manuals recommended women to take up watercolour painting, as its technique was easier to learn than that of oil painting and the kit was smaller and lighter to carry, suiting the fashionable idea of 'live painting' better. Lady Gregory's sketchbooks attest that she followed the London fashion, recording impressions of scenes as watercolours during the European trips. She was, in fact, so skilful that Sir William gladly reported to Sir Henry of the discovery of a new Italian-born painter: 'If you hear of a new painter called Augusta dei Sepoteri extolled in the Italian newspaper, you may guess who it is [...].'[74]

Besides providing a break from museum visits, the drawing classes at Heatherley's were also a form of schooling in social etiquette. Jan Marsh has pointed out that 'artistic skill in women was actively encouraged as a mark of class status'.[75] Bernard Denvir notes that by the mid-nineteenth century the 'interest in art had reached epidemic proportions', dominating London society conversations.[76] Kate Flint has underlined the importance of this artistic education, stating that having an 'opinion on artistic matters was increasingly an indication of one's achieved status'.[77] In fact, interest in art amongst women, not only among the gentility, had been growing steadily throughout the Victorian period. Lady Elizabeth Eastlake, Lady Emilia Dilke, Anna Jameson, Vernon Lee (Violet Paget), and Mrs Russell Barrington (Emilie Isabel Wilson) distinguished themselves as art critics; Hilary Fraser writes about a keen interest among women with regard to writing art history.[78] Art and travel books, authored or illustrated by women like Mariana Starke, had increased significantly in popularity.[79] Francina Irwin has noted that amateur women painters 'often chose to have their portraits painted holding a crayon or a brush, pointing to a sketch they had done, thereby demonstrating the importance of their artistic activities in their lives'.[80] Lady Gregory's decision to continue with the *Grand Tours* after the birth of her son pointed to this shift in the perceived roles of women among the educated classes. She may have felt resentment and regret at the early separation from her baby, as Judith Hill suggests, but her education in art matters had to continue if she expected to become a respected and influential member of cultivated high-class Victorian society and was to contribute to the aristocratic table talk in London.[81] Borrowing a line from Oscar Wilde, Lucy McDiarmid has astutely observed that Lady Gregory thoroughly 'understood the importance of dominating a London dinner table'.[82]

Art, Empire, and Critical Debates

The extent to which Lady Gregory and her husband were immersed in the visual arts signifies the profound importance of painting, drawing, and sculpture to Victorian English society among the ruling *élite*. Robert Hewison draws attention to the fact that, in conjunction with the growing interest in the arts, 'there was a rapid expansion in demand for visual imagery of all kinds'.[83] This growing interest in the visual arts in Britain and Continental Europe during the nineteenth century originated largely from Napoleon's obsession with amassing art works from territories that his troops had conquered. Napoleon's aim of filling the rooms of the Palais du Louvre (renamed as Musée Napoleon) with war booty from Italy initiated a general movement of Italian, French, and German art works across the European Continent. He transported invaluable paintings and statues to Paris in what can only be described as Roman triumphal processions.[84] Furthermore, due to French penal laws, the Italian nobility was forced to sell many works held in Italian *palazzos* to French officers.[85] After Napoleon's defeat and the dissolution of the Musée Napoleon, art works were put up for sale as some Italian families could not finance the return of their pictures and statues.[86] Prior to this, during the course of the French Revolution, the Orleans sale of 1792 that consisted of a fine collection of Italian and Northern paintings added to the artistic possession of the English nobility. In 1792, Louis Philippe Joseph of the Orleans branch sold his collection, and many of the paintings went into the hands of private English collectors. For the first time, English aristocrats were able to decorate their homes in the same style as that of the Italian nobility.[87] The selling of Napoleon's and his officers' war booty and the Orleans sale instigated a desire among British aristocrats to own homes decorated with works of fine art. So it happened that, as prominent members of the British establishment, Sir William's forefathers embellished the walls of Coole with valuable paintings by Italian masters and French artists. The acquisition of the bust of the Italian patron of arts Maecenas, from Italy, to decorate the grounds of Coole Park, underlined such aspirations. This is the context from which Coole Park came to acquire such importance not just to Yeats in later years, but to the host of other Irish writers, dramatists and painters who came to stay there, including George Russell (Æ), John Millington Synge, George Bernard Shaw, Sean O'Casey, and Lennox Robinson.

The art trade that emerged between English collectors and Continental European art dealers reached its climax during the Victorian era. As a result of the increasing activity in art trade among European countries throughout the nineteenth century, critics began to undertake the creation of a canon of art. Art works were assessed in relation to each other on the basis of the quality of workmanship, the originality of composition, and their significance in the given historical period. Based on the result of such investigations, a hierarchy was established among the artists. 'Scientific' canonisation of the fine arts, effectively undertaken by German art historians such as Johann Joachim Winckelmann and Gotthold Ephraim Lessing during the eighteenth century, not only led to the rediscovery and reappraisal of certain artists but also helped art dealers in their assessment of the value of art works. In England, the process of canonisation was continued by influential university professors and art critics, such as John Ruskin or Walter Pater, and by members and professors of the Royal Academy of Arts, such as John Constable, William Powell Firth, Charles Eastlake (who had studied at the Musée Napoleon), John Everett Millais, and Edward John Poynter. Over time, their words and thoughts came to be regarded as the most credible sources upon which to base the most enduring value of an art work. Sir William himself had helped to enrich the process by drawing attention to a particular artist's work or to a particular period of art in the course of parliamentary debates on the finances and the new acquisitions of the National Gallery in London. The high quality of Lady Gregory's own artistic education comes to light in this context, in that she learned the rules of painting in a studio frequented by members of the Royal Academy of Arts, and in the fact that she learned the art of painting favoured by the so-called Academic School. This school demanded care and precision in the handling of the artistic subject matter.

Napoleon's wars, the canonisation of art, and the opening-up of the art market generated intense and wide-ranging interest in the fine arts in Britain during the nineteenth century. All leading museums and galleries enriched their collections with invaluable art works and archaeological finds. The British Museum, for instance, acquired the Rosetta Stone (known for its significance in recording Ancient Egyptian history and language) and the bust of the Egyptian Pharaoh Ramesses II, from the Ramesseum in Thebes, along the River Nile. These acquisitions were taken from the French army's North African war booty, following their capitulation to British troops at Alexandria in 1801. Adding further to Britain's imperial status, the British Museum came to acquire works by the Greek master Phidias (including some of his sculptures from the Acropolis in Athens) following intense negotiations between the British Parliament, the British Museum, and former British ambassador to Greece Lord Elgin. These artefacts were put on public display almost immediately after acquisition, sparking widespread interest in ancient cultures. Stemming from a certain romantic nostalgia and appreciation of the past, the Gothic Revival brought Italian *trecento* artists (the so-called *Primitives*) into the limelight. The Oxford Movement, the Pre-Raphaelite Brotherhood, the impressive buildings of British architect Augustus Welby Pugin, and the writings of John Ruskin were culminations of this interest in the Middle Ages. Walter Pater and his circle successfully drew attention to the works of Botticelli, Michelangelo, and Giorgione. Proponents of the Hellenic Revival, Pater and his university friends incited a renewal of interest in the works of Raphael, Michelangelo, and Leonardo da Vinci. At the same time, Florentine and Venetian art works of the late Renaissance period became increasingly popular, including the works of Botticelli, Bellini, Tintoretto, and Titian. Following aggressive purchasing campaigns, the National Gallery amassed a series of paintings by these and lesser known artists, in addition to pictures by masters from the Low Countries, such as those of van Eyck and van der Weyden. Baroque art had become highly regarded by the end of the century (partly as a result of Sir William's sustained efforts), which was heralded by increasing interest in the works of two of his favourite artists, Murillo and Velázquez.[88]

Sir William was famous for his efforts to enrich the collections of London's National Gallery. He fought for the acquisition of the Peel Collection because he knew that this would make the Gallery strong in the Dutch School. He reasoned that the Gallery would have to spend its annual grant or it would be withdrawn and any unspent balance returned to the government.[89] As Director at the time, Sir William Boxall voiced concerns regarding financing. A new director, Sir Frederic Burton, was appointed upon Sir William's recommendation. Sir Frederic was a fellow Anglo-Irishman, member of the Arundel Society and of the Council of the Royal Irish Academy, and founding member of the Irish Archaeological Society. As artist and antiquarian, Sir Frederic supported Sir William's proposal to enrich the collection with works by Botticelli and Jean-Antoine Watteau.[90] Added to this, Sir William was often in direct conflict with the British government regarding financing the Gallery. He protested personally to Prime Minister Benjamin Disraeli, which resulted in the award of a Government Grant to the National Gallery in 1879. Later, he protested to Prime Minister William Gladstone (following the controversy over the purchase of the Blenheim pictures), which resulted in the re-establishment of the Government Grant in 1889.[91]

The question of whether or not it was worth paying high amounts for collections of paintings was part of a more general public debate around the social function of art. Ruskin was of the view that the expression of moral truth was the essence of a great work of art; hence his appraisal of *trecento* frescos and altarpieces, most prominently those of Cimabue,

Fra Angelico, and Giotto. He insisted that art was to be the 'devoted fulfilment of moral duty' which revealed 'the real God, though darkly'.[92] As church attendance had been in decline in England, he hoped that a growing interest in didactic, religious painting would reawaken an interest in religious values at a time when the profit motive and private interest dominated social relations. He praised *trecento* paintings for their capacity to elevate the soul, a quality he found missing in Hellenic art. Greek artists, in his view, 'could not conceive a spirit', as 'the entire Greek intellect, as compared to mediaeval intellect, was in a childish phase'.[93] His viewpoint lay in stark contrast to that of Pater, who praised Hellenism for its desire for beauty, rationality, blitheness, and repose.[94] At the beginning of his career, Ruskin considered Greek art a product of a childish phase of human history, only capable of producing representations of worldly Gods whom he regarded as 'finite' entities compared to the 'infinite' God of the Middle Ages.[95] As George Landow puts it, Ruskin conceived of beauty as the representation of divine nature and moral truths.[96] Sir William himself speculated on the possibility of using *trecento* paintings in devotional teaching because of the morality inherent in the works. He explained in his essay *Arundel Society* (1884/1887) that frescos from this period represented either a 'Scriptural story, a sacred legend, or an allegory inculcating the excellence of virtue'.[97] Both Ruskin and Sir William saw moral instruction as the main purpose of *trecento* art, a didactic attitude that made its mark on the early work of the Pre-Raphaelite Brotherhood, founded in 1848. Writing in defence of the Brotherhood in 1851, Ruskin considered their work worthy of praise for their intention to convey moral truths, something he thought lacking in the art of his contemporaries. Indeed, in 'Pre-Raphaelitism', a lecture delivered on 18 November 1853, he argued that art had lately lost its sight of its moral purpose, seeking instead to represent beauty and pleasure only.[98]

Such was the measure of Ruskin's influence on Victorian art and social criticism that during his 'Ten O'Clock Lecture' the US painter and essayist James McNeill Whistler felt it necessary to condemn his times as one in which, under Ruskin's influence, 'art has become foolishly confounded with education'.[99] Aimed at diverting his audience away from Ruskinian art criticism and its demand for a moral and social purpose to artworks, he suggested that the worthiness of a picture should be evaluated purely on the basis of the painter's poetry and not according to the 'noble philosophy in some detail of philanthropy, courage, modesty, or virtue'.[100] Whistler held that art had always existed quite simply as a natural product of the artist's imagination, and had been born out of the artist's pride to please himself. Robin Spencer has noted the influence of Théophile Gautier and Algernon Swinburne on Whistler's rejection of 'the explicit moralising of much Victorian art'.[101] Swinburne had formulated his art theory in his essay on William Blake in 1868, rejecting the idea that art should concern itself with 'moral, didactic, or religious ends'.[102] Alastair Grieve has remarked that Gautier's preface to *Mademoiselle de Maupin* (1835) had demonstrated a 'total lack of concern for Christian morality in favour of the pursuit of beauty for its own sake'.[103] This view was later disseminated by Pater, who frequented Swinburne's circles between 1868 and 1870. In the 'Conclusion' to the 1868 edition of *The Renaissance: Studies in Art and Poetry*, Pater voiced his belief in the 'love of art for its own sake', the appreciation of art independent of moral considerations.[104] Pater refused to accept the view that an artist ought to possess a desire to partake in a social or a moral mission. Swinburne, Whistler, and Pater set the artist apart from society, one who was to create beautiful objects solely for his own delight. Graham Hough observes that, in this regard, Whistler's rather elitist approach was anchored in French *fin-de-siècle* attitudes which the painter had encountered during his stay in Paris in the 1880s. 'Whistler became deeply imbued with the notion of artists as a class set apart', writes Hough, 'whose standards and aspirations were outside the comprehension of the vulgar'.[105] Whistler thus came to regard the task of an artist as that of capturing the ethereal moments of a world, described by Pater in his 'Conclusion' as 'unstable', 'flickering', and 'inconsistent'.[106]

The debate about the social function of the arts and the artist came to the fore during the 1880s, following the infamous Ruskin versus Whistler libel case of 1878. Whistler sued Ruskin for criticising his work and affecting its financial value in consequence, in what was the most high-profile court case of the period prior to Oscar Wilde's trials in 1895. Ruskin's argument, formulated in *Fors Clavigera* in July 1877, that Whistler's *Nocturne in Black and Gold—The Falling Rocket* was not worthy of its asking price at the Grosvenor Gallery, was proven right in the court case. Nevertheless, the jury's verdict was for the plaintiff.[107] The one farthing conferred for the assessed damages (instead of the thousand pounds that the plaintiff demanded) showed that the court deliberately diminished the seriousness of the crime. Still, Whistler heralded the court's decision as a clear vindication of his attitudes and he went on to promote his ideas more stridently. Following the court case,

Whistler took up a lecture tour of London, Oxford, and Cambridge, and Ruskin resigned his Slade Professorship of Art. Although the court case centred round one painting, the debate that ensued developed into a more general discussion of the social value of the visual arts. All London artists and art critics contributed to the discussion, including William Rossetti, Albert Moore, Edward Burne-Jones, William Powell Firth, Tom Taylor, William Morris, and, later, George Bernard Shaw.

These discussions were ongoing while Sir William and Lady Gregory were travelling around the European Continent. During the travels, Lady Gregory amassed an extensive knowledge of art history, gaining appreciation of the artistic legacy of European and Middle-Eastern antiquity and why it held such stature in the modern era. She familiarised herself with the characteristic features of European painters, sculptors, and architects. Travelling around the world, the cultural diversity of the largest empires—the Ottoman and the British—opened up to her, as she visited sites in Turkey, Egypt, and India. In the process, she became more acutely aware of the cultural significance of her own home at Coole Park in Co. Galway. She became an amateur painter in order to record the variety of experiences that she was amassing in her travels around the world and in Ireland. She made good use of her talent and her knowledge of art and art history in the artistic and aristocratic circles of Victorian England, where she also learned to familiarise herself with the many contesting views regarding the value of art, the function of art in society and the role of the artist in social formation. Her observations after a visit to the Jean-François Millet exhibition, held at the Musée des Beaux Arts in Paris in May 1887, are telling as regards her own views on these contemporary debates:

> [D]rawing and painting most beautiful—all simple subjects, labourers and their wives at work in the field, or in cottage homes, a girl feeding poultry, very graceful. The 'Angelus' a working man and woman bowing their heads in the sunset to say a prayer—most exquisite. We met E. Martyn and he going there. Then to the Salon—what a contrast! Nudity and horrors and scene painting throughout.[108]

Millet's idyllic rural genre paintings are contrasted here with the larger-scale, sensual, and historical canvases on display at the Salon in Paris. Her observations on the beauty of the picturesque rural landscape, depicted at a moment of religious reflection, and the aversion that she felt towards the more visceral artistic representations, are telling as regards her views on the function and value of the arts. This is very significant to understanding her role and her influence in the Irish Revival from the 1890s. Her reaction here indicates the extent to which she had, by temperament and by education, interiorised Ruskin's artistic and aesthetic principles. These principles regarding art and the artist turned into guiding threads as she began to involve herself in the cultural and literary renaissance developing in the British Isles.

NOTES

1. Lady Augusta Gregory, *Seventy Years* (Gerrards Cross: Colin Smythe, 1974), 16.
2. Judith Hill, *Lady Gregory: An Irish Life* (Stroud: Sutton, 2005), 15.
3. Qtd. in Brian Jenkins, "The Marriage," in *Lady Gregory, Fifty Years After*, ed. Ann Saddlemyer and Colin Smythe (Gerrards Cross: Colin Smythe, 1987), 75.
4. George Eliot, *Middlemarch* (Oxford: Oxford University Press, 1998), 176–211. Kohfeldt, Pethica and Hill observe that, later in her life, Lady Gregory fancied herself to some extent as Dorothea of Eliot's *Middlemarch*, remarking that she was reading Eliot's famous book during her courtship with Sir William. Mary Lou Kohfeldt Stevenson, "The Cloud of Witnesses," in *Lady Gregory, Fifty Years After*, ed. Ann Saddlemyer and Colin Smythe (Gerrards Cross: Colin Smythe, 1987), 69; James Pethica, ed. *Lady Gregory's Diaries, 1892–1902* (Gerrards Cross: Colin Smythe, 1996) xii; Hill, *Lady Gregory*, 25. Significant for the present consideration is Eliot's long-standing interest in the visual arts, her knowledge of contemporary aesthetic theory and her discipleship of John Ruskin. Eliot was a lifelong friend of Sir Frederic Burton of the National Gallery, London.
5. Mary Lou Kohfeldt, *Lady Gregory, the Woman Behind the Irish Literary Renaissance* (London: Deutsch, 1984), 276. On this matter, Kohfeldt quotes one of Lady Gregory's letters to John Quinn. Lady Gregory's finished manuscript was rejected by publisher Constant Huntington on the grounds that her memoirs dealt extensively with her life and acquaintances in London but revealed little about the Irish Literary Revival. Huntington failed to realise the importance Lady Gregory attributed to those early formative years. For the debate around the possible publication of the memoirs, see Colin Smythe, "Foreword," in Lady Augusta Gregory, *Seventy Years, Being the Autobiography of Lady Gregory* (Gerrards Cross: Colin Smythe, 1973), vii–ix.

6. Brian Jenkins, *Sir William Gregory of Coole: The Biography of an Anglo-Irishman* (Gerrards Cross: Colin Smythe, 1986), 205.
7. Gregory, *Seventy Years*, 142.
8. For the Gregorys' tradition of collecting, see Jenkins, *Sir William Gregory of Coole*, 206.
9. Jenkins, *Sir William Gregory of Coole*, 206. Sir William and John Ruskin were fellow students at Christ Church, Oxford.
10. Lady Augusta Gregory, *Coole* (Dublin: Cuala Press, 1931), 5.
11. Colin Smythe, *A Guide to Coole Park, Co. Galway, Home of Lady Gregory* (Gerrards Cross: Colin Smythe, 1973), 24. Smythe quotes a guest who remarked that the walls of the Breakfast Room were "lined with prints, engravings and lithographs—portraits of friends of the Gregory family since 1768 when they first came to Coole." Among the paintings were the portraits of Robert Peel and Lord Melbourne as well as the engravings of Reynolds's portrait of Edmund Burke. Jenkins notes that Sir William, an admirer of Robert Peel, was "the proud owner of a large collection of masterpieces." Jenkins, *Sir William Gregory of Coole*, 206.
12. Gregory, *Coole*, 14. See also *Catalogue of Printed Books formerly in the Library at Coole, the Property of the Lady Gregory Estate—Sotheby Auction Catalogue for 20 and 21 March 1972* (London: Sotheby and Co., 1972), 49, 53, 63.
13. Lady Augusta Gregory, *Hugh Lane* (Gerrards Cross: Colin Smythe, 1973), 116.
14. Sir William quoted in Jenkins, *Sir William Gregory of Coole* 205. Jenkins notes that the Gallery had a reasonable representation of European and English art, including works by Hogarth, Reynolds, Gainsborough, and Turner.
15. Jenkins, *Sir William Gregory of Coole*, 205. Sir William opposed the removal of the natural history collections at Bloomsbury to Kensington for the same reasons. See Jenkins, *Sir William Gregory of Coole*, 201.
16. For the Gallery of Modern Art as an educational project, see Lady Augusta Gregory, *Hugh Lane* (Gerrards Cross: Colin Smythe, 1973), 53.
17. John Ruskin, *The Guild and Museum of St. George*, in *The Works of John Ruskin*, ed. E. T. Cook and Alexander Wedderburn, vol. 30 (London: George Allen, 1903–1912), l–li. Further references to Cook and Wedderburn's multivolume work will be as follows: Ruskin, *Title of Individual Work*, volume number.page number. Example here: Ruskin, *The Guild and Museum of St. George*, 30.1 li.
18. Ruskin, *Time and Tide*, 17.316.
19. For more on his ideas, see Ruskin, *The Guild and Museum of St. George*, 30.5 and 30.53.

20. Sir William Gregory, *Arundel Society*, Pamphlet, May 1887, reprinted from *The Nineteenth Century*, April 1884, 5. Gregory Family Papers, Special Collections and Archives Division, Robert W. Woodruff Library, Emory University, Atlanta, GA.
21. Gregory, *Arundel Society*, 30.
22. Gregory, *Seventy Years*, 141. Sir Joseph Edgar Boehm was born in the Austro-Hungarian Monarchy, in Vienna, of Hungarian parentage. After studying in Vienna, Italy and Paris, he settled in England. He became a British citizen and a celebrated artist. He worked for the Royal Family; it was he who sculpted the marble statue of Queen Victoria at Windsor Castle. He became member of the Royal Academy in 1882.
23. For the first part of the Italian journey, see diary entries between 18 and March 30, 1880. *Lady Gregory's Holograph Diary, 1880–1882*. Gregory Family Papers, Special Collections and Archives Division, Robert W. Woodruff Library, Emory University, Atlanta, GA.
24. Ruskin, *Poems*, 2.233; *Modern Painters*, vol. 2, 4.xxx–xxxi.
25. Diary entry, March 29, 1880, Emory.
26. Ruskin, *Giotto and his Works in Padua*, 24.28. Ruskin writes: "Giotto was not indeed one of the most accomplished painters, but he was one of the greatest men who ever lived. He was the first master of his time, in architecture as well as in painting; he was the friend of Dante, and the undisputed interpreter of religious truth, by means of painting, over the whole of Italy. The works of such a man may not be the best to set before children in order to teach them drawing; but they assuredly should be studied with the greatest care by all who are interested in the history of the human mind."
27. Ruskin, "The Schools of Art in Florence; Lecture II: Cimabue," 23.207.
28. Ruskin, "The Schools of Art in Florence," 23.208. For Ruskin's evaluation of Giotto, see Ruskin, *Giotto and his Works in Padua*, 24.13–11; appendix 24.113–23; "Lecture on Cimabue" (1874) in "The Aesthetic and Mathematic School of Art in Florence," 23.197–209; and Ruskin, *A Joy Forever*, 16.75. Lady Gregory refers to these paintings as 'Poverty', 'Chastity', 'Obedience', and 'St. Francis surrounded by angels'. She was taken with the Taddeo Gaddi's and Cimabue's works, mentioned also by Ruskin in his Oxford lecture on Cimabue. Diary entry, March 29, 1880, Emory.
29. Ruskin owed his knowledge of Giotto's work to Sir Henry Layard. See Ruskin, *A Joy Forever*, 16.75.
30. Diary entries between March 31 and April 22, 1880, Emory.
31. Diary entry, April 13, 1880, Emory.
32. Diary entries between April 22 and May 7, 1880, Emory.
33. Diary entry, April 29, 1880, Emory.

34. Gregory, *Seventy Years*, 32.
35. The gold funeral mask attributed to Agamemnon, commander-in-chief of the Greeks during the Trojan War, was excavated by Schliemann near Mycenae in 1876. The attribution has been questioned since, but in 1880 the mask was considered to be one of the most significant archaeological finds. If, in Lady Gregory's words, Layard was 'the man who made the Bible true', then Schliemann's excavations made Homer's epic narration of the Trojan War believable. Agamemnon is a principal figure of Homer's *Iliad*, narrating the final stages of the Trojan War, and appears in Homer's *Odyssey*.
36. Ruskin, *Bibliotheca Pastorum*, 31.22.
37. Ruskin, *Modern Painters*, vol. 2, 4.118.
38. Michael R. Booth, *Victorian Spectacular Theatre, 1850–1910* (London: Routledge, 1981), 19.
39. Gregory, *Seventy Years*, 155. Gregory refers here to the 'Sweet Waters of Asia', a popular travel destination for the Ottoman and the Euroepan social *élite*, situated not far from Constantinople. For some of the Gregorys' trips around Constantinople, see diary entries for May 16 and 18, 1880, *Lady Layard's Journals*, Baylor University, Texas, http://www.browningguide.org/browningcircle.php.
40. G. R. Berrige, *British Diplomacy in Turkey, 1853 to the Present: A Study in the Evolution of the Resident Embassy* (Leiden: Martinus Nijhoff, 2009), 25.
41. Gregory, *Seventy Years*, 155.
42. Diary entry, May 13, 1880, Emory.
43. Diary entry, May 29, 1880, Emory.
44. Diary entry, June 17, 1880, Emory. The collection of sculpture, inscriptions, and architectural pieces were subsequently bought by the British Parliament and were presented to the British Museum.
45. Diary entries between June 16 and 26, 1880, Emory.
46. Diary entries between July 26 and August 23, 1881, Emory.
47. For Rossetti and Hunt's journey to France and Belgium in 1848 and the influence of Flemish painting on their art, see Graham Hough, *The Last Romantics* (London: Duckworth, 1983), 58–59. The Pre-Raphaelites borrowed the pictorial devices of mirrors and windows from Memling's *Virgin and Child* and van Eyck's *The Arnolfini Wedding*. The device was used to open up enclosed spaces in Hunt's *The Awakening Conscience*, *Fanny Homan Hunt*, *Il Dolce Far Niente* and *The Lady of Shalott*. See George P. Landow, *William Holman Hunt and Typological Symbolism* (New Haven: Yale University Press, 1979), 87 and Chapter 3.
48. Diary entries between October 28 and November 11, 1881, Emory.
49. Gregory, *Seventy Years*, 171.

50. Carla De Petris, "Lady Gregory and Italy: A Lasting and Profitable Relationship," 34, no. 1 (Spring/Summer 2004): 38. Here De Petris relies on Lady Gregory's own comments on Ca' Capello in *Seventy Years*. Gregory, *Seventy Years*, 285.
51. For Bellini's painting, see diary entry, November 2, 1881; for Carpaccio's, see diary entry, November 4, 1881, Emory.
52. For Giorgione's work, see diary entry, November 4, 1881; for the comments on Il Redentore, see diary entry, November 10, 1881, Emory.
53. Gregory, *Seventy Years*, 34.
54. Diary entries between December 17, 1881 and April 1, 1882, Emory.
55. See, for instance, Elizabeth Longford, "Lady Gregory and Wilfrid Scawen Blunt," in *Lady Gregory, Fifty Years After*, ed. Ann Saddlemyer and Colin Smythe (Gerrards Cross: Colin Smythe, 1987), 85–97; and Declan Kiberd, *Inventing Ireland* (London: Cape, 1995), 83–95.
56. Diary entry, November 26, 1881, Emory.
57. Diary entry, December 5, 1881, Emory.
58. Diary entries between April 1 and May 9, 1882, Emory.
59. Diary entries between October 10 and November 14, 1884. Lady Augusta Gregory, *Typewritten Diaries, 1882–1892*, Lady Augusta Gregory Papers, Albert A. and Henry W. Berg Collection, New York Public Library, New York.
60. Diary entries, October 13 and 16, 1884, Berg.
61. Diary entry, November 7, 1884, Berg.
62. Ingo F. Walther, ed. *Masterpieces of Western Art* (Köln: Taschen, 2002), 28–29.
63. Diary entry, November 8, 1884, Berg.
64. Diary entry, November 8, 1884, Berg.
65. Gregory, *Seventy Years*, 93.
66. Gregory, *Seventy Years*, 93.
67. Gregory, *Seventy Years*, 93–94.
68. Diary entries for the period between January and May 1888, Berg. Lady Gregory often writes of drawing or painting at various art historically significant sites, such as the Sta Maria del Popolo, the Sta Maria Maggiore or the Medici Gardens, suggesting that she was practicing 'live painting' as she travelled through Italy.
69. Diary entries, June 5, 12, and 18, 1886, Berg. Lady Gregory remarked in her diary: "Exhibition with 18 little boys," "Exhibition with 17 boys" and "19 boys to Ex."
70. Judith Hill, *Lady Gregory: An Irish Life* (Stroud: Sutton, 2005), 78.
71. Karen E. Brown, *The Yeats Circle: Verbal and Visual Relations in Ireland, 1880–1939* (Farnham: Ashgate, 2011), 9.

72. Melita Cataldi, "Lady Gregory's Sketchbooks," in *Roots and Beginnings*, ed. Pietro Deandrea and Viktoria Tchernikova (Venezia: Cafoscarina, 2003), 303–16.
73. Lady Augusta Gregory, *Sketchbooks*, 3032 TX-3039 TX, Prints and Drawings Collection, National Library of Ireland, Dublin.
74. Qtd. in Cataldi, "Lady Gregory's Sketchbooks," 311.
75. Jan Marsh, "Art, Ambition and Sisterhood in the 1850s," in *Women in the Victorian Art World*, ed. Clarissa Campbell Orr (Manchester: Manchester University Press, 1995), 37.
76. Bernard Denvir, *The Late Victorians: Art, Design and Society 1852–1910* (London: Longmans, 1986), 1.
77. Kate Flint, *The Victorians and the Victorian Imagination* (Cambridge: Cambridge University Press, 2000), 178.
78. Flint, *The Victorians and the Victorian Imagination*, 193; Hilary Fraser, *Women Writing Art History in the Nineteenth Century: Looking Like a Woman* (Cambridge: Cambridge University Press, 2014).
79. Francis Haskell, *Rediscoveries in Art* (London: Phaidon, 1980), 169–71; Francina Irwin, "Amusement or instruction? Watercolour manuals and the women amateur," in *Women in the Victorian Art World*, ed. Clarissa Campbell Orr (Manchester: Manchester University Press, 1995), 164–65.
80. Irwin, "Amusement or instruction?," 150.
81. Hill, *Lady Gregory*, 34–37. Hill has suggested that Lady Gregory had travelled *primarily* to please her husband. Of course, it is reasonable to expect resentment and regret at the separation from her child Robert, as sketches of a baby on the margin of her diary suggest. Nonetheless, a distinct voice of maternal longing is notably absent from Lady Gregory's diaries. Hill translates this silence as 'extreme reticence' on the maternal matter, coming from a desire not to displease her husband. This may be true, but it also assumes that the young woman did not herself relish the glamour of touring Continental galleries; that Lady Gregory may have actually enjoyed discovering a world of art and culture that was new to her.
82. Lucy McDiarmid, "Oscar Wilde, Lady Gregory, and Late Victorian Table-Talk," in *Oscar Wilde and Modern Culture: The Making of a Legend*, ed. Joseph Bristow (Athens, OH: Ohio University Press, 2009), 49. See also Lucy McDiarmid, "Lady Gregory, Wilfrid Blunt and London Table Talk," *Irish University Review* 34, no. 1 (Spring/Summer 2004): 67–80; and Lucy McDiarmid on table talk in *Poets and the Peacock Dinner: The Literary History of a Meal* (Oxford: Oxford University Press, 2014).
83. Robert Hewison, Ian Warrell, and Stephen Wildman, *Ruskin, Turner and the Pre-Raphaelites* (London: Tate Gallery, 2000), 11.

84. Niels von Holst, *Creators, Collectors and Connoisseurs* (London: Thames, 1967), 217.
85. Haskell, *Rediscoveries in Art*, 54–55.
86. von Holst, *Creators, Collectors and Connoisseurs*, 229.
87. Haskell, *Rediscoveries in Art*, 44.
88. Nineteenth-century interests in art are best described in von Holst's *Creators, Collectors and Connoisseurs*, 215–71 and Flint, *The Victorians and the Victorian Imagination*, 190.
89. Jenkins, *Sir William Gregory of Coole*, 208.
90. Jenkins, *Sir William Gregory of Coole*, 253–54.
91. Jenkins, *Sir William Gregory of Coole*, 272–73.
92. Ruskin, *Modern Painters*, vol. 2, 4.329.
93. For the Greek's inability to conceive a spirit, see Ruskin *Modern Painters*, vol. 2, 4.329; for Greek art belonging to a childish phase, see Ruskin, "Greek and Christian Art," 20.405 and 403–6.
94. Walter Pater, *The Renaissance*, ed. Donald L. Hill (Berkeley: University of California Press, 1980), 181.
95. Ruskin, *Modern Painters*, vol. 2, 4.329.
96. George Landow, *The Aesthetic and the Critical Theories of John Ruskin* (Princeton: Princeton University Press, 1971), 148.
97. Gregory, *Arundel Society*, 11.
98. Ruskin, "Pre-Raphaelitism," 12.145. See also Ruskin's pamphlet of the same title 'Pre-Raphaelitism' (1851) for the same views on the necessity of didacticism in art. Ruskin, "Pre-Raphaelitism," 12.348.
99. James McNeill Whistler, *The Gentle Art of Making Enemies* (London: Heinemann, 1919), 150.
100. Whistler, *The Gentle Art of Making Enemies*, 147.
101. Robin Spencer, "Whistler, Swinburne and art for art's sake," in *After the Pre-Raphaelites*, ed. Elizabeth Prettejohn (Manchester: Manchester University Press, 1999), 60.
102. Donald L. Hill, "Critical and Explanatory Notes," in Walter Pater, *The Renaissance*, ed. Donald L. Hill (Berkeley: University of California Press, 1980), 458.
103. Alastair Grieve, "Rossetti and the scandal of art for art's sake in the 1860s," in *After the Pre-Raphaelites*, ed. Elizabeth Prettejohn (Manchester: Manchester University Press, 1999), 17; Hill, "Critical and Explanatory Notes," 458. Grieve translates from Théophile Gautier's *Mademoiselle de Maupin* (Paris: Garnier-Flammarion, 1966), 45–46.
104. Pater, *The Renaissance*, 190; see also 189. The book's conclusion was edited out of second edition for fear of causing offence, but was re-included in the third edition in 1888, only a few years after Whistler's lecture.

105. Hough, *The Last Romantics*, 178.
106. Pater, *The Renaissance*, 187.
107. Stanley Weintraub, *Whistler: A Biography* (London: Collins, 1974), 215. For more on the trial, see Derrick Leon, *Ruskin, the Great Victorian* (London: Routledge, 1949), 518–30; Roy McMullan, *Victorian Outsider: A Biography of J. A. M. Whistler* (New York: Macmillan, 1973), 182–93; Weintraub, *Whistler*, 194–216.
108. Diary entry, May 14, 1887, Berg.

'The "whorl" of Troy': Celtic Mythology, Victorian Hellenism, and the Irish Literary Revival

UNEARTHING THE PAST

Lady Gregory remained an illustrious member of the London Victorian art world after Sir William's death in 1892. She dined with her late husband's old friends, attended private and public viewings of prestigious art exhibitions, and had classes at Heatherley's Art School in Newman Street. She socialised with Sir Henry Layard, Sir Frederic Burton, Sir Alfred Lyall, Sir Charles Robinson, Martin Colnaghi, and George Frederic Watts. By way of keeping her late husband's memory alive and strengthening her social position, she edited and published his memoirs, *Sir William Gregory K.C.M.G., An Autobiography* (1894), and edited the letters of his grandfather under the title *Mr. Gregory's Letter-Box* (1898). She dealt with the difficult Irish political and cultural challenges of the day in a sensitive manner, winning the respect of her husband's old friends.[1] She began to reflect more seriously on the experiences that she had accrued during the long museum tours of her married years, and on the critical debates that had emerged regarding the social value of art. Significantly, she began to look for ways through which some of the proposals emerging from those debates might be realised in Ireland. As she deepened her knowledge of the local culture around Coole Park, and more widely in the general Galway area, she discovered her interest in scientific antiquarianism. A result of this was her blending of *fin-de-siècle* Celticism with late Victorian Hellenism. Her participation in the rediscovery of the old Celtic legends for the modern age was motivated to a large extent by her desire to contribute to the broader Classical Revival of nineteenth-century England.

Lady Enid Layard continued to be a close friend and a companion in their archaeologically inspired fieldwork in the Irish countryside. The two women embarked on a folklore-collecting tour of the Burren on the Galway/Clare coast in the late 1890s. Their familiarity with archaeology and archaeological methods helped them discover the hidden treasures of the area. '[S]he had pragmatically questioned the household staff', writes Hill, 'searched for wells, and gone into a souterrain within the circular earthen ramparts of a ring fort, popularly believed to be places where fairies gathered'.[2] Hill is right in suggesting that the unfazed manner of Lady Gregory going into the *souterrain* points to her detachment from the taboos inherent in the local folk culture. Lady Gregory's attitude is interesting for another reason, as her new activity in Ireland and her earlier experiences in Continental Europe and Asia shared certain striking similarities. She entered the *souterrain* of the ring forts in Galway as she had once entered the Pharaoh's tomb in Egypt to discover ancient burial customs and hieroglyphic systems. During the process of familiarising herself with ancient Egyptian civilisation, she endeavoured to maintain a measure of objectivity towards the ancient culture, much in the same manner as she would do later when entering ringforts near Galway.

Her methods of gathering information on ancient pagan beliefs point towards the precedence of Sir Henry Layard, Dr. Heinrich Schliemann, and Emil Brugsch. Layard, Schliemann, and Brugsch had excavated burial grounds and entered the Pharaohs' tombs in order to discover valuable information about a particular historical period or a specific geographic area. Schliemann's methods in particular were considered to be unique for the way in which he had set out to unearth the remnants of the ancient city of Troy. He had an unfaltering belief in the authenticity of the ancient legend once sung by Homer and he granted significant credence to the local legends when determining the location of the walls of the city.[3] As a result, he unearthed the walls and remnants of an old city near Hissarlik, along the Greek-Turkish border, which he considered to be the ruins of the ancient city of Troy. Still believing in the authority of the literary text and local legends as his guiding lines, he discovered what was thought to be the ancient city of Mycenae, where Agamemnon, the leader of the Achaean army in Homer's *Iliad*, was believed to have been buried. The authenticity of the sites and of the finds has been disputed since; in fact, it has been proven that it was not Troy, nor was it Agamemnon's death mask that the German archaeologist discovered in Greece. At the time, however, Schliemann's excavations were a marvel for many of those working within the fields of archaeology, science, antiquarian studies, and literary studies.[4] The Victorian social *élite* as well as the general reading public considered Schliemann's discoveries to be a verification of the historical accuracy of Homer's legends. Lengthy conversations with Schliemann and other prominent archaeologists gave Lady Gregory deep insight into the archaeologist's profession as it was practised at the time. All she then had to do was to put her knowledge into practice in rural Ireland during the years following the death of Sir William.

Lady Gregory's archaeologically inspired field work continued when she embarked on a journey to find Anthony Raftery's grave around Craughwell, Co. Galway.[5] Raftery was a famous nineteenth-century Irish poet, singer, and fiddle player from the district around Coole Park. Douglas Hyde had already identified the house in which Raftery had spent his last days and Thomas Concannon mentioned the poet's unknown grave in the Gaelic League's journal *An Claidheamh Soluis*. After reading the Hyde and Concannon articles, Lady Gregory set out to find Raftery's unmarked grave. She finally located it in Killeeneen, outside the village of Craughwell, and published an open letter in *An Claidheamh Soluis* to raise money for a tombstone for Raftery.[6] Hill writes that, moved by her enthusiasm, the local stonemason's wife lent her a handwritten copy of Raftery's Irish songs. This was a valuable collection; Hyde had searched for it in vain. Lady Gregory translated the poems with the help of one of her tenants, Pat Mulkere, and published some of the material in an article in the English literary journal *The Argosy* in January 1901.[7] Between the discovery and the publication of the material she visited workhouses to collect information about the poet and his times. She discussed her findings with Hyde, who was himself in the process of compiling an anthology of the poet's verse, and who gave her hearty encouragement. Raftery's headstone was finally unveiled at the Gaelic League *Feis* on 26 August 1900.[8] It was a simple monument; Lady Gregory as patron of the gravestone project chose for it a simple inscription in honour of the Greek poet Homer.[9] 'In commissioning the stone with its gesture towards Homer', argues Hill, 'and celebrating Raftery in the article Gregory aimed to reclaim the poet for the next generation by giving him status in the modern world'.[10]

This same gesture, however, was also indicative of the extent to which the literary revival in Ireland was indebted to recent developments in British Hellenism. Her placement of the article on Raftery, 'the Irish Homer', in a London newspaper like *The Argosy* points towards Lady Gregory's keen awareness of the newly developing blend of Celticism and Hellenism in late Victorian England.

She experienced this blend in a very personal way. As her son Robert was growing up to become an educated young man, his relationship with his mother was intensifying. By the end of the decade he had left Harrow College and entered New College, Oxford, where the curriculum consisted of extensive readings of Homer's *Iliad* and *Odyssey*. Robert needed to study these works carefully as he began preparations for his degree in Classics. During this period he often travelled home to Coole Park to spend time there with his new Oxford friends, who enjoyed the hunting season in Ireland. Out of affection for her only son, Lady Gregory bought more land for shooting at Lisheen Crannagh, across Coole Lake, in spite of the family's rather precarious financial situation, from which Robert was sheltered.[11] Robert spent a considerable amount of time preparing for his examinations, and his mother helped him with this. As in earlier years, he asked his mother to read the *Iliad* with him, and he received not only a beautiful rendition of the epic poem but insights into the Greek culture that his mother had experienced during her early travels with her late husband.[12] Besides, Robert took advantage of his father's extensive library collection, which was at his disposal in the old library room at Coole. Sir William himself had spent much time during his last years annotating John Graham Cordery's translation of Homer's *Iliad* (1870/1886).[13] She herself had read Alexander Pope's translation of the *Iliad* and the *Odyssey* when she was still a young woman; she read the works alongside Ruskin's *The Stones of Venice*.[14]

As she was helping her son with his preparation for examinations in Greek drama and art, she started to work on a compilation of ancient Irish legends.[15] Pat Mulkere and Sean Connolly, an Irish teacher from Aran, assisted her in this work.[16] Since she supported the efforts of Douglas Hyde and the Gaelic League to revive the Irish language, she arranged with the local parish priest and the National School Master that the Aran man would instruct local schoolchildren in Irish.[17] She remembered in *Seventy Years* how helpful Connolly was to her when she was preparing her collection of Celtic legends. Connolly translated an English version of a legend into Irish, which Lady Gregory translated back to the Kiltartan dialect of Hiberno-English, a dialect that she employed for her compilation of the Celtic materials and subsequently for her Abbey plays.[18] Philip O'Leary notes the difficulties in comprehending these materials:

> [T]he most distinctive treasures of the early literature, in particular the Ulster Cycle tales about Cú Chulainn, were locked away in a language unintelligible not only to the general reader, but to the most informed students of Modern Irish as well. Thus for a knowledge of their own literary tradition, many fluent in the modern language were forced to consult the translations, especially those in English, accompanying editions prepared by their countryman Whitley Stokes or by foreigners like Meyer, Thurneysen, Windisch, de Jubainville, or Marstrander.[19]

O'Leary points here to an irony with which many Irish scholars were confronted at the time. This was their reliance on academic translations by Continental European philologists when Irish-born scholars were compiling new versions of Irish mythology. According to Lady Gregory's own records, she consulted a number of foreign translations, adaptations, and scholarly evaluations of the material, including those by Ernst Windisch, Kuno Meyer, and Marie Henri d'Arbois de Jubainville.[20] She complemented these works with English-language material, compiled and translated by Eugene O'Curry, Douglas Hyde, Whitley Stokes, and Eleanor Hull.[21]

Lady Gregory was an assiduous scholar. She read and compared various manuscripts of varying length and significance at the National Library of Ireland, the Royal Irish Academy, and the British Museum. Friends, old and new, helped her during the process. Sidney Colvin, former Slade Professor of Art and later Keeper of the Prints and Drawings Collections of the British Museum, granted her access to the museum's literary archives. W. B. Yeats directed her to the manuscript translation of the *Táin Bó Cuailgne* (the War of the Bull of Cooley) at the Royal Irish Academy in Dublin.[22] Trinity College Dublin refused to grant permission to view its holdings on the grounds that the Celtic material she wanted to consult was considered indecent, asinine, and unimaginative, and as such should be withheld from the general public. Robert Atkinson, Professor of Sanskrit and Todd Professor of Celtic Languages at the Royal Irish Academy, voiced these attitudes when he gave a speech at the Vice-Regal Commission on Intermediate Education: 'I would say it would be difficult to find a book in ancient Irish in which there was not some passage so silly or so indecent as to give you a shock from which you would never recover during the rest of your life'.[23] Atkinson and his colleague Rev. John Pentland Mahaffy, however, were ignorant or indifferent to the fact that some of the 'objectionable material' was 'being made known' to the public by the Gaelic League. Hyde's organisation, which Gregory wholeheartedly supported, called for the collection of old folk stories, some of which contained material related to Celtic legends. These stories, which had lived on in rural Ireland, were then published in popular bilingual journals, including *Fáinne an Lae* and *An Claidheamh Soluis*. At the *Oireachtas* of 1897, a new literary competition was launched to encourage native Irish speakers to submit for publication some of the old legends and folk stories that they knew. O'Leary argues that the annual *Oireachtas* and the local *feiseanna* encouraged many Gaelic speakers to share their stories with the wider public.[24] Eager to gather some stories for her second book of Irish legends, Lady Gregory herself commissioned a competition at the Galway *Feis* in 1902. This was for the 'best collection in prose or verse of unpublished legends relating to the Fianna of Erin'.[25] She had mentioned already in *Cuchulain of Muirthemne* that the stories of Finn and of the *fianna* were still known in Ireland, and she wanted to hear these stories before she embarked on the next literary project.[26] For *Cuchulain of Muirthemne* (1902) she compiled the legends of the Ulster cycle; for *Gods and Fighting Men* (1904) she decided to collect the stories of the Tuatha Dé Danann and of Finn, son of Cumhal. Lady Gregory's literary excavations bore fruit: she went on to publish another volume of Celtic legends that later defined the Irish literary movement and its development during the twentieth century.

With these new collections of legends, she contributed to the work of many scholars and academics who had been involved in publicising the old manuscript materials from the mid-nineteenth century onwards. Eugene O'Curry's *Lectures on the Manuscript Material of Ancient Irish History* (1861), based on a series of lectures he had delivered in 1855 and 1856, made public some materials held in library archives in Britain and Ireland. O'Curry made a point of providing a near complete account of the medieval annals, genealogies, poems, stories, legends, and ecclesiastical manuscripts, with the view to drawing attention to the forgotten history of Ireland.[27] As Professor of Archaeology, he insisted on including *facsimiles* of some of the original materials in the handwriting of medieval monks, one of whom was thought to be the Irish saint Column Cille. Some poems and stories were printed in the original, old Gaelic fonts and were accompanied by contemporary English translations. This was to facilitate the reading of old verse in the original language. O'Curry's desire to 'make known' the treasures of Gaelic antiquity to modern Irish people stemmed from the same educational purpose that had motivated Sir William and Ruskin to 'make known' *trecento* art to modern English people. Furthermore, O'Curry's method of publishing information in multiple languages for the purpose of allowing his readership to understand and internalise ancient words seem to reflect some of the motivations of those who inscribed the ancient Rosetta Stone. While one language on the stone (the most ancient of them all) bears a stamp of 'authenticity', the other language (the most recent of them all) allows the modern reader to access the information encoded on the surface of this monument of ancient history. O'Curry was not alone in his work; he was assisted by the philological and moral support of Rev. John Henry Newman, Rev. Charles Graves, Rev. James H. Todd, Dr. Robert D. Lyons, John Edward Pigot, and Whitley Stokes.

As the first Professor of Irish History at the newly established Catholic University of Ireland, O'Curry's aim was to use the fragmented manuscript material to write up a continuous and linear narrative of the 'General History of Erinn'.[28] Incorporating myths and legends into a single historical narrative was an idea that Lady Gregory's cousin Standish O'Grady took up in his multi-volume work *History of Ireland* (1878–1880). O'Grady's pseudo-scientific account of Irish history offers a wonderfully imaginative blend of a series of archaeological facts, mythological tales (as preserved for centuries in the Christian tradition), and his own evaluations of the social history of Irish feudalism. From *History of Ireland: Cuchulain and His Contemporaries* to *History of Ireland: Critical and Philosophical* the volumes cover an astonishing array of events ranging from the formation of the island's prehistoric landscape (through divine interventions of mythological gods and goddesses) to fictitious accounts of Cuchulain's return to his native land during the nineteenth century. Michael McAteer argues that throughout the writing process, O'Grady was struggling with the 'tension between the historical and imaginative approach' as he was trying to engage with and reflect on contemporary evaluations of Irish history and of Irish character.[29] McAteer mentions that one of O'Grady's aims was to challenge Matthew Arnold's view of the Celtic races as being temperamentally inferior to the

Teuton/Saxon, as Arnold had formulated it in his Oxford lectures, later published under the title *On the Study of Celtic Literature* (1867).[30]

Familiar with the Irish manuscript material through O'Curry's work, O'Grady directly questioned contemporary assumptions that the bardic literature of the Celts was inferior to that of the Greeks. As a Classics scholar, he sprinkled his account of Irish history with repeated references to Greek history, mythology, and literature in order to highlight the similarities and differences between the two literary traditions. O'Grady was adamant that the Celtic legends were at least equal in power, if not superior, to the ancient Greek sagas. O'Grady evaluated the relationship between the Ultonian (Ulster) and the Homeric legends as follows:

> In Homer, Hesiod, and the Attic poets, there is a polish and artistic form, absent in the existing monuments of Irish heroic thought, but the gold, the ore itself, is here massier and more pure, the sentiment deeper and more tender, the audacity and freedom more exhilarating, the reach of imagination more sublime, the depth and power of the human soul more fully exhibit themselves. [...] Through his [Cuchulain's] whole career, in war and peace, in the world and out of it, in spite of all the cold dictates of reason and logic, the heart of the reader is stirred and his imagination inflamed by the contemplation of all that terrible and superhuman heroism, and the knowledge of those deep wells of pity, tenderness, and love, whence sprang those gentle deeds and words which, even more than his heroism, go to the formation of the noblest character ever presented in literature![31]

O'Grady argued that the Celtic legends may have been stylistically less polished but they conveyed deeper and more powerful feelings out of which the heroic act sprang, and the emotional power inherent in the stories conveyed a deeper sense of the ancient world than the Homeric texts. Calling Cuchulain the 'noblest character ever presented in literature' was high praise indeed. It signalled that O'Grady considered not only Celtic bardic literature but also Celtic heroes superior to the ancient Greek gods and warriors. O'Grady conceived these home-grown heroes as role models for the young generations growing up in Ireland. Declan Kiberd writes in *Irish Classics* that with the tales O'Grady targeted those 'delinquent landlords who appeared on the verge of extinction under the land reforms of the 1870s and 1880s', those who had misused their power either through negligence or despotism over the centuries.[32] Kiberd draws attention to O'Grady's intense preoccupation with the state and behaviour of the landowning classes in Ireland at the time. This position was clearly evident in some of his later comments made in *Toryism and Tory Democracy* (1886). O'Grady was a graduate of Trinity College Dublin and a medallist of its Philosophical Society; it was inevitable that he addressed his thoughts first and foremost to the Protestant political and social governing classes of Ireland. Given the indebtedness of O'Grady's work to that of O'Curry, however, it is clear that he envisaged a wider readership for his works than that of the Anglo-Irish Establishment.

Lady Gregory acknowledged the value of her cousin's literary work, claiming that for readers of ancient Celtic legends 'Standish O'Grady's Homeric paraphrases had long been an inspiration and delight'.[33] However, both in concept and in style, her version of the Celtic legends differed significantly from other versions available on the literary market. Since her biographical writings had proven to be so successful, she decided to write up the stories of the Red Branch Knights of Ulster in the manner of a biography of the main hero, Cuchulain. *Cuchulain of Muirthemne* gives an account of Cuchulain's life from his conception by Lugh, the sun god, to his untimely death following the *Táin Bó Cuailnge*, the War of Cooley, which had commenced in defence of the honour and property of Conchubar, the High King of Ulster. Tales from the Ultonian cycle, including the *Feast of Bricrú* or the *Táin Bó Cuailnge*, were incorporated into the main thread of Lady Gregory's narrative describing Cuchulain's heroic life and his noble deeds.[34] Since the biographical approach was so significant, Lady Gregory considered it of foremost importance to build up the personality and character of the main hero and his warrior companions. Significantly, it is the continuous verbal interaction between the various characters that moves the action of the stories forward in *Cuchulain of Muirthemne*; and, even more significantly, it is through these verbal exchanges that the noble character of the heroes comes to the fore. The supernatural aspect of the tales (so pronounced in O'Curry's and in O'Grady's accounts) does not disappear altogether from her version but is significantly reduced. She remarks in *Seventy Years* that she was reading Charles Dickens's *Bleak House* while she was writing up the collection.[35] As Kiberd argues, the influence of Dickensian realism on the style of her narrative in undeniable.[36] Lady Gregory found Dickens's realism 'an immense relief', which was refreshing after 'those hours in that ancient world of heroism and of dreams' that she had spent reading manuscripts at the British Library or the Royal Irish Academy.[37] Her final version of the tales, therefore, belonged to the world of fiction rather than to the world of scholarly antiquarianism. Unlike her predecessors, she was less concerned with drawing up a pseudo-scientific account of the whole history of Ireland than in retelling the lives of the heroes of Ulster.

Celticism, Hellenism, and the Arthurian Legends

Lady Gregory revealed in the preface to *Cuchulain of Muirthemne* that she had left out many passages of the original Celtic material which she had thought her audience 'would not care about for one reason or another'.[38] Omitting material was a wise decision from many points of view. This way her work could acquire a wider readership in Ireland, given the conservative influence of both the Catholic and the Protestant churches in Irish society. By toning down the violent and sexual overtones characteristic of some of the original stories, she was able to avoid the censorship of the Roman Catholic clergy in particular. Her comments that she had done all 'from a peasant point of view' may have sounded patronising at the time but this approach was important in winning for her the approval of members and sympathisers of the Gaelic League, who had been involved in the collecting of old stories which had survived in the oral tradition of rural Ireland.[39] Furthermore, her rather sanitised version of the old tales conformed to the conservative tastes of those Catholic and Protestant revivalists who idealised the imagination of the rural people of Ireland; and it ensured the toleration of those sceptical about the Irish Revival (including those dons of Trinity College), who thought the materials were unsuitable for literary dissemination in their original form. As a devout Christian herself, she felt better about not including overtly violent and sexual passages in a book that was published under her own name. As her comments on the Jean-François Millet exhibition indicated from more than a decade previously, she was not disposed towards art works that were explicitly sexual or violent in their nature. More importantly still, as a widow and mother, she had to consider the implications of her actions for the legacy of the Gregory family as well as for the future career prospects of Robert. She had been careful to depict her late husband and his family in a positive light, describing them as benign statesmen and landlords of a very high moral esteem in her two biographies; much of which was done to assist Robert's advancement at Oxford and in the Civil Service of the British

Empire that Sir William and Lady Gregory had originally intended for the only heir of Coole Park.

Beside these, the main purpose behind the sanitisation of the legends was educational. Contrary to Whistler's attitude that art should not be confused with education, she took a Ruskinian approach on the matter, regarding her work on Irish mythology as educational material. She hoped that Irish children would read her book, learn about ancient times, and imbibe a certain kind of noble and chivalrous disposition that was characteristic of the heroes as presented in her tales. George Russell drew attention to the educational nature of the project in his review of *Cuchulain of Muirthemne*:

> I do not doubt that there will be a great change in the next generation, for the character of many children will have grown to maturity brooding over the memories of heroes who were themselves half children, half demigods.[40]

Hailing Lady Gregory's book in Arthur Griffith's *United Irishman*, Russell deliberately drew attention to the character-building nature of Lady Gregory's project. O'Grady himself had considered the Celtic heroes as role models for the new generations; likewise, Lady Gregory considered the Celtic characters as examples to follow.

She disclosed that she had modelled the characters of Cuchulain, Conan, and Usheen on Lord Talbot, Lord Wellesley, and Sir Robert Peel.[41] Besides providing a direct link between her book on the Rt. Hon. William Gregory (Robert's great-grandfather) and her first collection of Celtic tales, her comments are also indicative of the nature of the educational project that she had in mind. During his long years as Under Secretary, William Gregory served a succession of Lord Lieutenants, including Lord Talbot and Lord Wellesley. The compilation *Mr. Gregory's Letter-Box* contained a selection of letters between the Lord Lieutenants and the Under Secretary to which Lady Gregory added personal and political information relevant to the historical period in question. In the *Letter-Box*, Talbot, Wellesley, and Peel are depicted as men of honour who felt an immense sense of duty towards Ireland and the Irish people, and whose good intentions were severely hampered by the religious and sectarian conflict on the island and by the continuous political conflicts in the British Parliament. According to the correspondence published in the *Letter-Box*, these statesmen hoped to improve the living standards of Irish tenants. They made steps towards providing relief for the famine-struck rural population and they intended to further the cause of a new system of land tenure in Ireland. However historically accurate or not her accounts may have been, the sentiment inundating the text suggests that the main obstacles facing the plans were the people of Ireland themselves in their division along religious sectarian lines. Lady Gregory paints a picture of the turbulent decades during which William Gregory held his office: grave social and political demands were imposed upon the British administration by Orangemen, Ribbonmen, Tidewaiters, Repealers, and militant Catholics, hopeful of a French military campaign on Irish soil during Napoleon Bonaparte's rule in France.[42] Talbot, Wellesley, and Peel emerge in her account of those years as men with a real sense of *noblesse oblige* when it came to local matters. She emphasised the nobility of their character and the deep sense of duty that they felt towards the country during their short periods in administration. It is telling that in her rather Victorianised versions of the medieval tales of the Red Branch of Ulster, she conceived the characters of the main heroes as Gaelic antecedents of these nineteenth-century noblemen who embodied Ruskin's ideals of gentlemanly conduct.

Throughout *Cuchulain of Muirthemne* she emphasised the chivalric behaviour of Celtic heroes, who were loyal to their kinship and who defended the honour and property of the clan leaders. This was also the sentiment of Malory's *Le Morte d'Arthur*, a medieval legend widely popularised in Victorian art and literature. Chivalry was the very essence of the Arthurian legends and was used in various nineteenth-century adaptations of the tales, in Colin Graham's words, as a 'corrective on the present'.[43] The noble chivalric code of conduct determining the behaviour of King Arthur, Sir Lancelot, or Sir Gawain was noticeably emphasised in Victorian accounts of medieval tales. Of the many adaptations, Graham draws attention to Tennyson's *Idylls of the King* as a literary example in which heroic personae are melted into, and glorified by, the accounts of the mythical past. He remarks that the Arthur of the *Idylls* was an amalgamation of three historical characters: the spiritual Arthur Hallam, the military Lord Wellesley, and the monarchical Prince Albert, the Prince Consort.[44] Tennyson dedicated his poems to Prince Albert, who, as Graham points out, 'endorsed the valorised national past of Arthur when in 1847 he commissioned William Dyce to decorate the Queen's Robing Room in the Palace of Westminster with

Arthurian Paintings'.[45] Peter Denman stresses that during the long history of English nation building the original Arthurian legends became 'decelticised', and King Arthur was made a 'symbol of England and of things English'.[46] In order to comment on contemporary British society and on the politics of the British Empire, Tennyson continued this process of 'decelticisation'. In this process the Celtic origins of the Arthurian legend were almost entirely eradicated, surviving solely in some of the tales.[47] Graham goes on to say that as a corrective measure, O'Grady's family tutor and literary precursor Samuel Ferguson decided to 're-celticise' the tales. Graham argues that Ferguson's *Congal*, for instance, was written with the specific aim to replant the legends in their Celtic past and to recapture the old spirit of the *Mabinogion*. Both the *Morte d'Arthur* and the *Mabinogion* served as literary antecedents for *Cuchulain of Muirthemne* and *Gods and Fighting Men*. The *Mabinogion* was compiled and translated by Lady Enid Layard's mother, Lady Charlotte Guest, and it served as basis for Tennyson's *Idylls*.[48] Lady Charlotte Guest's son, Enid's brother, proudly remembered the literary impact his mother's translations made on Tennyson, the future Poet Laureate of Queen Victoria.[49]

Tennyson's *Idylls*, as Richard Jenkyns remarks, was 'composed under the shadow of Homer' and the Arthurian court was, in fact, 'a purified version of the Achaean camp'.[50] The importance that Victorians accorded to Homer's work, as well as the growing interest in ancient Greek civilisation during the eighteenth and nineteenth century, was openly declared on the statue erected in honour of Prince Albert in 1872. Homer is seated in the centre on the Frieze of Poets of the Albert Memorial, surrounded by the figures of Dante, Virgil, Corneille, Molière, Cervantes, Goethe, Schiller, Chaucer, Milton, and Shakespeare. This prominent place, argues Jenkyns, was a sign of 'Homer's sway over the Victorian imagination'.[51] Stefano Evangelista has claimed that during the Victorian period the ancient Greeks were seen as 'spiritual contemporaries of modern Englishmen'.[52] 'Victorian England, at the height of its prosperity and political primacy', he explains, 'came to see itself as a modern inheritor of the Hellenic values of civility and humanism'.[53] The Victorian political and military *élite* saw themselves as responsible men, loyal to friends and rulers, brave in war and generous in peace. Evangelista reminds us that in universities 'Homer and heroic literature were read as textbooks of the ethical codes of mature masculinity'.[54] As the ethical codes underwent alterations during the long nineteenth century, so were the perceptions of the ancient heroes modified. By the end of the nineteenth century the ancient heroes were no longer perceived as revengeful, barbarous, cruel and war-loving (as they were at the beginning of the century), but were thought of as thoroughbred, chivalrous, and gallant.

The study of ancient Greek culture and civilisation formed a central part of the educational curricula of the old universities during the nineteenth century. As a result, the sons of the social and political *élite* were fastidious readers of ancient literature. Ruskin himself had read Homer's *Iliad* and *Odyssey* in Alexander Pope's eighteenth-century translation. His father John James Ruskin handed him a copy of the *Iliad* when his son was still a young boy. Ruskin's views on both the translator and the translation changed significantly as his life and career progressed. In *Modern Painters*, he criticised the translator for his choice of a strictly formal, neo-classical style, and he condemned the frequent occurrence of pathetic fallacy in the translation of passages that describe landscape features.[55] He was of the view that the English poet had destroyed the musicality and the lightness characteristic of the original Homeric texts. Ruskin was not alone in his criticism. Around the middle of the century Pope's translation came under serious attack from various quarters of Victorian society, inducing a debate in which Pope's eighteenth-century and Chapman's seventeenth-century translations were compared zealously to establish the supremacy of one over the other.[56] As time moved on, however, Ruskin modified his views. During his *Lectures on Art* lecture series (1870) he recommended his students at Oxford to read Pope for his mastery of language.[57] Later, in *Fors Clavigera*, he disclosed his intention to write up the poet's biography to defend him against what he then saw was unjust criticism of an English literary genius.[58]

Dinah Birch writes that the change in Ruskin's opinion occurred during a period in which the art critic was reconsidering the 'moral and political ethics of writing'.[59] Earlier, Ruskin was spellbound by the romantic charm of Wordsworth, Coleridge, and Keats's poetic imagination, while rejecting the lyrical formalism of Pope's poetry. Later, however, Ruskin had come to regard Pope's neo-classical formalism as intrinsic to the aristocratic appeal of his poetry. By this time (around the third quarter of the nineteenth century) new social movements had begun to emerge intending to rectify social injustices felt by large segments of the British population. Some of these movements were more moderate in character, urging a substantial overhaul of the social order but not its dismantlement. Others, however, publicly proclaimed as their long-term aim the complete abolition of the long-standing class system of the United Kingdom. Although sympathetic towards initiatives which aimed at ameliorating the working and living conditions of the middle and working classes, Ruskin was adamant that the initiatives should not affect the old traditional social order of the country. As Edward Alexander points out, Ruskin turned his attention to Homer around this time because he was able to derive from the ancient texts 'specific political doctrines that committed him to the defence of a hierarchical system of class based on the theory of *noblesse oblige*'.[60] Ruskin believed that the hierarchical class system should remain intact; that the aristocracy as beneficiaries of the system should take an active role in its upkeep both by military and by financial means; and that it should be the duty of the aristocratic classes to protect and care for the less fortunate. Edward Alexander writes that, like Matthew Arnold, Ruskin recognised and asserted the link between the principles of aristocracy and the nobility of Homer.[61] However, while Ruskin principally considered the political applications of the Homeric text, Arnold was mainly interested in the aesthetic value of the work, which he then brought into connection with noble principles.[62] Such developments in Ruskin's later social and aesthetic philosophy led him to view Pope's eighteenth-century translations in a more favourable light. By the 1870s, the neo-classical formalism of Pope's poetry came to represent for him, as for Arnold, the grand style of eighteenth-century English aristocracy, the traditions of which he considered vital for retaining the social system of the nineteenth century.

Following his submergence in art circles in which an appreciation of the art and culture of ancient Greece ran deep, Ruskin reassessed his views of Greek civilisation. This led inadvertently to his re-evaluation of Pope's translations. The principle of *noblesse oblige*, which he had first detected as characteristic of the aristocratic societies of medieval Europe, he now perceived as intrinsic to the social values of ancient Greece. This proved to be a point of reconciliation between the system of values of the Gothic Middle Ages, perceived and hailed by Ruskin as essentially Christian, and the system of values of the ancient Greeks, condemned by Ruskin in his earlier writings as fundamentally polytheistic and pagan. Ruskin was influenced in his reassessment to a large extent by the Hellenic Revival of the late nineteenth century, which impacted heavily on the arts and literature of his beloved country. He gave voice to these new views in his *Art of England* lecture series (1883), presenting an overview of English art of the nineteenth century. Given his long friendship with William Holman Hunt and Dante Gabriel Rossetti, he dedicated his first lecture to the evaluation of their work and of the principles of the Pre-Raphaelite Brotherhood. He then gave two lectures on those contemporary artists whose work blended most masterfully the principles of late Pre-Raphaelitism with the ideals of the Classical Revival.[63] Sir Frederic Leighton, George Frederic Watts, Lawrence Alma-Tadema, and Edward Burne-Jones (themselves Ruskin's disciples) were singled out because the art critic saw their work as offering new readings of his own moral philosophy in the fields of the visual and the dramatic arts.

Hellenism, Art, Theatre

While Lady Gregory was familiarising herself with the Hellenic material in Greece, Sicily, and London during the 1880s, a new theatre movement was underway in England. Leighton, Alma-Tadema, and Watts were amongst those painters who partook in this movement as their knowledge had accrued for the staging of the new productions of classical plays. Katherine Newey and Jeffrey Richards have pointed towards Frank Benson's production of Aeschylus' *Agamemnon* as the performance that inaugurated the new movement of the amateur stage.[64] This theatre movement owed much to the work of classical archaeologists like Schliemann and Layard, as their discoveries generated new waves of interest in antiquarianism. This resulted in a series of educational reforms in Oxford and Cambridge, where the old philological approach was exchanged for a new material one that required a more direct engagement with ancient cultures.[65] The theatre proved to be the ideal location for student attempts to reconstruct the antique world. Benson's *Agamemnon* was the first of these productions; it premiered on 3 June 1880 at Balliol Hall, Oxford. Audiences had not been accustomed to hearing a Greek play performed in Greek, and this unique production was a great surprise for both the viewing public and the critical press.[66] The play was a success and was later taken to other educational institutions, including Harrow, Eton, London, and Winchester. This success catapulted Frank Benson, the play's young actor-producer, to fame in the circles of Ellen Terry and Henry Irving at the Lyceum.[67] Benson had always been keen to acknowledge Ruskin's influence on his work, and in order to realise his own theatrical vision, he often enlisted the help of

Ruskin's favourite painters.[68] Thus, Leighton, Alma-Tadema, and Burne-Jones were some of those who offered advice to Benson on the historical accuracy of costume and setting.

Leighton, Poynter, and Watts designed the scenery for the lavish production of *The Tale of Troy*, performed at Sir Charles James Freake's regal home in Kensington in 1883.[69] The text of the play was adapted and translated by George C. Warr, Professor of Classical Literature at King's College London, from Homer's *Iliad* and *Odyssey*. The performance consisted of a series of *tableaux vivants*, accompanied by music composed by Otto Goldschmidt, Malcolm Lawson, Walter Parratt, and W. H. Monk. The four-day event, during which two English and two Greek versions of the play were performed, was a fund-raising event for the benefit of the King's College Lectures for Ladies project, which aimed at finalising the purchase and the remodelling of the house of lectures for ladies. The architect, Sir Charles James Freake, engaged Sir George Alexander as art director of the lavish production. Alexander consulted Ruskin's good friend Sir Charles Newton, Keeper of Classical Antiquities at the British Museum, to ensure that the production was carried out with the utmost historical accuracy. Ruskin himself thought the performance enjoyable and congratulated Alexander on his theatrical achievement. *The Tale of Troy* was revived three years later, on a much smaller scale, alongside Warr's adaptation and translation of Aeschylus' *The Story of Orestes* at the Prince's Hall in Piccadilly, London. The Pre-Raphaelite Walter Crane supervised this production and asked Leighton, Poynter, and Watts to rethink the original designs of the play. The lyrical and musical materials of the plays were published in the following year under the title *The Echoes of Hellas*, with Crane's spectacular illustrations.

Another spectacular theatrical production of the year was John Todhunter's adaptation of Sophocles' *Helen of Troas*, which was performed as a benefit for the British School for Archaeology in Rome, following the Royal Academicians' Ball on the theme of ancient Greece the previous year.[70] E. W. Godwin was responsible for the staging of *Helena in Troas*; his innovative approach surprised both his critics and his admirers. He abolished the proscenium arch to allow for a continuous flow of action between the players and the audience. For the same reason, he placed the chorus in the midst of the audience. He covered the floor of the auditorium with a painted oilcloth resembling a marble mosaic and, to re-create the mystical ritual of a Greek performance, he placed an incense-burning altar in the middle of the arena. Todhunter reproduced the beauty of ancient versification and Godwin conjured up the spirit of the ancient productions. For this reason, Godwin robed the women of the chorus in unbleached linen, designed to resemble marble figures, and posed them as studies of the sculptures of the Parthenon frieze. Although Leighton, Alma-Tadema, and Watts were not directly involved in the staging of the play, their paintings undoubtedly stirred Godwin's artistic imagination. The figures of their paintings were admired for their statuesque dignity and the pictorial compositions likened to the figurative arrangements of the Elgin Marbles.[71]

Antiquarian accuracy combined with visual spectacle in Godwin's productions. Godwin conceived of the theatre as a space where painting, drama, music, and architecture come together to create the noblest form of art. As a young student of architecture, he was an avid reader of Ruskin's *The Seven Lamps of Architecture* and *The Stones of Venice*. Even though later in his life he lost much of his early enthusiasm for Gothic design, the idea that the various elements of an art work should only exist in their subjugation to the creation of a monumental design was derived from Ruskin's appraisal of Gothic architecture. Ruskin celebrated the marvellously elaborate medieval cathedrals as *Gesamtkunstwerks*, in the creation of which painting, sculpture, and even music were all combined under a larger architectural design, the ultimate aim of which was to praise God's glory. As Godwin began to find interest in the new aesthetic trends of the century—branded by Pater, Swinburne, and Wilde—he also began to disregard the religious message of Ruskin's early writings. Nonetheless, he remained faithful to the art critic's ideals relating to the intertwined nature of the Sister Arts and their role in the creation of monumental designs.

The Princess's Theatre in London was one of the venues used for Godwin's grand-scale artistic productions during the 1870s and 1880s. When W. G. Wills's melodrama, *Claudian*, a play which dramatised life in the ancient city of Byzantium, was put on at the Princess's in 1883, director Wilson Barrett asked Godwin's advice. Michael R. Booth notes that Godwin, with his love for archaeological accuracy and pictorial realism, turned the show into a sensual spectacle.[72] Godwin envisaged *Claudian* as a demonstration of all that he considered to be valuable in British theatrical spectacles, as he did with Todhunter's *Helena in Troas*. Given his antiquarian interests, Godwin frequently visited the archival holdings of the British Museum and the Burlington Arcade, in order to look for original artefacts or their reproductions. While the production process was long and troublesome as a result, Barrett and Godwin's efforts were rewarded: the play received warm praise from the press. After seeing the performance, Ruskin renewed his friendship with both men, inadvertently contributing to Ruskin's more serious involvement in the staging of classicist productions during the early 1880s.[73] On Ruskin's advice, Barrett began to stage a series of classical plays, in which pictorial realism combined with scenic monumentalism. A reviewer of a contemporary magazine, *The Era*, compared Godwin's productions to Barrett's series of 'toga plays', emphasising that both were theatrical representations of the antiquarian pictorial ideals of the Classical Revival.[74] Aside from organising archaeological trips to the Mediterranean to study ancient art, Leighton, Alma-Tadema, and Watts spent endless hours in the British Museum, taking down the sculptural and compositional details of the Elgin Marbles in order to ensure the historical accuracy of paintings and theatrical *tableaux*.

Watts, in fact, believed that with the Elgin Marbles safely secured in the British Museum, it was no longer necessary for art students to travel to Greece—a view with which Sir William Gregory and Lady Gregory fundamentally disagreed. Elizabeth Prettejohn reminds us that Watts admired the Parthenon marbles both in their ideal and material form, and 'regarded Pheidias, as Arnold did Homer: a living poet who spoke directly to the present'.[75] He observed the marbles closely and 'followed their form with the same richness in detail and flexibility of movement that he attributed to the draperies themselves'.[76] Phidias, Homer, and Arnold were linked together in his theory of art, argues Prettejohn, since he conceived of the marble statues as visual representations of the 'grand style' of the ancient texts.[77] Leighton's large-scale canvases and theatre *tableaux* were examples of the fusion of literary mastery, sculptural fluidity, and pictorial grandeur about which his contemporary was theorising. One of the painter's friends observed that his figures were 'draped rather than dressed', with his draperies belonging 'to a realm where Art […] has lost contact with life'.[78] Leighton first painted a nude figure which he then overlaid 'with a thick shapeless layer of something that he was eventually to work up into a form of clothing'.[79] Pictorial grandeur blended with historicism in Alma-Tadema's *Pheidias and the Frieze of the Parthenon* (1868–1869), depicting the sculptor at work in his studio awaiting questions from visitors. His later canvases displayed a fusion of his earlier interests in antiquarianism, taking the form of a fascination with realist representations of marble surfaces, and his slowly developing sympathy for late-Pre-Raphaelite idealism. His later work, painted with a significantly lighter colour scheme, demonstrated his ability to retain the statuesque stateliness of his Grecian figures while dressing them in overlaid, semi-translucent layers of flowing drapery. This, according to Ruskin, once allowed artists in ancient times to exhibit the action of the body simultaneously with the flow of the gesture in dignified perfection.

George Russell remarked how the lines of *Cuchulain of Muirthemne* conjured up for him images of ancient Greek statues. Under the title 'The Character of Heroic Literature' he wrote a sculptural appraisal of Lady Gregory's new book:

> As we read our eyes are dazzled by strange graces of colour flowing over the pages: everywhere there is mystery and magnificence. Processions pass by in Druid ritual, kings and queens, and harpers who look like kings. When the wind passes over them and stirs their garments a sweetness comes over the teller of the tale, who felt that delight in draperies blown over shapely forms which is the inspiration of the Winged Victory and many Greek marbles.[80]

Russell here forged an intriguing connection between the work of ancient sculptors and that of Lady Gregory. Not only did he refer to Paeonius' *Nike of Samothrace* as the Winged Victory, but he also brought the processional marbles of the Parthenon into connection with the literary work. Earlier in the essay, he established a link between 'the Phidian beauty which in Greece was a long dream for many generations' and the charm of Lady Gregory's version of Irish legends.[81] He stated at the beginning of the review that 'Lady Gregory, a fairy godmother, has given to Young Ireland the gift of her *Cuchulain of Muirthemne*, which should be henceforward the book of its dream'.[82]

The connection between art and literature established here was not unique in Russell's writings. Phidias and the marbles of his workshop return as points of reference in many of his discussions of ancient art and literature. Not long after the opening of the Abbey Theatre in Dublin, an exhibition was held in 1906 at the Royal Hibernian Academy of G. F. Watts paintings, in conjunction with which a three-event lecture series were organised for those interested. John B. Yeats and W. B. Yeats delivered the first two lectures; George Russell gave the third. In his lecture, 'Art and Literature', Russell praised the Phidian marbles, saying that in them 'we find human forms suggesting a superhuman dignity'.[83]

His reference occurs during his discussion of *Love Triumphant*, Watts's allegorical painting of 1900. Russell appraised the picture with the following words:

> What is the real inspiration we derive from that noble design by Mr Watts? [...] A revelation of the heroic dignity a human form can express. [...] There were immortal powers in Watts' mind when those figures surged up in it [...].[84]

Russell used this lecture as an extended comment on the debate that enfolded in the aftermath of the Ruskin-Whistler trial around the moral/immoral/amoral nature of art. Hence the lecture was generously peppered with references to Ruskin, Whistler and, of course, Watts, who sided with the ageing art critic during the debate. Russell emphasised that the inspiration of an artist like Watts was essentially spiritual and that an artist, 'as he creates a beautiful form outside himself, creates within himself, or admits to his being a nobler beauty than his eyes have seen'.[85] Although occasionally critical of the English artist, Russell praised Watts's artistic achievements; he especially liked his *Love Triumphant*, on which the figure of the central character was modelled on Paeonius' *Nike of Samothrace*, or the Winged Victory.

This blending of literature and the plastic arts was not uncommon in nineteenth-century culture. Edward Bulwer-Lytton's novel *The Last Days of Pompeii* was but a series of *tableaux vivants*, forerunners of Alma-Tadema's classical scenes.[86] The rich tapestry of Lady Gregory's *Cuchulain of Muirthemne*, in which the arts of sculpture, painting, and literature were entwined, was indicative of the typically nineteenth-century character of the publication. Yeats wrote very highly of the new book:

> I think this book is the best that has come out of Ireland in my time. Perhaps I should say that it is the best book that has ever come out of Ireland, for the stories which it tells are the chief part of Ireland's gift to the imagination of the world—and it tells them perfectly for the first time.[87]

Yeats praised Lady Gregory's version of the legends for the 'tender, compassionate, and complacent quality' of the writing, reminding him of the most endearing features of the Irish language.[88] Having developed a keen interest in classicist theatre during the 1880s, Yeats immediately recognised the inherently performative aspects of Lady Gregory's work and its indebtedness to the cultural *milieu* of late Victorian England. He, who had praised Godwin and Todhunter for their production of the story of Helen of Troy, recognised the theatrical potential of Lady Gregory's version of the Celtic tales. Yeats was taken by the pictorial beauty and verbal elegance of Todhunter's *Helena in Troas* for he saw it as the re-creation of the perfect form of art which was in itself 'both religious and aesthetic, both cultivated and popular'.[89] Jenkyns explains that Yeats admired the production for having 'the appeal of a scholar to the scholarly' while yet 'it filled the theatre with the ordinary run of theatre goers'.[90] For much of his dramatic career Yeats tried to re-create this perfect union of words, pictures, and movements which he first experienced, amongst others, in these late Victorian reproductions of Athenian theatre.

Yeats did modify some of his views when his collaborations with leading theatre specialists intensified as his career in the theatre progressed, but even his modernist experiments with Edward Gordon Craig, the son of E. W. Godwin, were rooted in Godwin and Todhunter's philosophy of the stage. Gordon Craig's idea of the unity of the stage not only owed much to his father's dramatic concept but it also carried Ruskin's artistic message through to the new century. For the time being, however, Yeats tried to persuade Todhunter, the son of an Irish Quaker, to turn his attention to ancient Celtic literature. Yeats admired Todhunter's beautiful versification and his thorough historical antiquarianism in all the projects that he had undertaken; he suggested to his friend undertaking the task of compiling the legends. As Todhunter turned down the offer, Lady Gregory stepped in and, to Yeats's surprise, she proved herself to be the perfect literary executor of the project. She had been in conversation with Hyde, and other members of the Irish literary scene based in London, over the collection of the ancient literary material contained in medieval manuscripts. She had a good knowledge of the German, French, and Italian languages, which enabled her to read the various nineteenth-century translations of the ancient tales. She had been taking lessons in Irish, facilitating her understanding of the original written materials, and she had been involved in the work of the Gaelic League. She had learned from her archaeologist and antiquarian friends, at home and abroad, the cultural significance of excavations and of the preservation of the ancient heritage. Hers was a sophisticated and cultured background; writing up the tales in a form that would please the refined tastes of the learned *élite* of Britain and Ireland came naturally to her. As a result, her books of Irish legends were, to quote Yeats, both 'cultivated and popular'. More importantly, *Cuchulain of Muirthemne* and later *Gods and Fighting Men* were literary testimonies of the entwined nature of the verbal, the visual and the dramatic arts, as witnessed in many nineteenth-century literary texts and theatrical productions. She believed that a play was 'but [a] conversation clipped and arranged' and her books of Irish legend bore out this maxim.[91] Narratives were heavily reliant on conversations clipped and arranged, scenes closely resembling *tableaux vivants* and stories composed in the musical vernacular of her local area, granting the tales that special lyrical quality.

Firmly rooted in British Hellenism while steeped in Celtic mysticism, *Cuchulain of Muirthemne* appealed to the refined tastes of the British aristocracy who attended the Greek plays. The Prince of Wales and *art connoisseur* friends whom Lady Gregory met from time to time at various social occasions were regular attendants of the Godwin, Todhunter, and Barrett productions of the 1880s. So too was the statesman William Gladstone, who had a lifelong passion for Greek literature and culture. He composed a series of articles, which were published later under the title *Studies on Homer and the Homeric Age* (1858). Throughout his early career he actively campaigned for increasing the amount of time to be allotted to studying Homer in the old universities, especially at Oxford, as he believed that the ancient texts could teach students the art of gentlemanly behaviour and of governance.[92] He promulgated this view in his lectures on ancient Greek culture and literature.[93] Similarly to Lord John Russell and Lord Derby, he undertook the translation of Homer's *Iliad* and *Odyssey* and he was still involved in this literary project when the theatrical productions revived the interest in Homer's work during the 1880s. During this period, as Lady Gregory recalled, her husband and Gladstone would converse on the topic of Greek art, Homer's works, and the appreciation of the ancient culture in Victorian England.[94] Like Browning, Jovett, Benson, Godwin, Todhunter, Ruskin, and Sir William, Gladstone also followed closely the archaeological developments of Schliemann's excavations at Troy and Mycenae. Later in his career, these archaeological discoveries enticed him to accept an insignificant political mission to Greece, for he saw it as an opportunity to renew his knowledge of Greek art and literature in the aftermath of the historical discoveries.[95] Given the fact that he spent many long decades analysing and translating the Homeric texts, his political speeches and comments were often interspersed with Greek cultural references.[96] He conveyed to Ruskin his firm belief in the aristocratic principle. Like Ruskin, he admired the ancient world for its aristocratic character. Schliemann's discoveries, which turned mythology into verifiable accounts of ancient history, only confirmed his views. His peculiar understanding of the cultural and political achievements of ancient Greek culture, and his efforts to translate these achievements to meet the social and political demands of nineteenth-century British society, undoubtedly formed his opinion on the Irish question in the 1880s.

Not everyone agreed with the dissemination of Hellenic ideals among younger generations for educational and didactic purposes. Marc-André Raffalovich, John Gray, Oscar Wilde, and their aesthetic circles were also present at the popular theatre performances. Oscar Wilde once claimed to be the first to suggest the Balliol production of *Agamemnon*.[97] Evangelista notes that these circles of the 'aesthetic movement turned the study of ancient Greece into a field of progressive thinking', changing 'the language of the academic, political and moral establishment, into a language of dissent'.[98] Wilde, Gray, Symonds, Swinburne, and their Paterite friends, believed that the appreciation of Greek culture had nothing to do with the conformism and social conservatism propagated in the writings of Gladstone, Ruskin, and Arnold.[99] Lady Gregory was in touch with these circles during her marriage and during the decade following her husband's death. She turned up occasionally at dinner parties given by Raffalovich, Gray, and their friends from the Rhymer's Club. By the time of Wilde's infamous trials, she had grown bored with the 'over-dressed women & shady looking man', and she temporarily disappeared from their circles.[100] The contact, however, was not lost and as soon as the trials were over she renewed her visits. Lady Gregory found 'the society there considerably changed', of 'chiefly [con]'verts', and '[t]he conversation very Papistical'.[101] She observed that 'Raffy [was] as full of fathers fasts & formulas as they used to be of the stage'.[102] By this time Raffalovich, Gray, and Beardsley had begun to flirt with Catholicism. Hence, the dinner talk turned from topics related to Dionysian Hellenism to devotional issues of the Roman Catholic faith. Even though the gatherings had lost their earlier hedonistic character of which Lady Gregory had been critical, the new dinner talk appeared to her dull and the evenings strenuous. Still, James Pethica points out that as a mark of her importance to the circle, John Gray—future parish priest of St. Peter's in Edinburgh—gave her one of the few, priceless, privately bound and privately circulated copies of his collection of devotional poems, which he had started to compose in 1895.[103]

CELTICISM AND THEATRE IN IRELAND

Meanwhile, back in Ireland, the modernisation and popularisation of the old Celtic legends was gaining momentum. During the last decade of the century the most successful and popular way of dissemination was the dramatisation of the tales. Alice Milligan, a Presbyterian from Belfast and a fastidious worker for the Gaelic League, staged her own dramatised versions of tales at the local *feiseanna* in various towns around Ulster, including Donegal, Letterkenny, and Belfast. Her biographer Catherine Morris emphasises that Milligan's mythological and historical plays and *tableaux vivants* served a very specific political nationalist agenda.[104] Beyond Ulster, Peadar Ua Laoghaire's politically less charged, naturalist *tableaux vivants* were the most popular adaptations of the old tales, staged also under the auspices of the Gaelic League. In his *Autobiographies*, Yeats commented on the positive influence of Milligan's *tableaux vivants* on the emerging dramatic movement in Ireland at the turn of the century.[105] Yeats's early play, *The Countess Cathleen*, undoubtedly owed much to her political artistry. Lady Gregory's comments from the period, however, are less complementary about Milligan's work. One of the first plays produced by the Irish Literary Theatre that had recently been founded by Lady Gregory, Yeats, and Edward Martyn, was Milligan's most popular piece *The Last Feast of the Fianna*. It was staged alongside George Moore's *The Bending of the Bough* and Edward Martyn's *Meave* at the Gaiety Theatre in Dublin in 1900. Lady Gregory was dismissive of the play, calling it a 'tawdry little piece' and its language 'intolerable'.[106] The following year the repertoire of the theatre included Hyde's *Casadh an tSugáin* (*The Twisting of the Rope*) and Yeats and Moore's *Diarmuid and Grania*. Having produced and acted in the famous performance of Aeschylus' *Agamemnon* at the Balliol Hall at Oxford, Frank Benson travelled to Ireland to astonish a new audience with his acting style.[107] The first performance of *Diarmuid and Grania* went well: Lady Gregory wrote that even the critical dons of Trinity College could not find anything objectionable in the manner through which the theatre was popularising the old legends.[108] Public opinion changed, however, as the theatre continued with the performances.¹⁰⁹ Benson was widely regarded as one of the principal actors of the times, one who excelled in contemporary productions of William Shakespeare's plays. The bard's cycle of history plays, which Benson staged at Stratford-upon-Avon, was immensely popular with both critics and the viewing public. Benson's fine elocution and his sophisticated manner of acting, however, came under heavy criticism in Ireland. The Gaelic League was the most critical of Benson's manner of acting, which they considered to be affected and theatrical, and altogether unsuitable for the performance of old Irish tales.¹¹⁰

Lady Gregory understood that the legends would need to be written up in a way that would make them suitable for the type of dramatisation that Yeats, Russell, Moore, and Martyn had in mind. She built the narratives of *Cuchulain of Muirthemne*, and to a lesser extent those of *Gods and Fighting Men*, on a succession of dialogues in order to facilitate the dramatisation of the tales. Yeats, Russell, and Synge were appreciative of her efforts. Yeats called *Cuchulain of Muirthemne* 'the best book to have come out of Ireland'; Synge wrote that the book was 'part of my daily bread'; and Russell claimed that her tales had given him new dreams.¹¹¹ Of course, Yeats and Russell had already gained knowledge of the ancient times from the works of Ferguson, O'Curry, O'Grady, and Alfred Nutt. Lady Gregory was also well aware of Yeats's and Russell's occultist perspectives on Celtic mythology—derived in part from the teachings of the theosophical circles of Dublin and London—when they visited her in Coole to discuss the possibilities of establishing a literary theatre in the late 1890s.¹¹² Yeats especially was much taken with the possibility of further dramatisations of the Celtic legends. After hearing the amateur company of the Fay brothers perform Alice Milligan's history play, *Red Hugh*, Yeats declared his desire to stage his early Cuchulain play, *On Baile's Strand*, in an Irish accent.¹¹³ He conceived of this play as a Greek tragedy, as he did later of the story of Deirdre, 'Ireland's Helen'.¹¹⁴ As R. F. Foster puts it, Yeats was of the view that 'the new Irish literature could learn from the Greeks and even the English'.¹¹⁵ Yeats conceived of the Kiltartan speech employed in Lady Gregory's version of the tales as marks of authenticity, employed in much the same manner in which the Greek language was used in Benson's productions of the old Greek tales, which initiated a new trend in Victorian theatre. It was hoped that Lady Gregory's authenticated rendition of the old material would contribute to the evolution of a dramatic movement in Ireland in much the same manner.

When *Cuchulain of Muirthemne* was finally published, it received a unanimous welcome from the prominent literary and political circles of the times, to which she was proud to draw attention in her autobiography.[116] By this time the literary interests of these circles had begun to shift from Hellenism to Celticism, and her book was received as a charming, new interpretation of the old legends. Her final version dismissed Hyde's earlier claims that a colloquial style would not be fitting for the old legends, and flattened Atkinson's and Mahaffy's first suggestions that the old material was not worthy of being published for its lack of idealism and decency. Professor York Powell, friend of the Yeats family, congratulated Lady Gregory on her literary achievement: 'Your *Cuchulain* is an abiding joy. Cuchulain is most beautiful; the Deirdre part one of the most beautiful stories in the world I should think now. How odd that no one in Greek times ever idealised Helen and Paris! All the poets speak of them with some severity, and most with definite hatred'.[117] In its idealism and its use of language Professor Powell found her text even superior to the ancient tales, writing to the author that '[y]ou have the gratitude of everybody who cares for poetry of the highest kind, and the noblest tradition of Epic story'.[118] 'Lady Gregory had done her work as compiler with a judgement', wrote George Russell, 'which could hardly be too much praised, and she has translated the stories into an idiom which is a reflection of the original Gaelic and is full of charm'.[119] Here he was clearly echoing Yeats's thoughts on authenticity and language. Russell went further than this, however, in emphasising the inherently dramatic and artistic qualities of the text: 'I never thought I would like to read anything about Cuchulain after O'Grady's old epic. But you have swept away my prejudices by a dream wind of beautiful pictures'.[120] His words here were shrewdly chosen to echo the remarks of an *An Claidheamh Soluis* reporter who had written of Milligan's Ossianic trilogy in 1900: that it was a 'set of beautiful pictures'.[121] By phrasing his praise in a manner similar to the published admiration of her rival's work, Russell claimed a public recognition for his friend's version of the tales, a recognition which had been attributed hitherto mostly to the artistic and dramatic work of Alice Milligan. Moreover, with these shrewd comments, Russell instantly expelled O'Grady's earlier damning remarks on contemporary dramatisation of the tales. O'Grady considered the many crowd-pleasing adaptations to be a public degradation of the old Irish ideals. In his view, the modern adaptations used the tales for a specific, populist nationalist agenda, which was dishonest to the original ideals of the tales.[122]

Lady Gregory's version was much in line with O'Grady's own propositions in that it too praised the noble traditions of Ireland, the dissemination of which O'Grady had first undertaken in *History of Ireland*. *Cuchulain of Muirthemne* or *Gods and Fighting Men* did not in any way, to use O'Grady's word, 'degrade' the noble ideals of the medieval tales, as did many of the popular contemporary adaptations, in his view.

In fact, Lady Gregory reclaimed the legends for the aristocratic tradition of which she, Ruskin, and O'Grady were undoubtedly proud. By aligning the Celtic legends with Sir Thomas Malory's *Le Morte d'Arthur*, with Lord Tennyson's *Idylls of the King*, and, most importantly, with Homer's *Iliad* and *Odyssey*, she rescued them from what she thought to be the clutches of populist nationalism with which she was decidedly uncomfortable at this point of her life. She disseminated in her versions of the old tales the principle of *noblesse oblige* that her aristocratic social circle held in high esteem as the mark of gentlemanly conduct. As part of what she considered to be an educational project for Irish society, she compiled the old Celtic tales into 'textbooks', to use Evangelista's term. The objective was to teach young Irish boys the moral codes of mature masculinity in the manner of Homeric texts as used in colleges and universities during the Victorian period. By modelling the Celtic heroes on leading nineteenth-century British politicians, she could shape their characters in such a way that the heroes became Victorian aristocratic prototypes, easily identifiable by anyone familiar with the Arthurian legends or the Homeric texts, or indeed by any of their many nineteenth-century adaptations. This undoubtedly meant the Anglicisation of the Celtic material; she had taken many a step further in this regard than many scholars of Celtic literature and culture, including Windisch, Meyer, O'Curry, and O'Grady. But she had often looked across the Irish Sea for sources of inspiration and she did consider what she saw as a general programme of cultural education that was being implemented in Ireland to be broader in its remit than the geographical borders of the island of Ireland. If Greek heroes, or, indeed, medieval knights could be considered 'spiritual companions to modern Englishmen', to cite Evangelista again, then there was a high probability that the champions of the Celts could act as role models for Irishmen, young and old. Enabling the dramatisation of Irish legend by compiling the old tales as a series of 'beautiful pictures' or *tableaux vivants*, she gave herself and her acquaintances involved with the literary movement in Ireland the opportunity to disseminate her artistic and social ideas to a wide audience.

Notes

1. Judith Hill, *Lady Gregory: An Irish Life* (Stroud: Sutton, 2005), 127.
2. Hill, *Lady Gregory*, 115.
3. Henry [sic] Schliemann, *Troja: Results in the Latest Researches and Discoveries on the Site of Homer's Troy, and in the Heroic Tumuli and Other Sites, Made in the Year of 1882* (London: Murray, 1884). Schliemann writes specifically about how measurements in Homer's *Iliad* had given him exact measurements to locate camps, walls and heroic *tumuli*, 283–84.
4. A. H. Sayce, "Preface," in Henry Schliemann, *Troja: Results in the Latest Researches and Discoveries on the Site of Homer's Troy, and in the Heroic Tumuli and Other Sites, Made in the Year of 1882* (London: Murray, 1884), v–xxx. Professor Sayce of Oxford hailed his contemporary's achievements in the following terms: 'The problem, from which the scholars of Europe had turned away in despair, has been solved by the skill, the energy, and the perseverance, of Dr. Schliemann. At Troy, at Mykenae, and at Orkhomenos, he has recovered a past which had already become but a shadowy memory in the age of Peisistratos. [...] The heroes of the Iliad and Odyssey have become to us men of flesh and blood; we can watch both them, and older heroes still, in almost every act of their daily life [...]'. Sayce, "Preface," vii.
5. For her trip, see Hill, *Lady Gregory*, 139–40 and Hill, "Finding a Voice: Augusta Gregory, Raftery, and Cultural Nationalism, 1899–1900," *Irish University Review* 34, no. 1 (Spring/Summer 2004): 21–36, especially 24–5.
6. Lady Augusta Gregory, "Letter," *An Claidheamh Soluis*, December 2, 1899, 605.
7. Lady Augusta Gregory, "The Poet Raftery," *The Argosy* (January 1901): 44–58.
8. Lady Augusta Gregory, "Raftery's Grave," *An Claidheamh Soluis*, (September 8, 1900): 406.
9. Lady Gregory quoted in Maureen Murphy, "Lady Gregory and the Gaelic League," in *Lady Gregory, Fifty Years After*, ed. Ann Saddlemyer and Colin Smythe (Gerrards Cross: Colin Smythe, 1987), 151.
10. Hill, "Finding a Voice," 25.
11. Hill, *Lady Gregory*, 113.
12. For Robert's earlier acquaintance with the material, and for his mother's help, see James Pethica, ed. *Lady Gregory's Diaries, 1892–1902* (Gerrards Cross: Colin Smythe, 1996), 12.
13. Hill, *Lady Gregory*, 77.
14. Hill, *Lady Gregory*, 19.

15. Gregory, *Seventy Years*, 393.
16. Gregory, *Seventy Years*, 393; Pethica, *Diaries*, 292.
17. Gregory, *Seventy Years*, 393.
18. Gregory, *Seventy Years*, 394.
19. Philip O'Leary, *The Prose Literature of the Celtic Revival, 1880–1921* (Pennsylvania: Pennsylvania State University Press, 1994), 232.
20. Gregory, *Seventy Years*, 391.
21. Lady Augusta Gregory, *Cuchulain of Muirthemne: The Story of the Men of the Red Branch of Ulster* (Gerrards Cross: Colin Smythe, 1975), 271–72.
22. Gregory, *Seventy Years*, 398.
23. Qtd. in O'Leary, *The Prose Literature of the Celtic Revival*, 223.
24. O'Leary, *The Prose Literature of the Celtic Revival*, 229.
25. O'Leary, *The Prose Literature of the Celtic Revival*, 229.
26. Gregory, *Cuchulain*, 5.
27. Eugene O'Curry, *Lectures on the Manuscript Material of Ancient Irish History* (Dublin: Duffy, 1861), vii.
28. O'Curry, *Lectures on the Manuscript Material of Ancient Irish History*, ix.
29. Michael McAteer, *Standish O'Grady, AE and Yeats: History, Politics, Culture* (Dublin: Irish Academic Press, 2002), 15.
30. McAteer, *Standish O'Grady, AE and Yeats*, 18.
31. Standish O'Grady, *Selected Essays and Passages* (Dublin: Talbot; London: Unwin, 1918), 88 and 92.
32. Declan Kiberd, *Irish Classics* (Cambridge, MA: Harvard University Press, 2001), 402.
33. Gregory, *Seventy Years*, 391.
34. A new, printed version of *The Feast of Bricriu/Fled Bricend* had just appeared on the literary market; the Irish Texts Society of London, with its President, Douglas Hyde, published one of the central tales of the Ulster Cycle in 1899.
35. Gregory, *Seventy Years*, 393.
36. Kiberd, *Irish Classics*, 406–7.
37. Gregory, *Seventy Years*, 393.
38. Gregory, *Cuchulain*, 5.
39. Gregory, *Cuchulain*, 9. Eleanor Hull and Peadar Mac Fhionnlaoich remarked in *An Claidheamh Soluis* that the Gaelic League welcomed any new adaptation of the old legends. O'Leary, 234–35.
40. Peter Kuch, ed. *G. W. Russell—A.E: Writings on Literature and Art*, in *Collected Works*, vol. 4 (Gerrards Cross: Colin Smythe, 2011), 72.
41. Gregory, *Seventy Years*, 393.
42. Lady Augusta Gregory, ed. *Mr. Gregory's Letter-Box, 1813–1830* (London: Smith and Elder, 1898), 14–53; see correspondence on the potato famine and its consequences in Gregory, *Mr. Gregory's Letter-Box*, 212–18.

43. Colin Graham, *Ideologies of Epic: Nation, Empire and Victorian Epic Poetry* (Manchester: Manchester University Press, 1998), 55.
44. Graham, *Ideologies of Epic*, 59.
45. Graham, *Ideologies of Epic*, 57.
46. Peter Denman, *Samuel Ferguson: The Literary Achievement* (Gerrards Cross: Colin Smythe, 1990), 116.
47. Graham, *Ideologies of Epic*, 111.
48. Graham, *Ideologies of Epic*, 103.
49. Montague J. Guest, "Introduction," in *Lady Charlotte Schreiber's Journals*, ed. Montague J. Guest (London: John Lane, 1911), viii.
50. Richard Jenkyns, *The Victorians and Ancient Greece* (Cambridge, MA: Harvard University Press, 1981), 211.
51. Jenkyns, *The Victorians and Ancient Greece*, 193.
52. Stefano Evangelista, *British Aestheticism and Ancient Greece: Hellenism, Reception and Gods in Exile* (Basingstoke: Palgrave Macmillan, 2009), 9.
53. Evangelista, *British Aestheticism and Ancient Greece*, 9.
54. Evangelista, *British Aestheticism and Ancient Greece*, 9.
55. John Ruskin, *Modern Painters*, vol. 3 in *The Works of John Ruskin*, ed. E. T. Cook and Alexander Wedderburn, vol. 5 (London: George Allen, 1903–1912), 207–8 and 216–17. Further references to Cook and Wedderburn's multivolume work will be as follows: Ruskin, *Title of Individual Work*, volume number.page number. Example here: Ruskin, *Modern Painters*, vol. 3, 5.207–8 and 5.216–17.
56. Chapman's first complete translations of the *Iliad* and the *Odyssey* were published in 1616, although his first translations of Homer's works date back to the end of the sixteenth century. Writers and poets of English Romanticism differed in their views on these translations. John Keats, for instance, favoured Chapman's work above all others. Towards the middle of the century, the intensity of the debate was such that a series of new translations were made available to the reading public.
57. Ruskin, *Lectures on Art*, 20.76. Birch tracks down the many changes in the art critic's evaluation of the poet's translation of Homer in Dinah Birch, "Ruskin's Revised Eighteenth Century," in *The Victorians and the Eighteenth Century: Reassessing the Tradition*, ed. Francis O'Gorman and Katherine Turner (Aldershot: Ashgate, 2004), 163–81.
58. Ruskin, *Fors Clavigera*, 27.586.
59. Birch, "Ruskin's Revised Eighteenth Century," 168.
60. Edward Alexander, *Matthew Arnold, John Ruskin and the Modern Temper* (Columbus, OH: Ohio State University Press, 1973), 156.
61. Alexander, *Matthew Arnold*, 156.
62. Alexander, *Matthew Arnold*, 156.

63. For Hunt and Rossetti, see Ruskin, *Art of England*, 33.267–86; for Burne-Jones, Watts, Leighton, and Alma-Tadema, see 33.287–326.
64. For production details, see Katherine Newey and Jeffrey Richards, *John Ruskin and the Victorian Theatre* (Basingstoke: Palgrave Macmillan, 2010), 88.
65. Michael Dobson, *Shakespeare and Amateur Performance: A Cultural History* (Cambridge: Cambridge University Press, 2011), 166. Dobson asserts that there was a direct link between the rapidly rising interest in outdoor performances in the last few decades of the nineteenth century and the archaeological discoveries of the period.
66. Don Chapman, *Oxford Playhouses: High and Low Drama in a University City* (Hatfield: University of Hertfordshire Press, 2008), 13.
67. Chapman, *Oxford Playhouses*, 14. Benson, who started his career as a Shakespearean actor, returned to the plays of the bard at the Lyceum, after a brief engagement with Greek theatre at Oxford.
68. Newey and Richards, *John Ruskin and the Victorian Theatre*, 88.
69. For more production details, see Newey and Richards, *John Ruskin and the Victorian Theatre*, 89–90; Jenkyns, *The Victorians and Ancient Greece*, 302; Jeffrey Richards, "John Ruskin, the Olympian Painters and the Amateur Stage," in *Ruskin, the Theatre and Visual Culture*, ed. Anselm Heinrich, Katherine Newey, and Jeffrey Richards (Basingstoke: Palgrave Macmillan, 2009), 31–33.
70. Jenkyns, *The Victorians and Ancient Greece*, 303; Newey and Richards, *John Ruskin and the Victorian Theatre*, 90.
71. Jenkyns, *The Victorians and Ancient Greece*, 301 and 310–11.
72. Michael R. Booth, *Victorian Spectacular Theatre, 1850–1910* (London: Routledge, 1981), 65–67.
73. Newey and Richards, *John Ruskin and the Victorian Theatre*, 76.
74. Newey and Richards, *John Ruskin and the Victorian Theatre*, 92.
75. Elizabeth Prettejohn, "Between Homer and Ovid: Metamorphoses of the 'grand style' in G. F. Watts," in *Representations of G. F. Watts: Art Making in Victorian Culture*, ed. Colin Trodd and Stephanie Brown (Aldershot: Ashgate, 2004), 56.
76. Prettejohn, "Between Homer and Ovid," 56.
77. Prettejohn, "Between Homer and Ovid," 50.
78. Jenkyns, *The Victorians and Ancient Greece*, 311.
79. Jenkyns, *The Victorians and Ancient Greece*, 311.
80. Kuch, *G. W. Russell*, 74.
81. Kuch, *G. W. Russell*, 72.
82. Kuch, *G. W. Russell*, 72.
83. Kuch, *G. W. Russell*, 262.
84. Kuch, *G. W. Russell*, 262–63.

85. Kuch, *G. W. Russell*, 263.
86. Jenkyns, *The Victorians and Ancient Greece*, 317.
87. William Butler Yeats, "Preface," in Lady Augusta Gregory, *Cuchulain of Muirthemne* (Gerrards Cross: Colin Smythe, 1975), 11.
88. Yeats, "Preface," 11.
89. Jenkyns, *The Victorians and Ancient Greece*, 304.
90. Jenkyns, *The Victorians and Ancient Greece*, 304–5.
91. Gregory, *Seventy Years*, 412.
92. Jenkyns, *The Victorians and Ancient Greece*, 201.
93. Jenkyns, *The Victorians and Ancient Greece*, 201.
94. Gregory, *Seventy Years*, 57.
95. Jenkyns, *The Victorians and Ancient Greece*, 200; Quentin Broughall, "A Careful Hellenism and a Reckless Roman-ness: The Gladstone-Disraeli Rivalry in the Context of Classics," in *Gladstone: Ireland and Beyond*, ed. Mary E. Daly and K. Theodore Hoppen (Dublin: Four Courts Press, 2011), 153.
96. Jenkyns, *The Victorians and Ancient Greece*, 200; Broughall, "A Careful Hellenism and a Reckless Roman-ness," 149.
97. Fiona Macintosh, "Viewing *Agamemnon* in Nineteenth-Century Britain," in *Agamemnon in Performance, 458 BC to 2004 AD*, ed. Edith Hall, Fiona Macintosh, Pantelis Michelakis, and Oliver Taplin (Oxford: Oxford University Press, 2005), 139–62. Macintosh questions the validity of Wilde's claim but asserts that '[w]hat is significant about these claims, of course, is the fact that retrospectively, at least, the undoubted success of the 1880 *Agamemnon* made it worthy of close association'.
98. Evangelista, *British Aestheticism and Ancient Greece*, 11.
99. On conformism and conservatism, see Evangelista, *British Aestheticism and Ancient Greece*, 11.
100. Pethica, *Diaries*, 100.
101. Pethica, *Diaries*, 140.
102. Pethica, *Diaries*, 144.
103. For notes and details on John Gray's poems, see Pethica, *Diaries*, 46.
104. Catherine Morris, *Alice Milligan and the Irish Cultural Revival* (Dublin: Four Courts Press, 2012). Morris gives a very detailed account of Milligan's political activism during the period of the Irish literary and cultural revival at the turn of the twentieth century.
105. Yeats establishes the influence through William Fay and his company of amateur actors, who staged Alice Milligan's *Red Hugh*, a performance that mesmerised him. Milligan's influence was, of course, far greater than acknowledged by Yeats in his essay. William Butler Yeats, *Autobiographies* (Basingstoke: Macmillan, 1992), 449.
106. Pethica, *Diaries*, 242.

107. For a detailed account of the troubled production process, see J. C. C. May, "Introduction," in *Diarmuid and Grania*, Manuscript Materials by W. B. Yeats and George Moore, ed. J. C. C. Mays (New York: Cornell University Press, 2005), xxxvii.
108. Lady Augusta Gregory, *Our Irish Theatre: A Chapter of Autobiography* (Gerrards Cross: Colin Smythe, 1972), 29.
109. Mays, "Introduction," xxxviii–xxxix.
110. The fact that Frank Benson could not pronounce Irish personal and place names did not help matters. Mays, "Introduction," xxxvii–xxxviii.
111. For Yeats's comments, see Yeats, "Preface," 11; Synge is quoted in Gregory, *Seventy Years*, 403; and Russell's comments are in Kuch, *G. W. Russell*, 72.
112. R. F. Foster, *W. B. Yeats, A Life: The Apprentice Mage*, vol. 1 (Oxford: Oxford University Press, 1998), 185.
113. Yeats, *Autobiographies*, 449.
114. For *On Baile's Strand*, see Yeats, *Autobiographies*, 449; for *Deirdre*, see Foster, *W. B. Yeats*, vol. 1, 321.
115. Foster, *W. B. Yeats*, vol. 1, 131.
116. For her own account of the reception of *Cuchulain of Muirthemne* and *Gods and Fighting Men*, see Gregory, *Seventy Years*, 400–4.
117. Lady Gregory, *Seventy Years*, 401.
118. Qtd. in Lady Gregory, *Seventy Years*, 401.
119. Kuch, *G. W. Russell*, 75.
120. Gregory, *Seventy Years*, 403.
121. Qtd. in Morris, *Alice Milligan*, 247.
122. See Standish O'Grady in the *All Ireland Review*, Kuch, *G. W. Russell*, 68. Kuch points out that in later years Russell grew less assured in his views regarding the dramatisation of the legends. Kuch, *G. W. Russell*, 330–31.

'Ní neart go cur le chéile': Education, Social Reform, and the Abbey Theatre

THE HOME INDUSTRIES AND THE CO-OPERATIVE MOVEMENT

Ní neart go cur le chéile—'no strength without co-operation' (old Irish proverb).

By the 1900s, Lady Gregory had become active in the agricultural movement that aimed at improving the quality of local Irish produce and its distribution abroad. The hope was that over time this would improve Irish farmers' living standards and working conditions. Lady Gregory believed that the comprehensive agricultural reform movement, fostered by Chief Secretary Gerard Balfour and Horace Plunkett, would prove beneficial for tenants and landlords alike. This movement, with its emphasis on character building and the central role that it attributed to the arts, bore the hallmarks of Ruskin's social and economic ideas. Lady Gregory and Plunkett met at Baron Monteagle's dinner party on 16 March 1897, and had a long conversation about the growing success of the Irish Agricultural Organisation Society (IAOS), founded in 1894, with Plunkett as its President, R. A. Anderson as its Secretary, and Fr. Thomas Finlay as the Editor of its newspaper, *The Irish Homestead*.[1] Gerard Balfour wholeheartedly supported the project because the grand-scale, government-financed road and railway projects that his brother, Arthur Balfour, had proposed earlier in the decade remained largely ineffective in developing the Irish countryside, and he appreciated the novelty of the IAOS's approach. Following the dinner at Monteagle's,

© The Author(s) 2018
E. Remport, *Lady Gregory and Irish National Theatre*,
Bernard Shaw and His Contemporaries,
https://doi.org/10.1007/978-3-319-76611-9_4

Lady Gregory compiled ideas from James Anthony Froude's *The English in Ireland in the Eighteenth Century* for Plunkett to use in the Irish Financial Relations debate at Westminster.[2] She then invited Plunkett, Yeats, and Barry O'Brien for dinner to talk about the agricultural movement, politics, and art.[3] She wrote in her diary that she had helped 'co-operation' among these people: she handed a pamphlet on agriculture to O'Brien; gave her notes on Froude to Plunkett (to help him prepare for the coming parliamentary debate); suggested that O'Brien send on his *History of Ireland* to Plunkett; and handed over a short collection of folklore material to Yeats, who was much engaged at the time in preparations for the centennial celebrations of the United Irishman Rebellion of 1798, to be held the following year.[4]

She continued to support the work of the agricultural movement throughout the summer of 1897. She invited Plunkett, 'working himself to death' for the movement, to give a talk to farmers at Gort in September.[5] Plunkett's visit paved the way for the establishment of an IAOS branch in Gort. Sr. Mary de Lourdes Fahy remembered that Lady Gregory pressed ahead with the move 'despite fierce opposition from the shopkeepers who knew that farmers could now buy seeds and fertilisers in bulk and at a cheaper rate from the co-operatives'.[6] Slowly, Plunkett began to find Lady Gregory's literary movement increasingly compelling, especially for its potential to assist the agricultural movement. Consequently, he invited Yeats and Edward Martyn to an IAOS dinner to give a talk on the literary movement, and he took an active role in the amendment of the Local Government Bill, which was to grant occasional licence for theatrical performances.[7] As Lionel Pilkington has pointed out, it was this amendment (which Gerard Balfour, the Chief Secretary administered upon Plunkett's strong advice) which created the legal framework for the establishment of the Irish Literary Theatre in 1899.[8]

Supporting Plunkett's agricultural movement, Lady Gregory wrote up an article for one of the most well-respected London newspapers, *The Nineteenth Century*. 'Ireland, Real and Ideal' championed the new idea of agricultural co-operation in Ireland, which was hoped to improve the working and living conditions of those in the agricultural sector. She wrote in favour of the idea of forming a chain of co-operative societies in Ireland and of establishing a new system of banking to resolve the credit crisis of the sector.[9] The proposed Raffeisen bank system was based on a highly successful European model. It was hoped that the new system of rural banks would help indebted small farmers to acquire new loans without sliding into a debt cycle. It was also hoped that the new system of rural banking would make the well-established joint stock banks (which usually advanced money only to better-off farmers) review their position on lending to the poorer small farmers.[10] Thomas Boylan and Timothy Foley explain how the Raffeisen system was the direct opposite of the *laissez faire* economic system dominant in England throughout the nineteenth century; hence, it needed some publicising in England.[11] The banking system of Ireland and its operation became topics of long-drawn debates in the British Parliament. George Russell himself had to give a talk on the system of money lending in Ireland to a Select Committee of the House of Lords. As Lady Gregory noted afterwards, Russell was:

> full of life & energy—evidently doing his work well—& feeling that he is doing so—He makes me more hopeful about the state of the poor—for tho' the famine is bad now he does not think there will be actual death from starvation—& he thinks this may be remedied in the future—by co-operation—rural bonds—co-op stores & poultry farming—the people suffering terribly now from the 'gombeen men'.[12]

Setting up the co-operative societies and stores was an important step in rescuing farmers from the clutches of 'gombeenism'. Emphasising the importance of her friend's claims, Lady Gregory stated in 'Ireland, Real and Ideal' that the new system of village banks and the newly established chain of co-operative societies were indeed viable solutions to many of the grievances of Irish farming. She stressed that besides the obvious long-term benefits of the new agricultural scheme, farmers could experience its many immediate positive effects. For instance, she pointed out that by excluding the gombeen men and their profits from the system, the prices of goods had already fallen.[13]

'Self-help by mutual help' was also the motto of the co-operative movement in England, although the aims of the movement in England and in Ireland differed significantly. Plunkett soon realised these differences and the Irish Sectional Board of the Co-operative Wholesale Society (CWS), with Plunkett as its President, resigned from the CWS in 1895. The Board did so in order to dedicate their time fully to the establishment of the IAOS in Ireland. The CWS was, as Carla King calls it, an 'overwhelmingly consumer-oriented parent body', which had been set up to safeguard the rights and needs of consumers.[14] It was at the July 1888 conference of the CWS in Ipswich that Plunkett succeeded in establishing the Irish Co-operative Aid Association (ICAA). The ICAA however, could not solve the three main problems that Plunkett identified in Ireland: the owners of small shops being forced to buy their goods from larger retailers and thereby support the monopolies of the latter; the poor farmers buying on bank credit from the small shops; the more affluent farmers buying their stock in England.[15] In rejecting the CWS-style retail, wholesale, and manufacture of goods, the leaders of the Irish co-operative movement followed in the footsteps of Ruskin, who voiced his own concerns about retail commerce in his 1867 work *Time and Tide*. Ruskin condemned retail industry because he associated it with the 'degradation of persons occupied in it'.[16] He believed that profit-driven competitive industry generated selfishness, gradually turning society into a mass of self-absorbed producers.[17] Separating the Irish Co-operative Movement from the British CWS meant losing the financial support of a powerful and influential organisation. However, Plunkett and the Irish Sectional Board felt that separating from the parent body was the only possible way to initiate the necessary structural and financial reforms in Ireland. As Plunkett wrote in his later book, *Ireland in the New Century* (1904), what was really needed at the time was 'the rehabilitation of Ireland from within', by which he meant the internal reform of the country's economic system.[18]

Ruskin was, of course, critical of the alienating and dehumanising effects of contemporary processes of mass industrial production in Britain. The situation in Ireland was quite different, for the problem there was not one of overproduction, but rather the lack of good-quality production of goods, especially of agricultural produce. Despite the fundamental differences between the economic structures of Britain and of Ireland, Ruskin's repeated calls to restore the home industries to their former social status resonated with social and political leaders on both sides of the Irish Sea. Ruskin thought that the revival of the home industries would be beneficial in terms of creating new-style working environments. He hoped that the workshops would foster comradeship among fellow labourers and raise the general level of compassion within society towards the manual labourer. Ruskin thought that this would counter the divisive impact of economic competition for ever greater private company profits, which induced workers to regard their work solely as a means of survival, a pattern that he observed in the larger industrial towns of Britain.[19] For this reason, as part of his plan for a Guild of St. George, he helped set up the Langdale Linen Industry at Westmoreland and helped build a water-mill, St. George's Mill, at Laxey.[20] Ruskin was not alone in his attempts to reform the working and living conditions of manual labourers. Robert Owen, the Chartist movement, and the Rochdale co-operatives in England; John Doherty (with his Owenite cotton mill in Larne, Co. Antrim), and John Vandaleur on his Ralahine estate in Co. Clare: each tried to 'extend the field of social improvement'.[21] The uniqueness of Ruskin's approach lay in his insistence on the prominence of art in the social reform movement. Hobson has noted that the success of the Home Arts and Industries Association, founded in 1884, was evidence of the broad influence of Ruskin's social teachings.[22]

Ruskin clearly indicated in the objectives of the St. George's Guild that the revival of home industries as well as the agrarian and social reform movement should be extended to Ireland.[23] Alice Rowland Hart's work in Co. Donegal can be seen as one of the first attempts to revive the cottage industries in Ireland during the 1880s. The Donegal Industrial Fund encouraged the revival of the arts of spinning, weaving, knitting and embroidery; it was established with a view to providing work for the rural population of the county during the winter months, when it was almost impossible to make a living within the agricultural sector.[24] The unique, embroidered decoration of the Donegal linen, with its designs inspired by the Book of Kells, made the hand-crafted fashion items popular with the genteel women of Britain and Ireland. Rowland Hart's endeavour was enthusiastically supported by Lord and Lady Aberdeen, who used their high-society connections to boost sales of the beautiful hand-crafted products. Due to the Aberdeens' unfaltering support, Hart's constant enthusiasm, and the Donegal women's exceptional craftsmanship, the small co-operative endeavour became very successful within a relatively short space of time.[25]

Lady Gregory herself took part in helping to revive the cottage industries in Ireland. Her proposal to introduce net manufacturing and carpentry at the Gort Workhouse fell through due to the opposition of the local parish priest, Fr. Jerome Fahey. Her suggestion about the expansion of the linen-weaving workshop in the Gort Convent industrial school, in contrast, was greeted with enthusiasm by the local clergy. The workshop at the Sisters of Mercy School began to supply embroidered linen and tennis dresses for Lady Aberdeen and Lady Cadogan's prestigious Textile Exhibitions in London.[26] 'The Irish Industries in London', explains Hill, 'was an organisation, set up by Lady Aberdeen in 1886, to sell products of Irish cottage industries'.[27] Lady Gregory also penned an article about convent industries for *Erin, an Illustrated Journal of Art and Industry* (1896) in order to increase the sale of the Gort products.[28] She continued to actively participate in fostering good relations between the emerging manufacturing and the co-operative movements in Ireland. She discussed the future of the cottage industries with Lady Fingall, Lady Londonderry, and Florence Burke; women who were involved in organising the annual meetings of the Irish Industries. She knew that the bazaars were vital for promoting hand-made Irish goods among those who had the means to purchase them, but she also felt fatigued at the end of the long market days:

> I feel it ignominious, all this talk & professions about helping the poor Irish—& then fashionable people come, & buy from other fashionable people, getting as much as they can for their money, either in goods, or other commodities—& the extravagance of their dress makes one think of the poor workers at home![29]

These bazaars took place in fashionable London residences, such as Londonderry House, Lansdowne House, and Chelsea House; those in attendance were mainly wealthy English and Anglo-Irish aristocrats. Lady Gregory knew that the bazaars were excellent venues for marketing Irish produce; newspaper reports of the events spread the news about the developing Irish home industries. Nonetheless, out of these experiences grew also the realisation that the substantial financial and material improvement of Irish agriculture and manufacturing could only really be achieved through direct and grass-roots level involvement in the sectors.

She talked to Plunkett about this after the Chelsea House Irish Exhibition.[30] 'Ireland, Real and Ideal' was penned not long after this meeting. Plunkett gave a talk on the future of co-operation and agriculture in Ireland at the Irish Industries meeting in Londonderry House, and about a year later Lady Gregory accepted the invitation for dinner at Plunkett's residence. Lady Balfour, Lord Lytton, and Florence Burke were invited to the dinner; alongside W. B. Yeats, Edward Martyn, and George Moore.[31] The guests may have disagreed on what the causes were of the many social problems in Ireland and what measures should be taken to address the many social grievances, but the event most certainly indicated the growing rapprochement between those at the forefront of the Irish literary, manufacturing, and agricultural revival during the last few years of the nineteenth century. Further signs of the increasing support for each other's work were Lady Balfour's financial interventions at bazaars and artistic exhibitions—she bought handmade dresses by Gort manufacturers at Lady Gregory's stalls at the Irish

Industries bazaar and she prompted the sale of a Jack. B. Yeats painting at the Watercolour Exhibition.[32] On Lady Fingall's advice, Lady Balfour arranged for a performance of Yeats's *The Countess Cathleen* at her residence in Phoenix Park, with her friend in the title role. Yeats did not attend the event as it was held at the Chief Secretary's Lodge, but Lady Gregory, Russell, and Yeats himself helped with the preparations.[33] For these aristocratic ladies, the primary theme of Yeats's play was that of *noblesse oblige*, and they were flattered to participate in a performance which, in their view, glorified the aristocratic traditions of Ireland in that it presented a sorrowful Countess willing to make the ultimate sacrifice, that of her own soul, to save the souls of her tenants from eternal damnation. For those present at the performance, the play re-evoked the sense of *noblesse oblige* which permeated nineteenth-century culture in Britain and Ireland. Ruskin held this principle in the highest regard. He asserted in *Fors Clavigera* that aristocrats should themselves be 'shepherd lords', responsible for the well-being of their 'herd'.[34] Evoking here the figure of Christ as he did in many of his writings, the passage intentionally brings to mind Christ's ultimate sacrifice on the Cross, when Jesus becomes the Sacrificial Lamb in offering up his own life to save the souls of men from eternal damnation.

At this time, Yeats was involved in preparations for the centennial celebrations to commemorate the United Irishmen Rebellion of 1798 and he was moving in circles promoting revolution as the only effective way to alter Ireland's position within the British Empire. Hence, it is understandable that he had reservations about the venue for the performance of *The Countess Cathleen*.[35] But at this point in time the Irish dramatic movement was still in its infancy, and it needed the support of those in influential positions. Lady Gregory was pleased to enter in her diary that, as a result of the growing support for the co-operative movement among those involved in the Irish Literary Revival, Plunkett himself was beginning to show interest in the literary and language movements.[36] Trevor West has suggested that a reason for this was the co-operative man's growing awareness of the beneficial effects of native literature and the teaching of folklore on social life in Denmark, a country whose example of economic progress he had hoped Ireland would emulate.[37] Hence, Plunkett agreed with Lady Gregory on the necessary role of the arts in the development of Irish society. But, of course, Plunkett's understanding of the social role of the arts also stemmed from his Oxford days: the period during which Ruskin was disseminating his social and aesthetic principles so emphatically. Like Ruskin, Plunkett enjoyed going to the theatre, so he readily accepted the art critic's proposition that the arts should be regarded as a means of facilitating social reform. For Plunkett, a student of history at Oxford, Ruskin's talks and writings on the use of Greek and Shakespearean drama for the teaching of history would have been particularly persuasive. So when it came to taking a stance on whether or not to support the emerging dramatic movement in Ireland, Plunkett was in favour of the idea of staging new plays in support of Irish social reform.

The Irish Literary Theatre and the Abbey Theatre

At this time the notion of creating an Irish literary theatre was in the air. Lady Gregory credited a meeting at the residence of Sir William's old friend Count Florimonde de Basterot as the starting point of the movement which would lead to the establishment of the Irish Literary Theatre in 1899 followed by the foundation of the Abbey Theatre in 1904. The meeting with de Basterot was followed by a longer and more significant gathering in the summer of 1897, when Yeats and Russell arrived at Coole Park. The two young men had known each other from their days at the Metropolitan School of Art in Dublin and the Royal Hibernian Academy, where they studied the principles of classical art. Yeats and Russell found themselves overwhelmed by the art collection in Lady Gregory's home. Yeats remembered seeing paintings by Canaletto, Velázquez, Murillo, Guardi, Zubarán; helmets, shields, and swords in ornamented sheaths from India and Persia; and East India Company and Grillon's Club memorabilia relating to Sir William's family. Besides relics deriving from the family's connections within the British Empire, there were mezzotints and engravings of William Gladstone, Lord Palmerston, Lord Wellesley, William Pitt, and Charles Fox; autographed engravings of William Thackeray, Lord Tennyson, Mark Twain, and Robert Browning.[38] Sir Frederic Burton's Irish landscape sketches added local colour to the surroundings.[39] Yeats remembered in his *Autobiographies* that 'every generation [of the Gregorys] had been highly educated, eldest sons had gone the grand tours, returning with statues or pictures'.[40] What Yeats found most impressive was the library of 'Greek and Roman Classics bound by famous French and English binders' along 'two great sweeping avenues each a mile or a little more in length'.[41]

Lady Gregory was pleased to share some anecdotes of her Grand Tours to impress and amuse the two men, taken as she was with their appreciation of the artistic heritage of her home.[42] Foster remarks that Yeats 'felt he had found sanctuary' and the 'less dramatic, more "civil" landscape of Coole would henceforth provide (as Sligo once did) the place where he could write poetry'.[43] Yeats had confessed earlier that, away from political concerns, he 'longed for pattern, for Pre-Raphaelitism, for an art allied to poetry, and returned again and again to our National Gallery to gaze at Turner's *Golden Bough*'.[44] Lady Gregory's home was a place where art *could* be allied to poetry. Here, Yeats and Russell found a suitable environment within which to share their most inner thoughts on the achievements of classical art, the masterful impressionism of William Turner, and the beautiful craftsmanship of Pre-Raphaelite painting. Coole Park had an artistic appeal and aristocratic charm at which the two young men marvelled. Beyond this, they appreciated the stability and permanence associated with the Irish Big House tradition, and they were fascinated by the extensive collection of art books which their own families had never amassed.

It was in this 'gallery of art' at Coole Park that many long conversations took place regarding the future for a new dramatic movement in Ireland. The manifesto of the emerging movement, as Lady Gregory remembered it, propounded the long-term aim 'to build up a Celtic and Irish school of dramatic literature' in order 'to bring upon the stage the deeper thoughts and emotions of Ireland'.[45] The plays were to be performed in the spring of each year to entertain and educate Irish audiences. Foster cites Yeats's own version of the original manifesto. He asserts that it pre-dated the version that Lady Gregory included in *Our Irish Theatre* as the official document of the movement. Foster writes that her version, for which she used the old typewriter of her friend Lady Layard, was recorded later, from dictation.[46] The two documents differ significantly as regards the original aims of the dramatic movement. *She* claimed that the aim was to entertain and educate audiences, while *he* emphasised the desire for the 'freedom to experiment <without which no man no longer> which <exists no longer in modern England> is not found in the theatres of England, & without which no new movement in art <is> or literature can succeed'.[47]

This difference between Lady Gregory's and Yeats's versions is very significant as it highlights a basic contrast in their understanding of Ruskin's social and art criticism. Expressing the thoughts of her genteel friends who came to act as guarantors of the Irish Literary Theatre, Lady Gregory asserted that the two aims of the new theatrical endeavour were to *entertain* and to *educate* the audience. At the time, however, Yeats conceived of the theatre primarily as a medium through which he and other theatre-makers could carry out artistic experiments with voice and verse. Like Edward Gordon Craig, John Todhunter, and Charles Ricketts, Yeats valued the antiquarian and archaic staging practices of late Victorian theatre. However, his primary hope was that they would be able to revolutionise the medium in order to restore the supremacy of poetic speech over monumental stage designs popular with theatre-makers at the time. This idea was to pave the way for the return of poetic speech to the Victorian stage, either in the form of *fin-de-siècle* Pre-Raphaelitism or under the guise of proto-modernist minimalism. Yeats first conceived of the literary scene in Dublin as one in which such experiments could be carried out without the fear of subjection to the critical scrutiny of the English press and its establishment values. As he said in *his* version of the dramatic movement's manifesto, with its ancient idealism and love of oratory, Ireland was to give him the 'freedom to experiment' which was 'not [to be] found in the theatres of England'.

For her part, Lady Gregory aligned her views more directly with those of Ruskin, who frequently commented on the educational value of the theatre. During the 1880s, Ruskin often noted that the museum and the theatre were 'means of noble education', to which he added that he 'held the stage quite among the best and most necessary means of education—moral and intellectual'.[48] Comyns Carr, who was Sir William and Lady Gregory's close friend and a dedicated Ruskinian, believed that at the *fin de siècle* the theatre's 'appeal as an educational force [was] even greater and more immediate' than earlier in the century and that it had the power to educate a broad mass of the population on the 'masterpieces of ancient art'.[49] Here Carr identifies one of the key educational aims which Ruskin assigned to the theatre: to develop the audiences' knowledge of art in its historical forms. Ruskin noted of Wilson Barrett's 'toga plays' produced at the Princess's Theatre (especially of *Claudian*) that with its beautiful scene painting and its *tableaux vivants*, the play enlightened audiences on the beauty of pictorial art.[50] *The Times* applauded the play for offering 'intellectual refinements of the people'.[51] Henry Irving of the Lyceum Theatre believed that the theatre was an ennobling place by its very nature.[52] Ruskin propounded his belief that the role of art was to elevate the soul of humanity, and he saw this maxim demonstrated in many *fin-de-siècle* productions. These used scene painting by the finest artists of the period, including Leighton, Watts, and Burne-Jones. Ruskin often attended these performances just to marvel at the pictorial beauty of the stage.

Ruskin, however, considered the theatre to be more than simply a speaking museum: he admired it for its ability to 'form character'. He held the theatre in high esteem as a medium of conveying moral messages to large audiences in an effective manner. For this reason, he praised the works of William Shakespeare, Walter Scott, and Lord Byron. Katherine Newey and Jeffrey Richards point out that during his teenage years, Ruskin had composed a five-act Venetian play entitled *Marcolini*, heavily influenced by Lord Byron's and Shakespeare's great tragedies.[53] Later, Molière joined his group of favourite authors, Ruskin being convinced that Molière's work was essentially Pre-Raphaelite, especially in its insistence on conveying moral truths in plays like *Tartuffe* and *Le Misanthrope*. He thought of Molière as an artist whose work conveyed a 'high sense of all nobleness, honour and purity' and which exhibited 'an exquisite natural wisdom' and 'a capacity for the most simple enjoyment'.[54] For Ruskin, Molière's plays were the perfect manifestations of the idea that 'all good art was didactic and should develop man's moral sense', an idea he developed from his earlier writings in *Modern Painters*.[55]

Anselm Heinrich has pointed out that in a debate at the Oxford Union in 1835 Ruskin proposed the following motion: 'Theatrical Representations are upon the whole highly beneficial to the character of a nation.'[56] Ruskin thus joined those who were calling for the establishment of a National Theatre, believing that theatre not only had an educational and a moral mission but also a *national* one.[57] Edward Bulwer-Lytton proposed a few years previously that a National Theatre, when it came into existence, should play a pivotal role in the intellectual and moral refinement of the nation.[58] A few decades later, William Gladstone contemplated the possibility of granting government subventions to aid theatres along the lines proposed by Bulwer-Lytton.[59] These government subventions would have allowed companies to become professional and theatres non-profitable, freeing the theatre from the market demands of nineteenth-century capitalist society in England. Half a century later, William Archer, another of Ruskin's disciples, drew up a plan for the establishment of a state-subsidised National Theatre in London. The National Repertory Theatre, as it was called, was to open in the year of the tercentenary of Shakespeare's death in 1916. It was to provide a moral guideline for the British nation, along the lines proposed by Ruskin at the Oxford Union in 1835. The National Repertory Theatre was to stage the greatest works of the European dramatic tradition, including those of Shakespeare, Johnson, Molière, Sheridan, Hauptmann, and Ibsen.[60] The inclusion of Yeats's *The Countess Cathleen* in the long list of plays approved for the theatre can be accounted for by Yeats's friendship with Archer and Harley Granville-Barker, and also in the light of the subject of Yeats's play. The theme of aristocratic sacrifice, carried out in the service of the poor, also added a dimension of virtue to Yeats's play. This dimension was absent from the plays that served as its basis: Marlowe's *Doctor Faustus* and Goethe's *Faust*. Memories of the Irish potato famine of the 1840s and of the more recent Irish famine of 1879 still disturbed the collective memory of the English aristocracy. A play in which a woman of aristocratic birth offers up her soul to save her distraught famine-stricken tenants struck a chord with the English nobility. Notwithstanding this, the play's subtle critique of the commercialist materialist culture of nineteenth-century English society also allowed it to be received as an artistic endorsement of some of Ruskin's economic and social principles.[61]

Archer and Granville-Barker took to promoting their ideas in *Schemes and Estimates for a National Theatre*, first published in 1904. The publication of this book coincided with the opening of the playhouse of the Irish National Theatre Society in Dublin, under the directorship of Lady Gregory, Yeats, and Synge. The road that led to the opening of the Abbey Theatre in the old Mechanics' Institute near the River Liffey in Dublin's city centre was a long and winding one; personal and political disagreements almost prevented the realisation of the project. Following heated political debates over the three-year pilot-run of the Irish Literary Theatre, disagreements with the Catholic Church over plays and productions, as well as personal differences between the poets and playwrights of the Irish Literary Revival in Dublin, Yeats began planning a return to London.[62] For a while he thought that the British capital would be a better place to realise his dramatic ambitions. Adrian Frazier argues that at this point Yeats 'was not committed to writing nationalist drama for Dublin' but to scripting 'literary drama laid in Irish scenes', earnestly hoping for theatrical successes akin to those of Wilde or Shaw on the London stage.[63] Foster also notes Yeats's 'new phase of theatrical activity' around this time, including plans for the establishment of a new theatre in London under the auspices of The Literary Theatre Club.[64]

'The Theatre of Beauty', as it was described, was to be realised by Florence Farr, Edith Craig, Laurence Binyon, George Moore, Charles Ricketts, and Yeats's other Pre-Raphaelite friends, with whom he had been in contact since his Bedford Park and Hampstead days in London. At the time, Yeats was calling for the foundation of a 'theatre of art', distinguished from the 'theatre of commerce' in its rejection of stage realism, which—in his opinion—had destroyed Victorian theatre. He was hopeful of the success of this 'Theatre of Beauty' in London because ever since Ruskin's first pronouncements on the matter, there had been a continuous demand for the de-commercialisation of the public medium, most recently repeated by his friends Archer and Granville-Barker.

Lady Gregory was critical of Yeats's plans to establish a new theatre in London and urged him to turn his attention back to Ireland.[65] Aware of the political and artistic discourse of the times, she felt that the possibility of establishing a theatre along lines proposed by Ruskin and his disciples was far greater in an archipelagic capital than in the centre of the British Empire, itself built upon the achievements of industrial capitalism. While she understood her friend's desire to establish a theatre for aesthetic ends, she also felt that any new theatre should be socially engaged and serve the people of Ireland. With the passing of the Wyndham Land Act in 1903, the remapping of the Irish rural landscape was taking place. The Wyndham Land Act provided that vast numbers of tenants could become land owners, requiring a rapid restructuring of the country's agricultural sector. Hence, the implementation of the co-operative ideals disseminated by Plunkett and the IAOS most certainly seemed timely and necessary. Lady Gregory had travelled widely around the world, deepening her understanding of land cultivation and farming, similar in kind to Plunkett's appreciation of rural life as he had experienced it during his stay in the mountainous region of Wyoming in Midwestern America. During her travels, Lady Gregory had read a number of books on land cultivation, farming, and taxation reforms. She saw for herself the state of agriculture in the countries that she visited, including the Low Countries, Switzerland, Germany, Italy, Spain, and Portugal.[66] She contemplated these countries' rural landscapes and the life of their farming communities. Seeing at first-hand what was possible to achieve in the agricultural sector made her appreciate the notion of 'better farming, better business, better living', one of the mottos of the Co-operative Movement that Horace Plunkett used. As P. J. Mathews notes, Plunkett's reform plans to help Irish farmers were outside conventional party politics. Most importantly, they lay outside the remit of militant nationalist politics, a feature of the Co-operative Movement that Lady Gregory particularly appreciated.[67] Thus, Lady Gregory saw the new theatre in Dublin as in large measure a platform for Plunkett's co-operative ideals that would serve the economic and social restructuring of Irish society.

COMEDIES OF THE IRISH COUNTRYSIDE

Performed in the same year as the passing of the Wyndham Land Act, *Twenty-Five* was her first attempt to draw attention to the problems faced by the rural population of Ireland. The theme of emigration is addressed in terms of the harsh circumstances of a particular farming household. Michael Ford is a farmer who is forced to sell his house due to '[b]ad seasons and debts'.[68] He and his wife Kate are about to leave Ireland for Manchester, where he hopes to find work with the help of a brother who has already emigrated to the city. Michael is a farmer working on his own, forced to repay his loans from his own resources as he is unable to borrow any more money. Kate, who had lost her first sweetheart, Christie Henderson, when he emigrated to America, must now face the prospect of married life away from Ireland. The play suggests that without any sort of secure, local economic structure, Irish families would continue to leave their country. It emphasises the need for a social safety network, such as that which the IAOS was seeking to create for rural Irish communities. The network of the village banks that the IAOS proposed, the so-called Raffeisen bank system, would help indebted farmers like Michael in *Twenty-Five* to acquire new loans to purchase the tools necessary for the cultivation of the land and the maintenance of livestock. Less than five years previously, Lady Gregory had written favourably about the proposed system of village banks and in her first staged portrayal of Irish rural life she returned once again to the problem of farmers' financial debt and the impossibility of acquiring new credits within the existing bank system.

Twenty-Five was first performed at the Queen's Great Hall in South Kensington; it was designed to inform London theatre-goers about the plight of Irish people and to seek the support of English upper-class society for the work undertaken by the new agricultural movement in Ireland. By depicting the harsh economic circumstances which had driven hundreds of thousands of people from the Irish countryside to seek work in Britain, Gregory sought both emotional sympathy and financial support for the new agricultural project. She championed the idea that farmers should be able 'to work out their own salvation', as she put it in 'Ireland, Real and Ideal', and she strongly supported Plunkett's idea of forming co-operative societies to help Irish farmers to develop more productive farming techniques of benefit to all members of rural communities. Plunkett and the IAOS disseminated the view that these newly established co-operative poultry farms and creameries would help farmers counter growing competition on the British market, especially competition coming from Denmark, where dairy production and distribution were of a much higher standard than in Ireland. As Plunkett's contemporary Edward E. Lysaght remarked, the co-operative leader understood that '[u]nder modern economic conditions, combination has been found necessary to the success of every industry'.[69] Lysaght wrote that '[i]solated action no longer pa[id]'.[70] Hence, co-operation was needed both among the various actors within the agricultural sector in the Irish economy but also between agricultural, manufacturing, and transportation sectors. The Raffeisen system was considered to be instrumental in bringing about co-operation between the various members of the agricultural sector and financing their development. As G. D. H. Cole has argued, the 'essential principle' of the new system, the Raffeisen Credit Society, 'should work on a basis of unlimited liability, and in the spirit of mutual trust, through a small group of farmers well known to one another personally'.[71] There were 'no individual shareholders and no common capital'. The society was 'to make advances of money to its members for limited periods and for definite approved projects', and the advancing of the money was based 'on the combined guarantee of all the members, who are all liable without limit in case of default'.[72] This system of co-operative loaning had been successful in other parts of Continental Europe. As Plunkett indicated in *Ireland in the New Century*, it was time that Irish farmers adopted 'methods successfully pursued by communities similarly situated in foreign countries'.[73]

In *Ireland in the New Century*, Plunkett propagated the co-operative motto of 'self-help by mutual help', also disseminated in Lady Gregory's 'Ireland, Real and Ideal'. Plunkett combined the economic and financial aspects of the co-operative ideal with personal and social aspects. His hope was that mutual help exercised between the members of a co-operative society would result in its members gaining self-confidence. R. A. Anderson, the Secretary of the IAOS, wrote of the beneficial effect of co-operation on the individual:

As time went on, borrowers, who had been granted loans, had applied them to the specific purpose stated and had repaid them punctually, began to feel a genuine pride in their established reputations for honesty and punctuality and have been known to boast that their credit was so good with their society that they could obtain from it all the money they needed. In short, these modest little institutions had not only succeeded in making money for their members but were also doing something even more beneficial—making *character*.[74]

The 'making of character', or, as Plunkett called it, 'the building of character', was central to the success of the co-operative project. Plunkett wrote that '[t]he building of character must be our paramount object, as it is the condition precedent of all social and economic reform in Ireland'.[75] The co-operative leaders believed that the movement would enable the development of self-assured individuals who would be released from what they regarded as the negative effects of narrow-minded parochialism and the controlling forces of *cooring*.

Performed on the opening night of the Abbey Theatre in December 1904, *Spreading the News* is a *tour-de-force* comedy in which the plot of the play revolves around a series of misunderstandings which drive Bartley Fallon straight into the hands of the local police and magistrate. Behind the veil of comedy, however, lies the playwright's subtle scrutiny of the Irish practice of *cooring*, and its effect on members of local communities. Conrad M. Arensberg and Solon T. Kinball describe *cooring* as the 'commonest form of [non-monetary] cooperation' in rural Ireland, one that involved lending tools *and* family members to help out in households or on the fields.[76] This system required a strict hierarchy in work practices and an unacknowledged consent both within the family and within the neighbourhood. *Cooring* was a system based on mutual aid, as was the co-operative system, but its success depended on the effectiveness of the control exercised by the community over its members. The community in *Spreading the News* resembles one that is accustomed to *cooring* rather than co-operation, its members defined entirely through their place in the local community. Mrs. Tarpey explains in her opening lines that the people of Cloon have 'no trade at all but to be talking'.[77] The majority of the local population has no work. Jack Smyth seems to be the only person contracted to a job but he appears to be a seasonal labourer only. Katie Donovan is right in summarising the plot as 'a word-of-mouth collective fantasy, woven of misunderstanding, jealousy and gossip', leading to the destruction of Bartley Fallon's life and marriage.[78] The word 'collective' here is apt as no character seems to have any degree of autonomy in the community of Fair Green. Each community member falls for the machinations of communal gossip-mongering. Bartley Fallon is seen at the end of the play sitting quietly and forlorn, lamenting and accepting the charges brought against him by the community. Fallon is unable (and unwilling) to fight the coercive power of local gossip. He is perfectly resigned to accepting fatalistically the external governance exercised on his character by the village community—even when it amounts to character assassination—rather than taking the weight of responsibility for his life on his own shoulders.

Lady Gregory's 1906 play, *Hyacinth Halvey*, centres on the formation of the protagonist's character. Lurking in the background of the main story, however, are some of the problems experienced at the time with regard to the Irish meat industry. Smith-Gordon and O'Brien explain that one of the advantages of bacon-curing co-operative societies was that they allowed for qualified and traceable meat supply: '[t]hese societies take their members' pigs, sheep, and cattle, slaughter them, produce bacon, and sell dressed meat'.[79] Co-operative societies of this type guaranteed to observe the quality of raw meat and promised high standards of production. In addition to their quality assurance, these societies were profitable because they put on the market all the by-products of meat-curing (from soap to sausage); nothing was wasted. Lady Gregory drew attention to these possibilities in *Hyacinth Halvey*. Quirke, the village butcher, has a family of seven to feed and has little money, so he buys up unwholesome meat from the poor who live in the countryside around the village. He buys any animal, dead or alive. Then he sells on the raw meat, without any quality certificate or proof of origin. It is only after British soldiers stationed at the Shannon Fort Barracks have fallen ill that military officials demand investigation and seizure of any suspicious unwholesome meat stored at the butcher's shop. Through this feature of the play, Lady Gregory put forward the view that the sale of unwholesome meat threatened both the butcher and the consumer in Irish villages and towns. The butcher lives in constant fear of being caught by the local police; the consumer is constantly at risk of contracting illnesses from eating poor-quality meat. Lady Gregory, who herself had encouraged the setting-up of a poultry farm near Gort, was well aware of these risks.[80]

'[T]he capitalisation of honesty' and 'the building of character' were combined in the ideology of the co-operative movement, both in Ireland

and in Continental Europe. As Anderson wrote, the co-operative credit scheme was highly respected in Germany, France, Holland, Belgium, and Italy because it was 'one of the most valuable institutions of honesty', and as such it 'had earned for itself the proud title of "the capitalisation of honesty"'.[81] Hence, as Anderson indicated, a co-operative society helped to develop a more assured basis for self-reliance among its members *and* contributed to their financial well-being, because the honesty and the punctuality required of its members had great capital value within the co-operative banking system. *Hyacinth Halvey* deals with a man whose character has been fabricated through a series of false testimonials, provided by his family members in order to enable him leave his native village. He himself confesses that he was 'not reared for labouring' and that he always enjoyed playing cards, having an 'odd spree' or a cursing match with his comrades, and poaching rabbits.[82] Still, he takes the job of a health inspector and arrives at his new post in Cloon, where the local population admire him on the basis of the virtuous character that the false testimonials portray. Unaware of their false nature, the local people accept the word of the National School Master, the Head of the National Hurling Club, and that of the parish priest at face value. Lady Gregory wrote of Cloon that it was a place where '"character" [was] built up or destroyed by a password or an emotion, rather than by experience and deliberation'.[83] The locals think Halvey's character immaculate and refuse to accept that he tries to commit crimes in Cloon precisely in order to kick away the pedestal upon which he has been placed. Placing the question of Halvey's character formation at the centre of the play, Lady Gregory discloses how the form of help provided by Halvey's family was an obstacle to Halvey's self-development. Halvey associates himself with a local criminal named Fardy, in order to deliberately tarnish his own 'virtuous' character. Halvey even resorts to stealing from a local shop and robbing a local church in an attempt to tarnish his pristine reputation. He does so because this admiration entraps him in a 'golden cage'. Being required to live near the local clergy and the local police seriously limits his freedom of movement around the village, so he decides to break out of the 'golden cage' by proving to the villagers that he is a bad egg. It is only due to the playwright's foremost desire to send a positive message to her audience that all his criminal deeds are forgiven by the end of the play.[84]

Plunkett's movement promoted the emergence of self-confident individuality, but only through work carried out in the service of the local community. Lady Gregory revisited the theme of character building in *The Jackdaw* (1908), her new rural play written after the *Playboy* riots of 1907.

In some respects it expresses her own reservations about Synge's play: it address the problem of financial debt in rural Ireland, completely ignored in *The Playboy of the Western World*. This is so, even though the hero-fool figure who believes his own lies is not a rural Irish vagabond (as in the *Playboy*) but a retired soldier of the British army, who bases a money-making plan on a story from a penny magazine. *The Jackdaw* is set in a 'broken little town', the inhabitants of which are poor. Mrs. Broderick, the town's shopkeeper, is summoned to court for owing money to creditors. Evidence of the playwright's awareness of the serious problems of the financial system as it existed in the Ireland of her time, Mrs. Broderick sighs in despair: '[t]here more die with debts on them in this place than die free of debt'.[85] She needs to turn to a banker for a loan but is unlikely to receive one, given the debt that she already carries. Mrs. Broderick turns to her brother for help. After much deliberation, Nestor decides to help out his sister but he wants his anonymity in the transaction guaranteed. Nestor fears that should his sister sense that he has money, she will pester him for more. Nestor considers himself to be a self-sufficient and a well-developed character. He has a special status in the town as a retired soldier in receipt of an army pension. However, he has never done anything for the community; the town-people's high regard for him is really based on nothing but his endless self-promotion. He boasts of never taking credit and never having incurred debts. Nestor might think himself above the rest of the community but the playwright makes it clear that Nestor's self-erected pedestal is shaking at its foundation. He continuously boasts about his education; yet, his plan to safely deliver the money to his sister goes astray, basing it as he does on stories from cheap penny magazines. He falls off his pedestal when he falls into his own trap, trying to catch jackdaws for a fictional South-African miner (whom he himself has invented) making him look like a jackdaw in the process. In *The Jackdaw*, Lady Gregory contrasts sharply the co-operative ideal of achieving a special status within a community through honest endeavour, and the inflated egotism displayed by the self-professed 'hero' of the community.

Proselytisation and Social Reform

Spreading the News, *Hyacinth Halvey*, and *The Jackdaw* were among the most popular pieces performed by the Abbey Theatre during the first decade of the twentieth century. Little wonder then that the growing success of the theatre coincided with a period of growing support for the Irish Co-operative Movement. Mathews explains this as follows:

The notion that cultural self-belief was fundamental to economic development was to become the vital informing principle of the revival. In the same way, the economic self-help ethos was to become central to most of the new cultural movements who actively advocated support for Irish industry.[86]

Plunkett himself noted in *Noblesse Oblige* (1908) that Ireland was undergoing a social revolution.[87] Some considered this social revolution to be proselytising in nature. Plunkett believed that the Roman Catholic Church and Irish people's Catholic faith were directly responsible for a deficiency of individualism within Irish society.[88] He conceded that British government policies of the previous centuries—depriving Irish people of land ownership, of proper and adequate education, and of civil rights—had contributed significantly to the lack of interest in matters relating to industrial and commercial progress within the majority population of Ireland. He accepted that the economic and financial *status quo* in Ireland had been 'the natural outcome of historical conditions' but he also believed that there was a tendency in the Irishman to act as if he was 'a mere sojourner upon earth whose true home is somewhere else, a fact often attributed to his intense faith in the unseen'.[89] In *The Protestant Ethic and the Spirit of Capitalism* (1905), Max Weber had made the same argument, stating that 'the greater other-worldliness of Catholicism, the ascetic character of its highest ideals' resulted in its followers showing 'a greater indifference toward the good things of this world'.[90] Both writers admitted, however, the overgeneralising nature of their remarks: examples from France, Germany, Austria, and Italy proved that economic success was possible in countries where the Roman Catholic Church had strong social influence.[91] Nonetheless, Plunkett believed that there was a certain aversion to economic progress emanating from the Roman Catholic Church in Ireland, partly because, as Plunkett's staunchest opponent Rev. O'Riordan asserted, 'the Catholic religious ideal [was] not the ideal of utilitarian industrialism'.[92]

Accepting Plunkett's pronouncements as essentially correct, yet holding a much greater degree of sympathy for the Irish Catholic perspective, Lady Gregory's position on the issue of social progress was, in fact, located somewhere between that held by Plunkett and that of Ruskin. Plunkett recognised that social progress in Ireland needed to have a commercial and mercantile dimension to ensure the development of high-quality production within the Irish agricultural, manufacturing, and transportation sectors. Writing in a country where industrial capitalism had become the dominant economic system during the nineteenth century, Ruskin was highly critical of competitive commercialism, viewing it as a degenerate offshoot of British industrial capitalism. Hobson argues that in Ruskin's thought, mercantile economics—dominated by an individualist philosophy—was the ruination of the nation.[93] Hence, in Ruskin's view, the ideal social system was organic, feudalistic, and communitarian. Communitarianism, he believed, would do away with rivalries which had been originally instigated by the evils of commercial competition and profit making. Communitarianism, he went on to argue, would allow the development of the community-conscious individual who would work for the accumulation of communal wealth and for the amelioration of communal life. Ideally, Ruskin argued, people should work 'without the stimulus of direct profit'.[94] Ruskin's thinking on society and economics was undoubtedly indebted to Karl Marx's social criticism but it was even closer to that of Christian Socialists, themselves rooting their social critique in the ideas of the Oxford Movement. John Henry Newman, John Keble, and Edward Bouverie Pusey were distinguished High Church Anglicans who promulgated the notion that some level of *rapprochement* between the Protestant and the Catholic faiths in religious and social concerns was more than necessary.

Lady Gregory took issue with the proselytising undercurrent of the character building project in Ireland. Although Plunkett never suggested that religious conversion was a feature of his ideas on self-help projects in rural Irish communities, his writings argued clearly that traditionalist, Catholic Irish character was a hindrance to economic progress and that only an assimilation of a Catholic to a Protestant disposition could realise the economic progress that he desired for Ireland. Lady Gregory was aware of the dangers such discourse could initiate in doctrinal and denominational debates. She had personal experience of proselytising in her own family, and it was a practice that she was determined to avoid.[95] Neither Sir William nor Lady Gregory herself had ever resorted to proselytising their Catholic tenants. Sir William was at one point a student of Christ Church College in Oxford when 'Anglo-Catholicism was gaining momentum' and when the 'charges of bigotry and popery were being hurled at the University'.[96] William was upset by the religious turmoil in Oxford; he 'deplored the violence and abuse of both sides, especially in a community where people were obliged to live so close together and had the time to dwell upon and foster real and imaginary wrongs'.⁹⁷ Coming from Ireland, where the Tithe Wars of the 1830s were accentuating denominational differences brutally, he was upset to find growing religious disquiet at Oxford. Low Church Anglicans feared their centuries-long social and political dominance weakened as High Church Anglicanism was growing in popularity and influence among pastors, scholars, and congregations. Newman, Keble, and Pusey promoted the revival of the ritual and spiritual mysticism of the Medieval Church, which included the reintroduction of candles, hymns, and surplices into Anglican religious services (in order to heighten their reverential quality). They also promoted the ascetic lifestyle for Protestant priests, the institution of the monastery, and the idea of celibacy for Protestant preachers; the practice of fasting and long periods in solitary prayer for both priests and members of congregations. Doctrinal debates accelerated in intensity after Newman, William Ward, and Frederick Oakeley converted to Roman Catholicism in 1845. Their conversions aroused suspicions that any further dissemination of High Church Anglicanism would only encourage the Romanising of the Reformed Church. Furthermore, it was feared that a nationwide spreading of High Church Anglicanism would contribute to the strengthening of the Roman Catholic Church not only in England but also in Ireland.⁹⁸ Undoubtedly, Sir William's familiarity with the doctrinal debates in England, originating in his Oxford days, contributed to his understanding of religious matters in a significant manner, making him more aware of and sympathetic to religious diversity in Ireland.

One of the ways in which Lady Gregory sought to avoid accusations of anti-Catholic prejudice was to write plays which 'hit impartially around', to use an expression she herself had employed in relation to the success of George Moore's play, *The Bending of the Bough*.⁹⁹ Accusations of this nature would have certainly hindered the success of her theatre, thwarting the cultural and educational objectives that she hoped to realise through the medium of the stage. Nevertheless, accusations of anti-Catholicism continued to be raised against the players and playwrights of the Abbey Theatre, especially in relation to Synge, and, to a lesser extent, the plays of Yeats. Pilkington addresses the controversy around the 1899 Dublin performance of Yeats's *The Countess Cathleen*, in which Cardinal Michael Logue played a crucial part; the controversy around the Irish Literary Theatre's production of the play was a clear indication of the aspirations both of advanced nationalists and of Catholic Church hierarchy in Ireland at the time.¹⁰⁰ Advanced nationalists continued to campaign against Synge and disrupt the performances of his plays because they considered *In the Shadow of the Glen*, *The Well of the Saints* and later *The Playboy of the Western World* disrespectful representations of Irish Catholic men and women. While Yeats thrived on these controversies and instigated public debates in the press and in the Abbey Theatre itself, Synge and Lady Gregory were against making public the disagreements that arose between theatre and sections of its audiences.[101] Yeats used the theatre to campaign for the freedom of the artist in artistic and political matters, as he had done years earlier when he first drafted a manifesto of an Irish dramatic movement with Lady Gregory. He conceived of the theatre as a podium from which to launch public debates and thundering attacks on those whose social and political convictions he regarded as dogmatic or phlegmatic. Lady Gregory, on the other hand, saw the theatre as a place in which to foster understanding between the various factions of Irish public life. Moreover, she never forgot the support provided by Catholic institutions, such as the Total Abstinence League of the Sacred Heart, which had provided venues for the first rehearsals and performances of the Irish Literary Theatre back in the early days of the Irish dramatic movement.[102]

In view of this it comes as no surprise that *Spreading the News* opens with a dialogue between a local policeman and a magistrate who has just arrived in his district to take up office, one who is a self-confident and presumptuous individual. He has recently returned from one of Britain's prison islands and penal colonies, the Andaman Islands, situated just off the coast of the Indian subcontinent. Lady Gregory paints him as figure of ridicule, one whose prejudice against the local people of Fair Green leaves him completely ignorant as to the reality of circumstances in the Irish village to which he is assigned. In *Hyacinth Halvey*, the title character is expected to stand in a *tableau vivant* on stage in the local village hall, opposite a group of local corner boys from Noonan's bar, brought together for this spectacle. He is to stand there as an example for others to follow. Upon the local Sergeant's request, he is required to wear a blue ribbon, implying that his superior character is due to his respectable background. The Sergeant's proposition only emphasises the farcical nature of the *tableau*: it is clear from the testimonials that the new health inspector's background is far from respectable. Nonetheless, Halvey is to stand there, in front of the villagers, wearing a blue ribbon, turning the moment into a local instance of political propaganda.[103] Nestor of *The*

Jackdaw presents himself as a respectable, self-contained individual who has dutifully served Queen and country in the British armed forces. Yet Lady Gregory deliberately presents him as even more dull-witted a character than the other residents of the village.

Crucial to the success of Lady Gregory's plays was her decision to employ comedy as a vehicle with which to transport ideas through to her audience. Eric Weitz remarks that Lady Gregory's short comedies seem to be modernised versions of the *commedia dell'arte* tradition of medieval and Renaissance Italy.[104] Weitz's observations highlight the debt of Lady Gregory's theatre to a dramatic tradition of which she knew much due to her extensive travels in Continental Europe and to the wide variety of experiences that she accumulated during those visits to France, Italy, and Spain. Lady Gregory had gathered together some of her ideas on Italian theatre in an article handed over to Yeats and the Irish Literary Society in 1898.[105] Weitz identifies the indebtedness of her theatre to the Italian tradition in 'her placement of character "type" at the centre of comic development'. In addition, he writes, 'her use of formal patterning as dramatic humour device, and her astute anticipation of performance through rhythm, reversal and escalation' help harbour her short comedies safely within the Italian tradition.[106] He argues that to consider her plays as merely 'farcical' and overlook their close connection to the Italian tradition seriously 'threatens to minimize the real value' of the plays.[107] Weitz observes how Lady Gregory's characters wear masks, inviting her audiences to look beyond the specific character present on stage to the 'character type' that he or she represents. This allows the playwright to move beyond the particular to the universal, reducing the 'social problem' aspect of her plays to a minimum, supplying just enough narrative content to communicate universal 'character types' to her audience through individual characters as masks.

She had some previous experience with this form of drama. During those long sea voyages, especially to faraway lands like India, she would entertain her fellow travellers with little sketches that she herself wrote and produced. Kohfeldt writes of Lady Gregory's success as writer, director, and stage manager of a short piece, *Cat-ass-trophy*, on board the *Nizam* from Brindisi, Italy, to India in 1885. Lady Gregory was 'the center of social life on the ship', writes Kohfeldt, 'which contained mostly Anglo-Indian officials and a British regiment on its way to a border war in Burma. […] She organized an evening of charades, writing, directing, acting in them, and finding a good cause to sanction their fun'.[108] While the evening's entertainment was designed specifically for British officers by themselves and their friends, her other play, *Marionettes* (in which men acted as living marionettes worked by strings), was applauded all round by a multifarious audience of officers, soldiers, arabs, and all classes of passangers, including those travelling on the deck of the ship.[109] These performances demonstrated not only that she had had good experience of putting together entertaining sketches before she started working for the Irish dramatic movement at the end of the nineteenth century. The performance of *Marionettes* on board the *Nizam* for India in particular showed Lady Gregory's skill in writing and producing a play that could provide comic entertainment for an audience composed of people from widely differing social, economic, and ethnic backgrounds, a skill that would be important to her dramatic work later at the Abbey Theatre in Ireland.

Lady Gregory's employment of characters on stage as masks and her composition of *Marionettes* raise the question of the relationship of her work to the proto-modernist theatre of Gordon Craig and its profound influence of Yeats's drama during the 1910s. However, as Weitz emphasises, the use of masks in modern theatre had its origins in ancient Greek drama, much admired by theatre-makers of the Victorian and Edwardian periods. Centuries earlier, a more modern use of mask and of the *commedia dell'arte* tradition influenced many a European playwright, including the French dramatist Molière. Little wonder, writes Richard Andrews, since Molière 'lived and worked cheek by jowl with Italian actors, had Italian playscripts in his personal library, and was subject therefore to a steady stream of influence from Italian dramatic material'.[110] Lady Gregory's close friend Bernard Shaw was amongst those who first observed the similarity between the dramatic technique of Lady Gregory and that of Molière.[111] Weitz explains that both Lady Gregory and Molière used quick and sometimes repeated dialogues, and a 'shrewdly wrought series of reversals and escalating variations, switching and building upon the angles of comic irony'.[112]

This identification of Lady Gregory's Irish drama with Molière's seventeenth-century French plays is significant with regard to the influence of Ruskin on her ideas and practice. As stated, Ruskin admired Molière's work for what he perceived as the nobleness and the purity of the Frenchman's theatre.[113] Andrew Tate has drawn attention to the fact that Molière was the only writer of note who enjoyed Ruskin's continuous appreciation throughout the decades.[114] Ruskin was particularly appreciative of the realism and didacticism of Molière's plays, especially *Tartuffe, Le Misantrope, L'Avare, Le Bourgeois Gentilhomme,* and *Le Malade Imaginaire*. In *Fors Clavigera*, Ruskin used Molière's *L'Avare* as a case study of avarice, pronouncing on what he regarded as the religious message of the play: 'everything you do should be done in love of God and your neighbour and in hatred of covetousness'.[115] Furthermore, Ruskin admired the French playwright's work for its Pre-Raphaelite quality, by which he meant its ability to display 'an exquisite natural wisdom' and 'a capacity for the most simple enjoyment'.[116] The Abbey players found it easy to execute Molière's comedies because their style of acting was similar to that which was required to execute the French plays successfully. Indeed, Yeats remarked that the Irish players put on better performances of Molière's *Les Fourberies de Scapin* than did the French company of the Théâtre de l'Odéon in Paris.[117] Undoubtedly, the didactic and educational nature of the plays, as Ruskin had perceived it, significantly contributed to Lady Gregory's appreciation of Molière's work.[118] She went on to translate Molière's *Le Médecin Malgré Lui, L'Avare, Les Fourberies de Scapin*, subsequently published in *The Kiltartan Molière* in 1910.[119] Ruskin's revealing comments on Molière and the Pre-Raphaelite ideal are telling as regards the relation between the artistic qualities of the Pre-Raphaelite artworks and the pictorial aspects of Lady Gregory plays that she wrote during the first decade of the twentieth century.

Notes

1. James Pethica, ed. *Lady Gregory's Diaries, 1892–1902* (Gerrards Cross: Colin Smythe, 1996), 133.
2. Pethica, *Diaries*, 134–35. She read Froude's book two years previously. Pethica, *Diaries*, 65. Lyons explains that the parliamentary elections of 1895 (the year after the IAOS was founded) had great implications for the future of Ireland and of Irish social politics. Plunkett became an MP when he won a seat for South Dublin; Gerald Balfour, Arthur's brother, was appointed as the new Chief Secretary for Ireland; propositions about a new Board of Agriculture for Ireland were also put on the new Government's table. Within a year a new Land Act was passed, to replace the Land Act of 1891. It was hoped to incentivise tenant land purchase. Within two years of the Land Act, Gerald Balfour successfully carried through the Irish Local Government Act, giving Ireland a new system of local government based on the British model, with elected

urban and rural district councils. F. S. L. Lyons, *Ireland Since the Famine* (London: Collins/Fontana, 1982), 212. Lady Gregory was well aware of these changes, which only strengthened her resolve to support improvement of conditions for those working in the Irish agricultural sector.
3. Pethica, *Diaries*, 135–37. The length of this diary entry is very suggestive of the importance that she attributed to this meeting.
4. Pethica, *Diaries*, 135–37; for Yeats, see R. F. Foster, *The Irish Story* (London: Penguin, 2002), 221 and 223.
5. Pethica, *Diaries*, 152.
6. Sister Mary de Lourdes Fahy, "Lady Gregory—A Local Habitation and a Name," in *Lady Gregory Autumn Gatherings, Reflections at Coole*, ed. Seán Tobin and assoc. ed. Lois Tobin (Galway: Lady Gregory Autumn Gathering, 2000), 8.
7. 'And he [Plunkett] has been very kind about the Theatre—& rushed to see the Attorney Genl. & to see me on his one day over here—And he has taken George Russell out of Pim's & made him an organiser of rural banks.' Pethica, *Diaries*, 158.
8. Lionel Pilkington, *Theatre and the State in Twentieth-Century Ireland: Cultivating the People* (London: Routledge, 2001), 7.
9. Lady Augusta Gregory, "Ireland, Real and Ideal," *The Nineteenth Century* (November 1898): 762–82, especially 772.
10. Patrick Bolger, *The Irish Co-operative Movement* (Dublin: Cahill, 1977), 163 and 174.
11. Boylan and Foley observe that the political and financial circles in England considered the *laissez faire* system to be *the*, and possibly *the only* successful combination of the individual's self-interest and social utility, and great efforts were made to apply the system to Ireland. Thomas Boylan and Timothy P. Foley, *Political Economy and Colonial Ireland* (London: Routledge, 1992), 117.
12. Pethica, *Diaries*, 184. Bolger, Smith-Gordon, and O'Brien explain that those to whom Russell referred as 'gombeen men'—publicans, shopkeepers, produce-buyers and money-lenders—held a strong economic grip on rural communities and a great influence in politics and in the churches. Bolger maintains that, with its origins dating back to the seventeenth century, 'gombeenism' was a part of a 'gradual degenerative process' arising from the repression of Irish manufacturing industry, plus the fact that agriculture was becoming progressively inefficient and 'only sporadically profitable.' Nonetheless, given the secrecy of the transaction, farmers preferred to approach 'gombeen men' for loans in order to keep their financial circumstances hidden. Due to the reluctance of banks to advance money to indebted farmers, the middlemen

had acquired a privileged status in rural Irish society, in spite of the fact that the 'gombeenmen' often used the information gathered about families for their own social, financial, and political interests. Providing financial assistance to indebted farmers, 'gombeen men' added to local communities' control over its individual members. Bolger, *The Irish Co-operative Movement*, 162. For the grip of 'gombeen men' (publicans, produce-buyers, and money-lenders) on social, political, and religious affairs, see Lionel Smith-Gordon and Cruise O'Brien, *Co-operation in Ireland* (Manchester: Co-operative Union Ltd, 1921), 20.

13. Gregory, "Ireland, Real and Ideal," 773. Sr. Mary made reference to this when discussing Lady Gregory's keenness to set up a co-operative society in Gort after Plunkett's visit. Fahy, "Lady Gregory," 8.
14. Carla King, "Co-operation and Rural Development: Plunkett's Approach," in *Rural Change in Ireland*, ed. John Davis (Belfast: Institute of Irish Studies, 1999), 48.
15. Horace Plunkett, "Co-operative Stores for Ireland," *The Nineteenth Century* (September 1888): 411–12.
16. John Ruskin, *Time and Tide*, in *The Works of John Ruskin*, ed. E. T. Cook and Alexander Wedderburn, vol. 17 (London: George Allen, 1903–1912), 427. Further references to Cook and Wedderburn's multivolume work will be as follows: Ruskin, *Title of Individual Work*, volume number.page number. Example here: Ruskin, *Time and Tide*, 17.427.
17. For more on Ruskin's views, see J. A. Hobson, *John Ruskin, Social Reformer* (London: Nisbet, 1899), 130.
18. Horace Plunkett, *Ireland in the New Century* (London: Murray, 1904), 148–49.
19. Sarah Atwood, *Ruskin's Educational Ideals* (Farnham: Ashgate, 2011), 152.
20. Hobson, *John Ruskin*, 299–300.
21. Bolger, *The Irish Co-operative Movement*, 9–13. See also Louis P. F. Smith, *The Evolution of Agricultural Co-operation* (Oxford: Blackwell, 1961), 58. For Rochdale, see Hobson, *John Ruskin*, 299. John Vandaleur's Ralahine Commune was a rather short-lived endeavour due to the extravagant lifestyle of its founder.
22. Hobson, *John Ruskin*, 301.
23. Ruskin, *The Museum and Guild of St. George*, 30.5
24. Janice Helland, "Embroidered Spectacle: Celtic Revival as Aristocratic Display," in *The Irish Revival Reappraised*, ed. Betsey Taylor FitzSimon and James H. Murphy (Dublin: Four Courts Press, 2004), 97.
25. Helland, "Embroidered Spectacle," 98.
26. Fahy, "Lady Gregory," 8–9 and Judith Hill, *Lady Gregory: An Irish Life* (Stroud: Sutton, 2005), 104–5. For the achievements of the Gort

Convent Industry, see Joseph A. Glynn, "Irish Convent Industries," *The New Ireland Review*, June 1894: 239–40.
27. Hill, *Lady Gregory*, 104–5.
28. Pethica, *Diaries*, 119. Here Pethica explains that '[n]o issues of this publication appear to have survived.'
29. Pethica, *Diaries*, 180.
30. Pethica, *Diaries*, 134.
31. Pethica, *Diaries*, 205. Plunkett's guest list and the relations between Ruskin, Plunkett, the Balfours, and the Bulwer-Lyttons require some explanation. The Rt. Hon. Edward Bulwer-Lytton (1803–1873) was Secretary of State for the Colonies (1858–1859) and was a literary figure, whose novels were very popular during the nineteenth century, partly because of his employment of the dramatic *tableaux vivant*. Ruskin was a friend of Bulwer-Lytton, with whom he promoted the idea of establishing a National Theatre in London (see below). His son, Robert Bulwer-Lytton (1831–1891) served as Viceroy and Governor General of India (1876–1880). Robert had many children but significant in the present context is his son, Victor Bulwer-Lytton (1876–1947). Born in British India, Victor later became the Acting Viceroy of India (1926) and Governor of Bengal (1922–1927). Robert's daughter and Victor's sister, Elizabeth, married Lord Gerard Balfour (1858–1945), Chief Secretary for Ireland (1895–1900). The Bulwer-Lyttons were intimately familiar with the life and career of their family friend John Ruskin. Florence Burke was the sister of Lady Fingall (née Elizabeth Burke), wife of Arthur James Plunkett, Earl of Fingall (1859–1929). With Lady Balfour, Lord Lytton, and Lady Gregory (widow of the former Governor of Ceylon) present at Plunkett's dinner, the momentous occasion clearly marked the intertwined nature of local and imperial politics between India and Ireland.
32. Pethica, *Diaries*, 219 and 242.
33. See letter from Yeats to Lady Gregory on December 22, 1898 and to Susan Mary Yeats December 25, 1898 in William Butler Yeats, *The Collected Letters of W. B. Yeats; Volume Two: 1896–1900*, ed. Warwick Gould, John Kelly, and Deirdre Toomey (Oxford: Clarendon, 1997), 323–24 and 325–26. For notes to the Lady Gregory letter, see Yeats, *Collected Letters*, vol. 2, 324. For the reference to the performance, see Pethica, *Diaries*, 210.
34. Ruskin, *Fors Clavigera*, 27.161.
35. Letter from Yeats to Susan Mary Yeats, December 25, 1898, Yeats, *Collected Letters*, vol. 2, 325.
36. Pethica, *Diaries*, 215.
37. Trevor West, *Horace Plunkett: Co-operation and Politics, An Irish Biography* (Gerrards Cross: Colin Smythe, 1986), 25.

38. William Butler Yeats, *Autobiographies* (Basingstoke: Macmillan, 1992), 390–91.
39. Yeats, *Autobiographies*, 391.
40. Yeats, *Autobiographies*, 389.
41. Yeats, *Autobiographies*, 390.
42. Hill remarks that, at the time, Lady Gregory was trying to attract Yeats's attention. Yeats was a handsome, intelligent, and knowledgeable young man, but someone who was infatuated with the radical political activist Maud Gonne, known for supporting militant Irish nationalist politics. Hill, *Lady Gregory*, 114–15.
43. Foster, *W. B. Yeats*, vol. 1, 182.
44. Yeats, *Autobiographies*, 81.
45. Lady Augusta Gregory, *Our Irish Theatre: A Chapter of Autobiography* (Gerrards Cross: Colin Smythe, 1972), 20.
46. Foster, *W. B. Yeats*, vol. 1, 571.
47. Yeats's manifesto quoted in Foster, *W. B. Yeats*, vol. 1, 184.
48. Ruskin's quote is taken from his letter sent to the May 1888 issue of *The Young Man*, Ruskin, 34.549.
49. Comyns Carr, *Some Eminent Victorians* (London: Duckworthe, 1908), 245.
50. Ruskin in conversation with M. H. Spielmann from 1884, qtd. in Anselm Heinrich, "Ruskin and the National Theatre," *Ruskin, the Theatre and Victorian Visual Culture*, ed. Anselm Heinrich, Katherine Newey, and Jeffrey Richards (Basingstoke: Palgrave Macmillan, 2009), 100.
51. Heinrich, "Ruskin and the National Theatre," 101.
52. Katherine Newey and Jeffrey Richards, *John Ruskin and the Victorian Theatre* (Basingstoke: Palgrave Macmillan, 2010), 31–34.
53. Newey and Richards, *John Ruskin and the Victorian Theatre*, 4.
54. Ruskin, *Modern Painters*, vol. 3, 5.375.
55. Heinrich, "Ruskin and the National Theatre," 98.
56. Henrich, "Ruskin and the National Theatre," 98. Ruskin here refuted his mother's main claims against the theatre, namely that the theatre was a frivolous place. See for this, Newey and Richards, *John Ruskin and the Victorian Theatre*, 3.
57. Heinrich, "Ruskin and the National Theatre," 98.
58. Heinrich, "Ruskin and the National Theatre," 102. For Bulwer-Lytton, the national theatre project meant the foundation of the National Theatre in England.
59. Heinrich, "Ruskin and the National Theatre," 103.
60. William Archer and Harley Granville-Barker, *Schemes and Estimates for a National Theatre* (New York: Duffield, 1908), xi and 149–62, for *The Countess Cathleen*, see 145 and 156.

61. For more on the subtle social criticism in Yeats's *The Countess Cathleen*, see Michael McAteer, "A Currency Crisis: Modernist Dialectics in the Countess Cathleen," *The Irish Revival Reappraised*, ed. Betsey Taylor FitzSimon and James H. Murphy (Dublin: Four Courts Press, 2004), 187–204.
62. Ben Levitas's, *The Theatre of Nation* (Oxford: Oxford University Press, 2002) offers a detailed evaluation of the various debates during the three-year run of the Irish Literary Theatre.
63. Adrian Frazier, *Behind the Scenes: Yeats, Horniman, and the Struggle for the Abbey Theatre* (Berkeley: University of California Press, 1990), 45. See also Ronald Schuchard, "W. B. Yeats and the London Theatre Societies, 1901–1904," *The Review of English Studies* 29, no. 116 (November 1978): 415–46.
64. Foster, *W. B. Yeats*, vol. 1, 257.
65. Foster, *W. B. Yeats*, vol. 1, 258.
66. Among other works, Lady Gregory read Matthew Arnold's *Irish Essays* on the landlord-tenant relationship in Ireland and Henry George's *Social Problems* on possible new forms of taxation to alleviate the tax burden on tenants. Lady Augusta Gregory, *Excerpts from her readings*, Lady Augusta Gregory Papers, Albert A. and Henry W. Berg Collection, New York Public Library.
67. P. J. Mathews, *Revival: The Abbey Theatre, Sinn Féin, the Gaelic League and the Co-operative Movement* (Cork: Cork University Press, 2003), 29.
68. Lady Augusta Gregory, *The Collected Plays*, vol. 1 (New York: Oxford University Press, 1970), 5.
69. Edward E. Lysaght, *Sir Horace Plunkett and His Place in the Irish Nation* (Dublin: Maunsel, 1916), 43.
70. Lysaght, *Sir Horace Plunkett*, 43.
71. G. D. H. Cole, *A Century of Co-operation* (London: Allen and Unwin, 1944), 248.
72. Cole, *A Century of Co-operation*, 248–49.
73. Plunkett, *Ireland in the New Century*, 181.
74. R. A. Anderson, *With Horace Plunkett in Ireland* (London: Macmillan, 1935), 254.
75. Plunkett, *Ireland in the New Century*, 176.
76. Conrad M. Arensberg and Solon T. Kinball, *Family and Community in Ireland* (Cambridge, MA: Harvard University Press, 1968), 69.
77. Gregory, *Collected Plays*, vol. 1, 6.
78. Katie Donovan, "Let Us Now Praise Famous Women," in *Lady Gregory Autumn Gatherings, Reflections at Coole*, ed. Seán Tobin and assoc. ed. Lois Tobin (Galway: Lady Gregory Autumn Gathering, 2000), 13.
79. Smith-Gordon and O'Brien, *Co-operation in Ireland*, 64.

80. The Co-operative Wholesale Society of Britain too counted consumer protection and quality assurance among its most important aims.
81. Anderson, *With Horace Plunkett in Ireland*, 254.
82. Gregory, *Collected Plays*, vol. 1, 39–40 and 50.
83. See the playwright's notes in Gregory, *Collected Plays*, vol. 1, 255.
84. Speaking of eggs in *Hyacinth Halvey*, in the play the Department of Agriculture and Technical Instruction (DATI) is said to have sent a man with magic lantern slides to give a lecture on character building to the villagers of Cloon. Transported in the same carriage as the eggs, the slides break on their way to the village. The farcical incident reveals Lady Gregory's belief in the need for better modes of transportation in rural areas. Nevertheless, it indicates also her acknowledgement that the DATI would have been much better employed in developing the transport system around Ireland than exercising itself in arguments with the IAOS. At the time, the government-run DATI was involved in heated disputes with the IAOS over matters relating to the Irish agricultural sector. In *Hail and Farewell!* George Moore gave a sarcastic account on how DATI instructed rural people, using magic lantern slides, on improving the local egg and poultry industries. Lady Gregory implies in *Hyacinth Halvey* that character development should not be a result of some sort of a scientific experiment with slides and lanterns, but the outcome of a natural process of co-operation between people, as propagated by Plunkett and the IAOS. George Moore, *Hail and Farewell!* (London: Heinemann, 1947), 156.
85. Gregory, *Collected Plays*, vol. 1, 74.
86. P. J. Mathews, "The Irish Revival: A Reappraisal," in *New Voices in Irish Criticism*, ed. P. J. Mathews (Dublin: Four Courts Press, 2000), 18. See also Mathews, *Revival: The Abbey Theatre, Sinn Féin and the Co-operative Movement*, 8.
87. Horace Plunkett, *Noblesse Oblige: An Irish Rendering* (Dublin: Maunsel, 1908), 6.
88. Plunkett, *Ireland in the New Century*, 102. For more on Plunkett's thoughts on the Roman Catholic Church, the Irish economy, and the Irish character, see 94–112.
89. Plunkett, *Ireland in the New Century*, 54.
90. Max Weber, *The Protestant Ethic and the Spirit of Capitalism*, trans. Talcott Parsons (London: Routledge, 2000), 40.
91. Plunkett, *Ireland in the New Century*, 103.
92. Rev. M. O'Riordan, *Catholicity and Progress in Ireland* (London: Kegan Paul, 1906), 16.
93. Hobson, *John Ruskin*, 82.

94. Ruskin, *Time and Tide*, 17.36. This view was generally held by Ruskin, although in this particular instance he was writing specifically about those who worked in retail commerce.
95. Elizabeth Coxhead, *Lady Gregory: A Literary Portrait* (London: Macmillan, 1961), 3–4; Mary Lou Kohfeldt, *Lady Gregory, the Woman Behind the Irish Literary Renaissance* (London: Deutsch, 1984), 12; and Hill, *Lady Gregory*, 6. See also Lady Gregory's comments on her fear of being suspected of proselytisation in Lady Augusta Gregory, *Seventy Years, Being the Autobiography of Lady Gregory* (Gerrards Cross: Colin Smythe, 1973), 16. The Evangelical attitude of the Persse family, argues Kohfeldt, 'contained a good deal of aggression, self-interest, and fear.' Kohfeldt, *Lady Gregory*, 13. Desmond Bowen records that after the Disestablishment Act of 1869, those from Anglo-Irish backgrounds feared that the Church of Ireland would lose its influence on the island unless the membership of the Anglican Church was to increase significantly; hence, many families took to proselytising their tenants. Bowen notes that '[m]any Evangelicals reminded one another that not only were the Irish peasants in as much physical misery as the slaves in the colonies, but their spiritual destitution was, perhaps, even greater because of the power of Rome in Ireland.' Desmond Bowen, *The Protestant Crusade in Ireland, 1800–1870* (Dublin: Macmillan, 1978), 67–68. Bowen discusses the connections between the spiritual and the political side of proselytising in Ireland during the second half of the nineteenth century also in *Souperism: Myth or Reality* (Cork: Mercier, 1970), where he investigates the question further, examining the 'Second Reformation' in Ireland following the Great Famine of the 1840s. Bowen argues that Protestant fears increased after the failure of forceful conversion of Roman Catholics to the Protestant faith following the famine years of the 1840s.
96. Brian Jenkins, *Sir William Gregory of Coole: The Biography of an Anglo-Irishman* (Gerrards Cross: Colin Smythe, 1986), 39–40.
97. Jenkins, *Sir William Gregory of Coole*, 40.
98. Pope Pius IX issued a Papal Brief (1850) which strengthened the position of the Roman Catholic Church in England. It declared the creation of 12 dioceses within England and established the position of the Archbishop of Westminster as Head of the Church. This briefly amplified tensions between the Catholic and Protestant denominations in England. Partly as a result of the papal move, perceptions of papal aggression and the question of Catholicism in Ireland continued to dominate public debates in England, leading to anti-popery riots throughout the country. The situation was not helped by the fact that

High Anglicanism was growing in popularity. The tensions between High Church Anglicans, or 'Tractarians,' and Low and Broad Church Anglicans intensified as a result. The 'Tractarian' doctrine of apostolic succession only aroused feelings of unease for it was seen to undermine the centuries-long relation between the Church and the State in England. The doctrine was considered dangerous not only to England's status as a pre-eminent Protestant nation, but also for political circumstances in Ireland, where the minority Church of Ireland had been granted a position of privilege through the Act of Union of 1800. See David Morse, *High Victorian Culture* (London: Macmillan, 1993), 225.

99. Lady Gregory wrote: 'The play hits so impartially all round that no one is really offended, certainly not the Nationalists and we have not heard that Unionists are either.' Gregory, *Our Irish Theatre*, 28–29.
100. Pilkington, *Theatre and the State in Twentieth-Century Ireland*, 6 and 21–27.
101. W. J. McCormack, *Fool of the Family: A Life of J. M. Synge* (London: Weidenfeld & Nicolson, 2000), 318.
102. For more on the venues, see Adrian Frazier, "The Ideology of the Abbey Theatre," in *The Cambridge Companion to Twentieth-Century Irish Drama*, ed. Shaun Richards (Cambridge: Cambridge University Press, 2004), 39–40; Nelson O'Ceallaigh Ritschel, *Productions of the Irish Theatre Movement 1899–1916, A Checklist* (Westport, CT: Greenwood, 2001), 11; and Máire Nic Shiubhlaigh, *Splendid Years: Recollections of Maire Nic Shiubhlaigh as Told to Edward Kenny* (Dublin: Duffy, 1955), 12 and 14.
103. This instance of the play can also be seen as a subtle criticism of the type of 'in-yer-face' political propaganda, promoted by Alice Milligan and her theatre group as well as Maud Gonne and the *Inghinidhe na hÉireann*, who used *tableaux vivants* for very specific and radical nationalist purposes.
104. Eric Weitz, "Lady Gregory's 'Humour of Character': A *Commedia* Approach to *Spreading the News*." *Irish University Review* 34, no. 1 (Spring/Summer 2004): 144–56.
105. Pethica, *Diaries*, 196. Lady Gregory's article, "An Italian Literary Drama" was published in *The Dublin Daily Express* on April 8, 1899 to 'prepare the way' for the Irish Literary Theatre.
106. Weitz, "Lady Gregory's 'Humour of Character'," 144.
107. Weitz, "Lady Gregory's 'Humour of Character'," 145.
108. Kohfeldt, *Lady Gregory*, 73.
109. Diary entry, November 30, 1885. Lady Augusta Gregory, *Typewritten Diaries, 1882–1892*, Lady Augusta Gregory Papers, Albert A. and Henry W. Berg Collection, New York Public Library, New York.

110. Richard Andrews, "Molière, *Commedia dell'arte*, and the Question of Influence in Early Modern European Theatre," *The Modern Language Review* 100, no. 2 (2005): 444.
111. Dan H. Laurence and Nicholas Grene, eds. *Shaw, Lady Gregory and the Abbey* (Gerrards Cross: Colin Smythe, 1993), 64. See Shaw's eulogy for Lady Gregory's work (a speech delivered in London in 1910) on 63–64.
112. Weitz, "Lady Gregory's 'Humour of Character'," 151.
113. Andrew Tate writes in detail about the historical and religious factors behind Ruskin's appreciation of Molière's theatre. Tate locates Ruskin's interest in the theatre of Molière (1622–1673) and of Jean-François Marmontel (1723–1799) in Ruskin's idealisation of pre-revolutionary France. Tate argues that Ruskin idealised feudal France in the same way that he idealised feudal England or feudal Italy. In Ruskin's fantasy, the labourer was 'content to work hard for his family and to serve the noble man of his country,' while 'the patrician landowner rule[d] with mercy, justice and wisdom.' Andrew Tate, "The First Theatrical Pre-Raphaelite? Ruskin's Molière," in *Ruskin, the Theatre and Victorian Visual Culture*, ed. Anselm Heinrich, Katherine Newey, and Jeffrey Richards (Basingstoke: Palgrave Macmillan, 2009), 125.
114. Tate, "The First Theatrical Pre-Raphaelite? Ruskin's Molière," 114.
115. Ruskin, *Fors Clavigera*, 28.518.
116. Ruskin, *Modern Painters*, vol. 3, 5.375.
117. For Yeats's comments on the Odéon performance of Molière's *Scapin* in Paris in December 1908, see Gregory, *Our Irish Theatre*, 60.
118. See, for instance, the similarity between Molière's *L'Avare* and Lady Gregory's *Damer's Gold* (1912) in relation to Ruskin's denunciation of avarice in *Fors Clavigera*. In his *Academy Notes* (1875) Ruskin compared the naturalism of Molière's plays to that of Pre-Raphaelite paintings, including William Holman Hunt's *The Scapegoat* and Millais's *The Return of the Dove to the Ark*. Ruskin, *Academy Notes*, 14.267.
119. In later years, Lady Gregory translated *Le Bourgeois Gentilhomme* (1926).

'See a play as a picture': The Pre-Raphaelite Brotherhood, the Sister Arts, and the Irish Plays

THE ABBEY THEATRE AND THE PICTURE STAGE

In her notes to *Damer's Gold*, Lady Gregory wrote that the Abbey was to be a theatre 'with a base of realism' and 'with an apex of beauty', echoing some pronouncements of Yeats from the time of the foundation of 'The Theatre of Beauty' in London with Florence Farr, Edith Craig, and Charles Ricketts.[1] Her comment is misunderstood if taken as referring to her own work solely in terms of theatrical realism and to Yeats's plays in terms of theatrical aestheticism, that 'apex of beauty'. This wrongfully assumes a separation in her drama of the two main objectives of the theatre that Ruskin had so strongly advocated: the *education* and the *entertainment* of audiences. Lady Gregory herself adhered to aesthetic and pictorial principles with as much enthusiasm as Yeats or Synge. Nonetheless, the pictorial ideal that informed the staging of her plays was markedly different from those ideals employed by fellow dramatists and directors of the Abbey Theatre. Plunkett and Russell's social reform movement developed from the beginning of the twentieth century in conjunction with the efforts of the Abbey Theatre to promote new social ideas and to deepen artistic appreciation in Ireland.

The Abbey Theatre on Lower Abbey Street in Dublin, the house of the Irish National Theatre Society, was indeed a 'Palace of Art', to borrow the title of one of Tennyson's poems. Annie Horniman, Yeats's fellow member of the Hermetic Order of the Golden Dawn and daughter of a

© The Author(s) 2018
E. Remport, *Lady Gregory and Irish National Theatre*,
Bernard Shaw and His Contemporaries,
https://doi.org/10.1007/978-3-319-76611-9_5

successful Manchester tea merchant, had offered to provide the financial support for the renovation and refurbishment of an old building. The refurbishment turned the hall of the Mechanics' Institute into a modern 'Palace of Art'. The interior of the building was tastefully decorated with 'rich carpeting', stained-glass windows, ornamented wallpapers, and portraits of some of those who had been the driving forces behind a cultural renaissance in Ireland.[2] A small piano was placed neatly in a corner to provide musical entertainment for guests gathering in the entrance hall. On the ground floor, the auditorium contained rows of comfortable scarlet leather seats with 'polished brass work separat[ing] each seat'. At the back of the auditorium, wooden benches were installed for those with cheap tickets. On the large gallery, as well as on the ground floor, the rows of seats were arranged on a slope in order to allow the audience to have a 'perfect view of the stage'. On the walls, 'painted in colours to harmonise with interior', there were two large medallions and copper and brass-framed mirrors. German electric lamps were installed to light up the auditorium during the intervals, while the lights were dimmed during performances. These modern electric lights allowed the audience to enjoy a more comfortable and intimate viewing experience in the theatre hall through which they could remain more attentive during performances. The use of these electric lights broke with the more widespread practice of lighting the theatre space with gas or candle chandeliers, which tended to burn up the air of the auditorium by the end of a performance (no doubt leaving some audience members slumbering). With the audience seated in darkness and their ears attuned to the melody of the players' words, the Abbey Theatre made radical inroads into restoring the supremacy of the spoken word over monumentalist staging practices that were popular with early twentieth-century stage designers both in Dublin and in London. More significantly, this new theatre allowed playwrights, players, and stage managers to experiment with a number of different theatrical concepts.

The popularity of the *tableau vivant* during the Victorian and the Edwardian periods impacted significantly on the theatrical practices at the Abbey. Four years after the opening of the theatre, Yeats delivered an animated speech at a British Association matinée, in which he criticised *fin-de-siècle* staging practices and praised the new theatrical approach of the Abbey Theatre:

> We believe words more important than gesture, that voice is the principle power an actor possesses; and that nothing may distract from the actor,

and what he says, we have greatly simplified scenery. [...] Good realistic scenery is merely bad landscape painting, an attempt to do something which can only be done properly in an easel painting; but if you are content to *decorate* the stage, to suggest, you create something which is peculiar to the stage, for you put before your audience a scene that only wakes into life when the actors move in front of it.[3]

These comments were addressed to theatre practitioners of his time, people for whom the stage was nothing more than an enlarged painting. Taking their inspiration from nineteenth-century narrative paintings (abounding in pictorial details), designers of the times tended to overcrowd their stage with an unnecessary amount of props and people. Over time, the platform stage of the early nineteenth century evolved into three-dimensional stage sets, giving designers the opportunity to create the illusion of reality on the stage. Live animals and real trees often decorated the stage for forest scenes, and large water containers were used for water scenes in order to impress the illusion of reality onto the audience.[4] While on the platform stage the actor and his delivery of monologue dominated the performance, in these so-called 'Victorian realist sets' the actor was almost entirely lost in enormous and elaborate designs. In fact, in these sets, the actors' artistry was almost entirely subordinated to the pomposity of the stage design. Throughout much of his dramatic career, Yeats worked hard on restoring the supremacy of the actor's verbal artistry over monumentalist stage designs; his early public pronouncements on the theatre indicate how seriously he considered the matter.

Yeats's concerns regarding contemporary staging practices were understandable. In his famous 1766 work, *Laokoon*, Gotthold Ephraim Lessing had advocated the idea that a play was effectively a 'living picture', a perspective that was to exert a major influence on theatre practice in Europe during the course of the nineteenth century.[5] Developing Lessing's notion, *fin-de-siècle* practitioners advanced very far in their employment of the theatrical *tableau*. Martin Meisel remarks, for instance, that the Haymarket Theatre in London went as far as putting a golden border around the stage in order to create the required picture-frame effect.[6] During the nineteenth century, various older forms of the *tableau vivant* were revived and numerous new forms invented. These ranged from the 'curtain *tableau*'—the grouping of the actors at the end of a scene—to the '*tableau* of situation': that moment in which actors paused to 'form a picture'. This was to create the illusion that a play was in fact nothing but a series of pictures. Under French influence, *tableaux vivants* became popular in genteel companies; the re-enactments of famous paintings became a popular form of entertainment in the homes of English aristocracy. The *entr'acte tableau* took this form of private entertainment to the public sphere. *Entr'acte tableaux* were static re-enactments of famous paintings during the intervals of plays, designed to keep the attention of the audience while the next scene was being set up on stage behind the closed curtains.[7] In his review of the *Living Pictures* show performed at the Palace Theatre in London in 1894, Shaw wrote enthusiastically on the popularity of the *tableau vivant* in late Victorian theatre.[8]

Yeats conceived of his early play *The Countess Cathleen* as a series of *tableaux vivants*. The play was performed by an aristocratic ensemble at the Chief Secretary's Lodge in Dublin in 1899 and it was included in the list of plays recommended for the repertoire of the National Theatre in London in 1904. Popular as his play was, Yeats's scenic concept was not of the contemporary, popular narrative kind. James Flannery uses the phrase 'patterned scenic decor' to describe the playwright's early ideas for stage design.[9] During the late 1880s Yeats made friends within an artists' circle in London's Bedford Park, artists who were experimenting with new staging practices under the directorship of Charles Ricketts.[10] Flannery writes that in Ricketts's productions, '[t]he actor was not seen as a three-dimensional, flesh-and-blood figure. Instead, he was but another element in the overall stage pattern—a symbol of human perfection rather than a reflection of life as it existed in the stalls and pit of the theatre'.[11] What caught Yeats's attention was the fact that the actors seemed to perform a ritual in front of the painted scenery; their costumes and movement blending in with the overall design. Flannery argues that Yeats conceived of this very ritualistic form of theatre as reminiscent of the type of performance that was popular amongst his fellow members of the Hermetic Order of the Golden Dawn; hence his interest in Ricketts's designs.[12] True as this is, there was also another aspect to Yeats's interest in these new designs: their debt to the theatrical ideals of the Classical Revival in England. Godwin, Todhunter, and Barrett's concepts of ritualised theatre and patterned scenic décor—displayed in productions of *Helena in Troas* and *Claudian*—owed much to the pictorial ideals of the 1880s. Working towards the reinvention of Athenian life for the Victorian age, Alma-Tadema, Leighton, and Watts drew their inspiration from the compositional and structural arrangements of the ancient marble friezes of the Parthenon of Athens. The statuesque quality of their sceneries reminded audiences of the figurative arrangement and elegant draperies of the Elgin Marbles that were on view at the British Museum in London. The pictorial realisation of the classical sculptural ideal on stage created a beautiful blend of ritual and sensual artistry that Yeats, Godwin, Todhunter, and Barrett much admired.

As Godwin's son, Henry Irving's stepson, and Yeats's friend, Edward Gordon Craig had inherited his father's love of sculptural splendour and noble refinement as well as his stepfather's appreciation of large-scale architectural structures. Craig worked these into his own blend of scenic decor, for which he used a series of movable screens lit by an assortment of coloured lights. His accomplice in minimising scenic décor was his friend J. M. Whistler, who became famous by his court case against Ruskin in 1878. Whistler himself was inspired by certain strands of Pre-Raphaelite art, as witnessed in the works of Dante Gabriel Rossetti. This is perceptible in Whistler's early work, *Symphony in White No. 1: The White Girl*, painted between 1861 and 1862; it is reminiscent of Rossetti's *Ecce Ancilla Domini!* (1849–1850). Whistler's painting is a portrait of a young woman who is holding a white lily in her left hand; her loose brown hair is falling down onto her white dress. Whistler painted the portrait when he was experimenting with minimalist colour schemes during his first stay in Paris. Thus, the influence on his work of the French painters Edgar Degas, Édouard Manet, and Claude Monet is also evident. Finding ideal colour combinations to convey particular moods and feelings had been his lifelong preoccupation; during the Ruskin court case he had famously declared that the creation of 'harmon[ies] of colour[s]' had always been his artistic aspiration and that he had disagreed with Ruskin over the use of colours as symbols.[13] Ruskin tended to impose a colour-coded allegorical interpretation upon the medium of representation for he believed that individual colours and selected colour schemes should be indexed to ideals, often religious ideals. Whistler disagreed with such a response to paintings; in his view, a painting should be judged purely on the basis of the artist's poetry and not on a 'noble philosophy in some detail of philanthropy, courage, modesty, or virtue' that might have been suggested to the viewer by the colour scheme of a painting.[14] Oscar Wilde shared the painter's thoughts, declaring in his lecture 'The Value of Art in Modern Life', delivered at the Gaiety Theatre in Dublin in 1885, that painters should be able to use colours as they wished, free of religious didactic purposes.[15] Richard Ellmann writes that Wilde used this lecture to voice his own dislike of Victorian narrative painting, a genre which he considered to be the by-product of the Victorians' interest in storytelling. Wilde disliked narrative paintings because they encouraged a certain moralist response to art, according to which the merit of a painting was granted on the logic of the narrative rather than on the mode of artistic expression or the selection and execution of colours.

Whistler's desire to create 'harmonies of colours', or rather 'harmonies of moods', and his particular indexation of his paintings with musical titles—such as symphony, arrangement, nocturne—points towards his unique sensitivity to the hierarchy of the Sister Arts. Drawing on the writings of Georg Friedrich Hegel, Walter Pater argued that '[a]ll art constantly aspires to the condition of music' because '[i]t is the art of music which most completely realises this artistic ideal, this perfect identification of form and matter'.[16] Pater defined music as the 'perfect art form' because in it form and matter were in perfect harmony. Ingo F. Walther argues that Whistler's choices of titles which conjure up musical scores perfectly illustrate the painter's desire to 'capture the poetic mood of pictorial and musical harmony'.[17] Whistler realised his pictorial ideal by using one main colour and its different tones, or one main colour and the many shades of its complementary colours in a given painting, as illustrated by his *Symphony in White No. 1: The White Girl*; *Harmony in Green and Rose: The Music Room*; *Arrangement in Grey and Black: Portrait of the Painter's Mother*; and *Nocturne in Black and Gold: The Fire Wheel*.

Yeats himself was touched by the stylistic simplicity and minimalist colour schemes of Rossetti, Burne-Jones, and Whistler's paintings. Yeats was very particular about the colour schemes employed for the production of his plays because he intended to realise the perfect identification of form and matter—of which Pater and Whistler spoke—in the medium of the theatre. Flannery emphasises how Yeats wished to stage his poetic plays using no more than two or three complementary colours in order to heighten the poetic quality of his work.[18] Only a few colours were used to create the required dramatic effect for the March 1903 production of *The Hour-Glass*, which bore the designs of Robert Gregory for costumes and Thomas Sturge Moore for staging.[19] An olive-green curtain decorated the back of the stage, in front of which the pupils and the Wise Man wore costumes of different shades of purple. The Fool wore a costume of a red-brown colour, with touches of green in order to harmonise with the colours of the drapery hanging at the back of the stage. Yeats asked for an indigo-blue cloth to cover the back of the stage for the January 1904 production of *The Shadowy Waters*. The sail of the boat was to be blue-green and the mast and bulwark were to be painted deep indigo-blue. The costumes were of blue material with touches of green.[20] Green, purple, and black were used for the main scene of *The Green Helmet*, the reworked version of *The Golden Helmet* from two years previously.[21] The sea in the background was painted a shady green colour to harmonise with the green robes of Cuchulain's tribesmen, the Green Men. The stage props were of purple black to match the dark purple robe of the Black Man, while the interior of the cottage was painted orange-red to highlight the startling red colour of Red Man's robe in the play. Yeats liked using the colour green in its numerous shades and tones, bringing to mind the green reveries of Rossetti's famous *The Day Dream*, *Veronica Veronese*, and *Beata Beatrix*; and of Burne-Jones's celebrated *Green Summer* and *Spring*. Burne-Jones's pictures especially inspired many stage pictures for Yeats's *Deirdre* plays during this period. Yeats received Chaucer's *Canterbury Tales*, illustrated by Burne-Jones's designs, in 1905; this book became a major source of inspiration for Yeats in subsequent years.[22] Yeats, who conceived of Deirdre as a Celtic Helen of Troy, marvelled at Burne-Jones's artistry in blending late Pre-Raphaelite sensitivity with a *fin-de-siècle* appreciation of Greco-Romanism. Yeats's admiration of this blend was clearly evident in the staging of *Deirdre* in Dublin in 1906 and in London in 1908; on all occasions the play bore the marks of Yeats's continuous interest in Celtic mysticism in terms of Victorian Hellenism.[23]

Staging Pictorial Ideals

Whistler and Burne-Jones belonged to Lady Gregory's circle of artist friends; yet her ideas on the pictorial were markedly different to theirs, and likewise to those of Yeats. Like many theatre practitioners before her, she continued to adhere to the theatrical convention of the *tableau vivant* and to the realist, narrative type of picture making. She confessed in her notes to *Damer's Gold* that she first saw a play as a picture: 'I pictured to myself, for I usually first see a play as a picture, a young man, a mere lad, very sleepy in the day time. [...] I placed him in the house of a miser, an old man who had saved a store of gold. I called the old man Damer [...]'.²⁴ Damer was living in a typical Irish country cottage with a typical Irish cottage interior. Ensuring the authenticity of the stage scene was paramount for Lady Gregory. For her most successful plays, *Twenty-Five*, *Spreading the News*, *Hyacinth Halvey*, and *The Jackdaw*, she collected props and clothing items in and around the Coole Park area. Brenna Katz Clarke writes that for her first Abbey play, *Spreading the News*, 'Lady Gregory brought actual market bills or fair bills for the walls of the set and there were people who came up from the country to see the plays and saw their names written on the set walls'.²⁵ In this aspect, the stage picture of *Spreading the News* was strikingly reminiscent of a famous Victorian painting, John Orlando Parry's *A London Street Scene* (1840). Parry's painting was a narrative watercolour of one of the streets in the imperial metropolis, conveying a sense of recognisable social reality to the viewer by displaying famous theatre bills and advertisements on a wall. Richard L. Stein has commented that during the Victorian period 'street scenes' were 'common forms of urban genre painting, [...] records of actual life'.²⁶ Stein argues, however, that Parry's painting was a strange early example of the genre in being 'material' and 'nonhuman' as opposed to the usual 'street scenes' depicting people walking along streets.²⁷ Stein adds that the Hogarthian detail of the pickpocket in *A London Street Scene*, to the left of the poster man putting up the newest advertisement, was not enough to create a substantial degree of urban mass in the painting. In this respect it differed from other street scenes such as they appear in the allegorical painting *Work*, by Ford Madox Brown, which has the figures of Thomas Carlyle and John Ruskin looking on a crowd of London working men.²⁸ Nonetheless, as Stein writes of Parry's *A London Street Scene*, 'it is a site we can imagine actually seeing; nothing in the image is extraordinary, as the title promises'.²⁹

In pursuit of this type of visual realism for her plays, Lady Gregory continued to gather props and clothing items for performances. Katz Clarke argues that '[i]t became a kind of obsession for Lady Gregory to get accurate properties'.³⁰ The illustrated programme of the Abbey Theatre tour in England in 1906 laid emphasis on the company striving for stage authenticity when pointing out that 'the properties used by the company are all taken direct from the cottages of the peasantry'.³¹ The little wooden vessels and the cowskin sandals, the 'pampooties', were brought from the Aran Islands, while the turf baskets and the panniers had been taken from various locations in Co. Kerry. For Synge's *Riders to the Sea*, Lady Gregory was asked to acquire four red petticoats, a number of Aran caps and an original spinning wheel, props which were used later in other Abbey Theatre plays.[32] Frank Fay asked Yeats to sketch him cottage interiors in Sligo in order to be able to reproduce the interior scenes accurately at the Abbey.[33] Lady Gregory's drawing of a cottage interior in her sketchbook of Inisheer and the setting of *Cathleen ni Houlihan* or *The Pot of Broth* is significant in this regard.[34] Her drawing depicts the interior of a peasant cottage with a fireplace in the middle surrounded by a pot and a wooden spoon, clothes, and hats on the walls. Food is boiling in the pot on the fire and there is a window in the top left corner of the sketch. Her efforts to reproduce rural cottage interiors authentically were much appreciated. The review of *Twenty-Five* in D. P. Moran's newspaper *The Leader* propounded that '[t]he game was a perfect genre picture, a Connaught idyll', which 'won the sympathies of the audience, and came as a pleasing contrast to the more sombre hints of the earlier part of the programme'.[35] The review echoed some of the playwright's own comments on the need to write comedies to lift the audience's spirits after Synge's more tragic or Yeats's more mystical plays.[36] Her ability to write comedy was most certainly needed to make the Abbey Theatre a successful enterprise, financially and culturally. However, the reviewer's comments were also striking for the connection that they established between genre painting and Lady Gregory's *Twenty-Five*. This suggests that the playwright was successful in realising the genre that she so much admired, as revealed, among others, by her diary entry on the Jean-François Millet exhibition in the Musée des Beaux Arts, Paris in 1887.[37] The European Grand Tours during which she studied the history of rural genre painting in the Low Lands, in Germany, and in France, shaped her artistic vision to a significant degree for much of her later career as dramatist.

John Millington Synge, too, was known for an interest in genre realism. Maurice Bourgeois, Synge's friend and supporter in France, wrote of the playwright's admiration for the work of the French artists Monet, Manet, Renoir, Poitevin, Maxence, and Duffaud.[38] Above all, wrote Bourgeois, Synge admired the work of Jean-François Millet, 'in whose work the artistic possibilities of peasant life—which Synge himself was to express—were fully revealed and utilized'.[39] Synge had tried his hand at painting and he was a regular visitor to the Louvre and the Luxembourg Gallery in Paris; he 'had an eye for colour' and he used to explain to his friends 'the function played by the various tints in the harmony of a picture'.[40] Lady Gregory and Synge shared their admiration of Millet's work but it sprang from different sources. While Lady Gregory liked the religious contemplative nature of Millet's paintings—like that of his *Angelus* (1857–1859)—Synge admired Millet's work for its 'image[s] of labour', an admiration that he shared with the painters Paul and Grace Henry, who had travelled to Achill Island, County Mayo, after reading Synge's *Riders to the Sea*.[41] Paul Henry's early images, explains Síghle Bhreathnach Lynch, focused on the everyday activities of the islanders, such as working the land and digging for potatoes, the staple diet on the Achill Island at the time.[42] Henry held the Millet-like quality of Synge's drama in high esteem, especially *Riders to the Sea*, which had inspired much of Henry's paintings of Achill Island inhabitants.[43] As Sinéad Garrigan Mattar notes, what Synge found intriguing about the islanders was their 'primitive' way of life as he observed and evaluated it through his comprehensive knowledge of nineteenth-century anthropology, evolutionary theory, and comparative Celtology.[44] Synge saw the islanders and their civilization as 'moved by strange archaic sympathies with the world', and being 'more moral and more pure than civilization itself'.[45]

Nicholas Grene has argued that beneath the surface realism of *Riders to the Sea* lie images with biblical, mythical, and literary origins.[46] Grene, however, warns against reading Synge's work symbolically for 'it is not a symbolic work which takes us beyond its own reality'.[47] Props and clothes do not point beyond a representation of 'the ordinary continuum', and are devoid of 'special or heightened significance'.[48] The nets, the oilskins, the pots on the turf fire help create a realistic sense of a rural Irish cottage in *Riders to the Sea*, indicating that the inhabitants live off the sea. The spinning-wheel and the bread, which is being prepared through the course of the play and which is finally offered to the coffinmakers, sustain the continuum that Grene observes, providing the time frame of the play. When first performed, the poverty of the scene, the bareness of the stage, and the naturalness of the acting truly heightened the tragedy of the Aran island family depicted in Synge's play. A mother and her daughters lose the only two remaining male members of their family, having already lost the father and four sons to the sea. Otherwise critical of Synge's work, even Joseph Holloway praised *Riders to the Sea*, writing in his diary that the audience 'was so deeply moved by the tragic gloom of the terrible scene on which the curtains close in, that it could not applaud'.[49] The curtains closed on the image of the mourning mother, keening the sons who would have been able to carry on the name and keep the legacy of the small fishing family.

Katz Clarke observes the simplicity of the acting and the stillness of the stage picture in this and other productions at the Abbey Theatre; many complaints appeared in newspapers at the time that the actors were not acting at all.[50] The simplicity of the style, however, was down to a technique that the director of actor training Frank Fay invented for the Abbey productions, one that made the company's productions popular with audiences in Britain, Ireland, and America. Fay derived the technique, in part, from the work of French actor and director Benoît-Constant Coquelin, whose company visited Dublin on several occasions between 1899 and 1905.[51] Fay visited the performances religiously and filled a notebook with comments on the company's performances of Molière's plays, including the French playwright's most famous play *Tartuffe*.[52] Fay developed his own work at the Abbey Theatre by using some of Coquelin's theoretical works, including *L'art de dire le monologue* (1884) and *L'art du comédien* (1894). Coquelin's insistence on naturalism and simplicity in acting greatly appealed to the man whose intention was to bring to life the true character of rural Ireland.[53] According to Fay, actors were to move very little on stage and were to concentrate mainly on delivering their dialogues in the most spontaneous and unaffected manner. Lighting was then used to accentuate the significance of a character in a particular moment of the play. This simplicity of style particularly suited the production of Lady Gregory and Synge's plays because of the genre realism intrinsic to their work. It also suited the early production of Yeats's plays, even though his work had much more in common with Aurélien Lugné-Poe's symbolist theatre than with Coquelin's naturalist endeavours.[54] Fay's staging, however, allowed Yeats's poetic texts to come alive and their lyrical beauty to gain audience appreciation.[55]

'Speaking pictures' as these productions were, the stage pictures of the early rural plays at the Abbey resembled little miniature paintings, also noted by contemporary critics. Holloway commented on William Fay's performance of Peter Gillane in *Cathleen ni Houlihan*: 'As a miniature portrait painter of humble Irish country folk he is unsurpassed'.[56] The remark recalls Lessing's original comments on the actor's pictorial art, comments that went on to define nineteenth-century practices of the *tableau vivant*. As *tableaux vivants*, these early plays were 'living pictures', or even 'speaking pictures'. Fay put great emphasis on the actors perfecting the dialect-speech from the part of Ireland in which the story of the play was set. Hence, actors and actresses worked with dialect coaches who were natives of a particular area. Máire Nic Shiubhlaigh, who played Maurya in Synge's *Riders to the Sea*, remembered that she had visited an old woman native to the Aran Islands who lived off Gardiner Street in North Dublin.[57] Dressed in a red petticoat and a large shawl, this woman taught the Abbey actress how to deliver the *caoin*, the traditional lament which appears at the end of the play, in an authentic manner. Players then perfected the Wicklow dialect for *In the Shadow of the Glen*, the Mayo dialect for *The Playboy of the Western World*, and the Galway (Kiltartan) dialect for *Spreading the News*, *Hyacinth Halvey*, and *The Workhouse Ward*.[58] Appreciating the immense time and effort put into realising the plays, Synge preferred to describe them as 'dialect plays' rather than 'rural plays'.[59] For the illusion of reality to be perfect, the proscenium opening of the Abbey stage was narrowed down to the scale of a peasant cottage during the rural scenes; the interiors were, as the directors confirmed, 'unique fac-similes [*sic*] of the originals'.[60] What the audience received in the end were little pictorial facsimiles of cottages out of which actors and actresses created 'living pictures'.

Some affinities notwithstanding, the simplicity and stillness of the Abbey's theatrical realism was markedly different from the spectacular realism of the late Victorian and Edwardian theatre made famous in the work of Henry Irving, Frank Benson, and Herbert Beerbohm Tree. Lady Gregory in particular was very critical of contemporary preoccupations with spectacular realism. As founder of Dublin's newly established Literary Theatre, she attended a number of the famous Shakespeare productions at the Lyceum Theatre in London during 1900 and 1901. Lady Gregory was critical of the productions, remarking on the poor quality of dialogue-delivery and on the constant changing of scenery which completely distracted the mind of the audience.[61] Yeats's friend, Frank Benson, put on a special performance of Shakespeare's *Richard III* at the Lyceum in honour of the Irish Literary Society. Lady Gregory was underwhelmed by the production. She wrote in her diary that there was too much spectacle and the acting was 'overdone & jerky'.[62] Neither did she share Yeats's enthusiasm for Benson's performance in the role of Hamlet in March 1900. 'Benson jerky & laboured', she wrote, '& his soliloquies those of a flea—hop—skip—wriggle—tho' in the quiet scenes & at the end, perhaps from being a little tired he grew better'.[63] Of course, Yeats was of a different opinion, visiting Stratford-upon-Avon to see Benson's production of Shakespeare's history plays. This experience turned out to be formative in relation to his own cycle of history plays of Cuchulain and the *fianna*, as Philip Edwards remarks.[64]

Lady Gregory made one exception with regard to contemporary productions of Shakespeare's plays. She liked Tree's *Midsummer Night's Dream* at Her Majesty's Theatre that she went to see with Edward Martyn in January 1900. This performance combined the two elements that Ruskin had considered the most valuable in a theatrical production: *educating* and *entertaining* audiences. Tree's version of the Shakespeare classic had all the essentials of Victorian spectacular realism. For the forest scenes, the stage was decorated with an array of live trees and was dressed in a carpet of scented herbs and wildflowers on which live rabbits were 'scurrying' from mount to mount.[65] For the illusion of the 'fairy reality' to be perfect, Tree used sophisticated stagecraft to move about his actors dressed as forest fairies, creating the illusion that the 'fairies' were flying effortlessly around the stage of the magic forest. Much in line with the requirements of Victorian theatrical antiquarianism, Tree employed historical realism for the Athenian scenes of the play. Scenery and costumes were used to bring back the beauty of the ancient world of the Greeks. Beerbohm Tree was critical of the kind of Continental realist theatre that Benoît-Constant Coquelin was popularising at the time.[66] He defended his own view of the theatre in two famous speeches. One of these was given at the Oxford Union in 1900, and was entitled 'The Staging of Shakespeare—A Defence of Public Taste'. The other one was delivered at the Imperial Restaurant in Regent Street in London, on the occasion of the gala dinner of British scenic artists in January 1904, less than a year before opening the Abbey Theatre in Dublin.[67]

Lady Gregory's theatrical realism was much closer to Synge's naturalism than to Benson's, Irving's or Tree's spectacular realism. Yet she relied far more deeply on those pictorial ideals that Ruskin had propagated than did Synge, or indeed Yeats. *Tableaux vivants* as her plays were, they were of the narrative type, which owed much of their artistic principles to those of the early Pre-Raphaelites. Chris Brooks coined the term 'symbolic realism' to describe the art of the early Pre-Raphaelites, especially that of William Holman Hunt and John Everett Millais. 'Symbolic realism' means that there are two artistic trends blended in a single painting; in other words, seemingly realist parts of a painting acted symbolically. Ruskin applauded this blend of realism and symbolism when he wrote that the young painters combined 'watchfulness to nature' with the 'highest imaginative power'.[68] Ruskin was much impressed with the young painters' determination to exercise the practice of 'live painting', a practice that he himself had recommended to young artists in order to improve their craft. Millais, Hunt, Collins, and Rossetti were more than willing to spend long hours in the open air to record the exact colour combinations and the precise lighting arrangements of a particular scene. They then attached symbolic meaning to the natural objects appearing in the scene, as seen in Collins's *Convent Thoughts*. Millais's *Christ in the House of His Parents* (1849–1850) is an early Pre-Raphaelite work in which realism is blended with symbolism for didactic purposes. The painting is of a carpenter's workshop with the carpenter's family appearing in the scene as various figures. Millais used the workshop of a carpenter and his family whom he knew in London as models. According to Elizabeth Prettejohn, it was a widespread practice among painters to use working-class models for their paintings.[69] The representation of the family with their distraught bodies and shrunken faces as they are labouring in the workshop is realistic; in fact, the painting was first conceived of as a commentary on child labour. Robert Upstone explains, however, that 'social realism' is 'combined with an interlocking, fully integrated symbolism', revealing the hidden message of Millais's painting.[70] A careful reading of the picture reveals that it depicts a scene from Jesus's life. The elder couple are his parents, Joseph and Mary; the young boy on the right is his cousin, John the Baptist; the young boy in the middle, whose hand had been pierced by a nail, is Christ himself.[71]

The 'symbolic realism' of the early Pre-Raphaelites had become famous in the form of the popular *narrative tableaux* during the Victorian era. Robert Braithwaite Martineau and Leopold Egg, for instance, were two followers of the Pre-Raphaelites who went on to develop some of the original pictorial concepts of the Pre-Raphaelite Brotherhood. Martineau and Egg employed the 'painting-in-the-painting' pictorial device in order to elaborate on certain aspects of the main scene unfolding in the foreground of the painting. Julia Thomas has described *Last Day in the Old Home* (1862) as Martineau's Firthian criticism of the upper classes who 'had spent their lives in indolence and wasted their fortunes'.[72] Thomas explains that the two pictures in the background of the painting help Martineau tell the story unfolding in the foreground. Those pictures, argues Thomas, serve to emphasise 'the fault of the man and the effects of his action on the rest of his family'.[73] Egg's triptych, *Past and Present* (1858), is another Victorian narrative painting in which the paintings in the background help the viewer decipher the story in the foreground. The picture of the biblical story of the 'Fall of Man', Clarkson Stanfield's *The Abandoned* (in the first plate of the triptych) as well as the posters for Tom Taylor's *Victim* and Tom Parry's *A Cure for Love* (in the third plate of the triptych) perfectly describe the main female character's dilemma about her future: should she stay abandoned in London or go searching for a new life in Paris.[74] This type of dramatic interchange between the foreground and the background of a painting was also characteristic of the celebrated eighteenth-century painter William Hogarth. His narrative pictures, especially his series *Marriage à-la-Mode* (1743–1745)—which left a decisive mark on the early works of the Pre-Raphaelite Brotherhood—had been widely popularised in Victorian England in forms of engravings, copies of which were kept even in the library of Coole Park.[75] Oscar Wilde had a point when he complained that Victorian narrative *tableaux* encouraged a moralist approach to art, a moral (and often religious) message being placed at the heart of many paintings, especially those whose painters followed the artistic principles of the Pre-Raphaelite Brotherhood. Lady Gregory, for her part, certainly did not object to this didactic approach, especially as she perceived the presence of Ruskin's artistic principles in those painterly endeavours.

Composing Plays as Paintings

Lady Gregory received Edward Moxon's edition of Lord Tennyson's *Poems* (1857) as a present while still at Roxborough.[76] This book was one of her first encounters with the Pre-Raphaelite notion of interacting the background and foreground of a painting. Amongst others, Hunt, Millais, and Rossetti contributed illustrations to this edition of Tennyson's poems. For Rossetti, this was one of his first adventures into the realm of *peinture* and *poésie*. Tennyson himself was somewhat puzzled by Rossetti's illustrations of his poems: he thought that some of the designs only loosely followed the original lines in his verses. He felt that Rossetti's wood-carving for 'The Palace of Art' was more of an *interpretation* than an *illustration* of the original poem. William Rossetti revealed the nature of his brother's artistic approach: 'It must be said also that himself only, and not Tennyson, was his guide. He drew just what he chose, taking from his author's text nothing more than a hint and an opportunity.'[77] Also critical of Rossetti's wordcarving, Tennyson preferred Hunt's visual artistic response to poetry as illustrated, for example, in his engraving for 'The Lady of Shalott'. Hunt's engraving captured the moment when, fighting the curse that falls upon her, the imprisoned woman struggles to break free from the entangled threads of the web that she has been condemned to weave. His admiration for the work as a whole notwithstanding, Tennyson still disliked some particular features of Hunt's design. He thought that the woman's flowing hair looked as if it had been 'struck by a tornado', and he criticised also the design of the web, which looked 'like the threads of a cocoon'.[78] Hunt defended his pictorial representation of the scene by saying that he 'had wished to convey the idea of the threatened fatality by reversing the ordinary peace of the room and of the lady herself; that while she recognised that the moment of catastrophe had come, the spectator might also understand it'.[79] In an earlier sketch, Hunt had employed a series of round tablets to narrate the lady's story as told by the poet. These tablets decorated the back wall of the lady's room. There was a large cracked mirror, placed in the centre of the wall; in it was the knightly figure of Lancelot, the cause of the lady's torments. Then there was a series of smaller, circular pictures around the mirror which narrate the rest of the story of the poem. The figure of the crucified Christ of the Moxon version, which looks down on the scene of the tormented lady, reminded the viewer of Lancelot's last words in the poem: 'God in his mercy lend her grace.'[80] Both Prettejohn and Upstone have suggested that the illustrator intended to open up the story in order to convey a religious message—the lady's sufferings and self-denial in the prison tower offered an opportunity for atonement or redemption.[81]

Foreground and background explain each other with the help of the 'painting-in-the-painting' compositional device in two of the most famous paintings from the period of the Spanish Baroque: Velázquez's *Las Meninas* (*Maids of Honour*, c. 1656) and *Las Hilanderas* (*The Spinners*, c. 1657). Velázquez was one of Sir William Gregory's favourite painters. Velázquez's biblical *bodegón*, *Kitchen Scene with Christ, Martha and Mary* (1618), was in Sir William's possession until his death in 1892, when it was bequeathed to the National Gallery in London.[82] Sir William was very particular that his wife Augusta saw the paintings of the Spanish master exhibited in the Prado Museum in Madrid.[83] Velázquez's *Las Meninas* depicts Philip IV and his wife Maria Anna in the company of Margarita Teresa and the *infanta*'s maids of honour. Philip IV and Maria Anna appear as figures reflected in a mirror placed in an ornamented frame on the rear wall. As in the case of Hunt's engraving, the masterly expansion of the scene towards the observer was an echo of Jan van Eyck's *The Arnolfini Portrait* (1434). One of the finest early examples of the 'picture-in-the-picture' compositional schemes, it was in the Spanish royal collection and served as an inspiration for Velázquez's royal portrait.[84] Later, the painting became a part of the collection of the National Gallery in London, where it inspired many young artists, including the Pre-Raphaelites. Copies of Rubens's *Pallas and Arachne* and Jordaens's *Apollo and Marsyas* decorate the back wall of Velazquez's royal group portrait. According to the royal inventories of 1686 and 1700, Juan Bautista del Mazo, Velázquez's son-in-law, had painted copies of these paintings, which hung side-by-side on the wall of the royal chamber of Philip IV.[85] Ovid's *Metamorphoses* was the source of the two stories, which help the painter accentuate the main messages of the picture: his desire was to convey the superiority of art and the artist over the ordinary man and the sadness of an artist whose work was unjustly criticised.[86]

Using Ovid's story of Pallas and Arachne from his *Metamorphoses*, Velázquez employed the 'painting-in-the-painting' compositional device in an even more sophisticated manner in *Las Hilanderas*. The painting depicts a group of women working in a tapestry workshop. Titian's *The Rape of Europa* hangs on the rear wall of the workshop in the form of a tapestry. Again, Titian's *The Rape of Europa*, one of Velázquez's favourite works, was in Philip IV's royal collection in a copy by the Baroque master Peter Paul Rubens.[87] According to Ovid's *Metamorphoses*, the rape was the theme of the first tapestry that Pallas Athena made during the weaving contest with Arachne, which was to determine whether the goddess or the common woman was a more skilful artist. The decision fell in favour of Arachne and, as an act of revenge, Athena condemned the young girl to the chore of eternal weaving. Charles de Tolnay identifies the fact that the foreground of the painting depicts the scene of the contest in the painting on the rear wall. According to Tolnay, Pallas Athena is seen disguised as an old woman sitting on the left of the picture and Arachne is seen on the right, sitting with her back to the viewers.[88] The arrangement of the female figures is repeated in the alcove situated at the back of the workshop. Standing before *The Rape of Europa*, Pallas Athena and Arachne are seen in the same compositional arrangement as their seated versions in the foreground, the arrangement revealing the identity of the spinners situated in the foreground of the painting. Such a compositional arrangement was a development from the painter's use of the device in his early *bodegóns*, including *Kitchen Scene with Christ, Martha and Mary* in which the identity of the two female figures is revealed by the small picture depicting the biblical story of Jesus's visit to the house of Martha and Mary.

Lady Gregory was familiar with the 'painting-in-the-painting' compositional device through her study of art works by van Eyck, Velázquez, and the Pre-Raphaelites. She was aware of the wonderful possibilities that this offered those painters who desired to play with compositional arrangements between backgrounds and foregrounds. As someone with a keen eye for painting and as a skilful playwright who first saw her plays as pictures, Lady Gregory set out to experiment with the possibilities offered by the aforementioned pictorial device when it came to creating the compositional schemes for her plays. Her use of this narrative device distinguished her plays conceptually from those of her fellow playwrights in the Irish Dramatic Movement, especially Synge and Yeats. *The Image* (1909) is a play that she structures through the interaction between an everyday situation that unfolds in the foreground action and a story of whales lying beached on an Irish shore that forms the background to the play. At the beginning of *The Image*, Coppinger (a stonecutter) and his wife are seen engaged in one of their regular conversations about life when various locals appear with news relating to the events of the previous night. Malachi Naughton, a mountain dweller, appears on stage and describes the surrounding rural landscape after a stormy night. Brian Hosty, a local farmer, then recounts the story of the beached whales. Darby Costello, a seaweed hawker, reports on the arrival of country people who want to get their hands on the expensive whale oil. Lastly, Peter Mannion, a carrier, informs the small group about the visit of the waterguard and the priest to the beach where the whales lie in order to acquire oil for the local community.[89] Each of the stories reveals new details of the events of the night before and makes the story more complete. In pictorial terms, the local men's verbally generated pictures finally come to fill the entire imaginary back wall of the main stage, extending the spatial and temporal boundaries of the stage as representing the main scene of a painting, such as we find in Velázquez's paintings *Las Meninas* and *Las Hilanderas*. Naughton, the mountain-man, first appears to be an insignificant *repoussoir* figure, introduced to fill the foreground of the stage picture, but his tale of Hugh O'Lorrha, about whom nobody seems to know anything, begins first to penetrate and then to take over the main story of the play.

The Full Moon (1910) is another of her comedies in which a background story infiltrates the main story developing in the foreground. This play is a continuation of an earlier one, *Hyacinth Halvey*; many of the playwright's favourite characters appear in the opening scene. Mrs. Broderick, Bartley Fallon, Shawn Early, and Hyacinth Halvey are seen waiting for a train in a shed in the village of Cloon, conversing idly. Night falls, the full moon appears, and the sound of a barking dog is heard from a distance. A woman known as 'cracked Mary' comes on stage and takes her fair share in recounting the story of a mad dog which is rumoured to be making the roads of Ireland unsafe for travel. As Mary's depiction of the mad dog develops into a full-blown story, more and more signs of madness are observable in Hyacinth Halvey's behaviour; the background story of the supernatural dog begins to take over the foreground story of the young man waiting for the train to leave the village. This, in turn, turns the young man into a raging, barking, mad dog by the end of the play, suspended between myth and reality. In this way, *The Full Moon* brings to mind one of the pivotal stories in the legend of Cuchulain as recorded in Lady Gregory's *Cuchulain of Muirthemne*.[90] This is the story of the boy Setanta killing the fierce hound of Culan, a deed by which he acquires the name of Cuchulain, the Hound of Culan. In the figure of Hyacinth Halvey barking like a mad dog by the end of the play, *The Full Moon* recalls the madness of Cuchulain at the end of Yeats's 1904 play *On Baile's Strand*. There Cuchulain is seen fighting the waves of the sea with his sword after having killed his own son, unknowingly.[91] In contrast to the mythical nature of these pieces, Somerville and Ross's short-story 'A Conspiracy of Silence' (1905) is a literary realist source of influence on *The Full Moon*. Written for their series *The Irish R.M.*, it was initially prompted by a suggestion made by Lady Gregory and Yeats to Somerville and Ross that the duo might write a play on 'shoneenism' for the Abbey Theatre.[92] Centred upon the question of the ownership of a hunting hound called 'Playboy', the story carries undercurrents that relate to the supernatural dog of Lady Gregory's *The Full Moon*. As a white hound that is embroiled in secrecy, 'Playboy' derives from a breed nicknamed 'the Whiteboys' in another tale from *The Irish R.M.*, the name of a secret agrarian rebel group in rural Ireland.[93] Furthermore, Halvey's barking like a mad dog recalls the ending of Synge's *The Playboy of the Western World*, a play in which the protagonist, Christy Mahon, acts like a barking mad dog, biting Shawn Keogh's leg after he is confronted with the reality of his murderous deed following the return of his father, Old Mahon.[94]

Spreading the News is another Lady Gregory play in which the realism of the main foreground action is gradually overtaken by a fictional story. Ingeniously, the entire stage picture acquires the aspect of a narrative painting such as Lady Gregory herself had encountered in the likes of Velázquez's *Las Hilanderas*. Just as the image of women weaving in the foreground of Velázquez's painting unwittingly alludes to the ancient fable of the weaving competition that is depicted on the tapestry hanging behind them, so the characters and the events of *Spreading the News* are overtaken by the background fiction—that Bartley Fallon has killed Jack Smith with a hayfork. The comedy of Lady Gregory's play derives from the characters' unfortunate misreading of the narrative elements, elements that the audience can observe perfectly well. Tim Casey believes Mrs. Fallon's upturned basket to signify a fight that supposedly has taken place between Bartley Fallon and Jack Smith. 'Jack Smith and Bartley Fallon had a falling out', says Tim, 'and Jack knocked Mrs. Fallon's basket into the road, and Bartley made an attack on him with a hayfork, and away with Jack, and Bartley after him'.[95] As the story gathers pace, Jack Smith's hayfork, which he is taking to the Five Acre Meadow, is mistakenly read as a murder weapon, and newly washed sheets that Kitty Keary—Jack Smith's wife—is laying out to dry on the hedge are mistaken for sheets being prepared for her husband's wake. 'Laying out a sheet for the dead!' cries Mrs. Tarpey, 'The Lord have mercy on us! Jack Smith dead, and his wife laying out a sheet for his burying!'[96] Through these and other confusions in *Spreading the News*, the actual occurrences in the play are overtaken by a narrative picture of Bartley Fallon killing Jack Smith with a hayfork after an argument at the local fair. With this fictitious story triggering an actual confrontation at the end of the play, and the living Jack Smith arrested by the police in the mistaken belief that he is impersonating the dead Jack Smith, the foreground realism of *Spreading the News* becomes the fulfilment of the background fable.

Words point beyond what is readily perceivable on stage in her more serious plays. In *The Gaol Gate*, two women are seen arriving at the gates of a jail, full of hope that their loved one will be released from prison. One is the mother of the prisoner, the other is his wife. There they find out that they have arrived too late: their loved one had been executed for murder the day before. The villagers seem to know that another man committed the act but no one dares to say a word about this. No one, least of all the condemned man Denis Cahel, dares to disclose this to the authorities for fear of being labelled an informer, placing the lives of his family members in danger. Cathy Leeney, Lucy McDiarmid, and James Pethica have highlighted some of the important political intimations of the situation in relation to Irish rebel nationalism.[97] However, the play carries equally important socio-political implications that point to the playwright's concern for those pressing social issues in rural Irish life that the leaders of the Co-operative Movement in Ireland sought to address. Denis and Mary Cahel are heavily indebted small farmers who cannot even entertain the hope of emigrating.[98] The only solution for them is to sell their holdings and for the mother to move into a workhouse after her son's release from prison.[99] As in the case of *Spreading the News*, what is addressed here, first of all, is the controlling power of communal gossip over members of small local communities. Both of them illiterate, the mother and the wife in *The Gaol Gate* decide against showing their neighbours the letter which they have received from the prison, the letter informing them of the pending execution of Denis. This happens because they are ashamed to ask their neighbours for help, fearing that their lack of education would make them vulnerable to the disgrace generated by local gossip. Sadly, as a consequence, they miss the last chance to talk to their loved one before the execution. So when they arrive at the jail gate, they only hear the news of his trial and execution. From the beginning of the play, the biblical story of Jesus Christ slowly penetrates the story of Denis Cahel unfolding in the foreground of the scene. Denis is falsely accused of having committed a crime, has refused to speak when interrogated, and is then sentenced to death with no justification.[100] From this perspective, Denis Cahel appears as Christ-like in being sentenced to death for the sins of others. His sacrifice, however, is devoid of the redemptive meaning that is inherent in the biblical story, revealing the ambivalence of Lady Gregory's attitude to the (un)worthiness of self-sacrifice. While Jesus returned to his disciples after his execution, Denis would only live on through the loving memory of his mother and wife, who promise to spread the news of his heroic sacrifice.[101]

First performed in 1910, Lady Gregory's *The Travelling Man* revolves around the King of the World's visit to the house of a woman and her young child. Seven years previously a man, calling himself the 'King of the World', led the woman of the house out of servitude into a new world, where she had found security in marriage.[102] Ever since that time, this woman has been waiting for the return of this 'King of the World'.

A bareheaded, barefooted beggar, wearing a ragged white flannel shirt and mud-stained trousers, comes to visit her house on the occasion in which the play is set, one in which the woman happens to be absent. The woman's young child greets the visitor and together they build a beautiful garden, using the mother's best plates. After her return, the mother scolds her child for letting the beggar into the house, allowing him to play with her special plates and offering him a cake that she had kept for her special guest. However, in the closing moments of the play she comes to realise that the beggar man *was* the special guest for whom she been waiting throughout the previous seven years. In *The Travelling Man*, words and objects acquire symbolic meanings to reveal the identity of the visitor. Biblical passages and Christian imagery lead the audience to understand the main story unfolding in the scene: the return of Jesus Christ to the world after his Resurrection, something he had promised to his disciples before the crucifixion. Like this travelling man, Jesus sought conversation with children. 'Let the little children come to me', says Jesus in one of the most often cited passages of the Bible, 'and do not hinder them, for the kingdom of God belongs to such as these. I tell you the truth, anyone who will not receive the kingdom of God like a little child will never enter it'.[103] The travelling man talks of a beautiful garden of peace where flowers and fruits grow on the same branch, bringing to mind the Christian belief in Paradise, God's bountiful and beautiful land of eternal peace.[104] The man and the child ride to the secret garden on a toy horse, a subtle allusion to the mule on which Jesus entered Jerusalem on Palm Sunday.[105] At first, when still in ignorance of the travelling man's true identity, the mother wishes that this beggar man should be taken out of society. This is reminiscent of the wish of the Pharisees, and of many who stood outside Pontius Pilate's palace during Jesus's trial.[106] If still in doubt as regards the traveller's identity, the young child's final remarks clearly indicate the figure of Jesus. The child informs the audience and his own mother that, astonishingly, the travelling man is walking on water.[107] The mother finally realises that this man was indeed the 'King of the World', as Christians refer to Jesus, who walked the roads as an ordinary-looking travelling man and who returned as such to his disciples after his Resurrection.[108]

As is the case with *The Gaol Gate*, *The Travelling Man* also brings to mind a Pre-Raphaelite painting. Hunt's *The Scapegoat* is alluded to in the figure of Denis Cahel as the scapegoat in *The Gaol Gate*, while Millais's *The Return of the Dove to the Ark* is inferred in *The Travelling*

Man. Hunt's *The Scapegoat* was painted on the shore of the Dead Sea in 1854–1855, in keeping with Ruskin's principles on 'live painting'. The painting depicts a white goat standing amid skeletons of dead animals in front of a distant range of hills illuminated by the light of the setting sun. Reading the symbols of the picture carefully, Mary Bennett has concluded that the goat was the sacrificial goat used in the Jewish ritual of atonement and was a 'type of Christ taking on the sins of the world'.[109] Landow, who has written about Hunt's 'typological symbolism', has observed that *The Scapegoat* combined the 'powerful physical image of suffering' with the image of the goat placed 'in its proper spiritual context', enabling the observer to see 'how wonderfully God structured sacred history to inform man of coming salvation'.[110] The gilded frame of the picture helps placing it in the 'proper spiritual context', with two quotations from the Old Testament, one from Isaiah 53:4, the other from Leviticus 16:22.[111] The dove holding an olive branch on the left of the picture frame recalls another Old Testament story, that of the Great Deluge from the Book of Genesis. Millais's *The Return of the Dove to the Ark* from 1851, which Ruskin intended to buy after its completion, tells the story of the dove which returns to Noah's Ark after the Great Deluge.[112] According to the biblical story, the returning dove is seen as the sign of the fulfilment of God's promise to Noah that there would be life after the Great Deluge. Therefore, in this context, the dove symbolises hope, amplified by the painter's dominant use of the colour green in the picture. The New Testament story of Jesus's baptism in the River Jordan is reminiscent of this moment from the Old Testament. After John the Baptist submerges Jesus in the Jordan, God's Holy Spirit is seen descending upon Jesus in the form of a bird. This bird has been depicted as a dove in pictorial representations of the scene, reminding viewers of the renewed fulfilment of God's promise that there would be life after death. Jesus's resurrection after his crucifixion is the final reminder and the final fulfilment of God's promise to mankind. Millais's *tableau* of the returning dove and of the children who hold in their hands the living branch that the dove has brought resonates strongly with the closing *tableau* of Lady Gregory's *The Travelling Man*. The final *tableau* of the play is that of a young boy who is holding a living branch, one that has been brought to his mother's house by the travelling man from his own father's eternal garden. Children wearing robes of white and green, symbolising innocence and hope, greet the dove and hold the branch in their hands in Millais's painting. Likewise, a young child is seen at the end of

The Travelling Man holding a living branch. The moment carries a theological double meaning in both Millais's painting and Gregory's play: the divine fulfilment of a given promise and the earthly hope for a better future. Millais's painting found its resting place in Thomas Combe's collection, where it was hung next to Collins's *Convent Thoughts* and Hunt's *A Converted British Family Sheltering a Christian Missionary from the Persecution of the Druids* (1849–1850), a companion piece to Millais's *Christ in the House of His Parents* (1849–1850).

IRISH PRE-RAPHAELITISM

Lady Gregory understood Yeats's interest in late Pre-Raphaelite ideals; she herself had attended the double exhibition held in honour of Dante Gabriel Rossetti in 1882–1883.[113] The exhibition of the recently deceased painter's work was one of the most anticipated events of the London season. During his lifetime Rossetti had refused to display his paintings at the exhibitions of the Royal Academy where the wider public could have viewed them. Consequently, the Rossetti double exhibition hosted by the Academy and the Burlington Fine Arts Club became the talk of the season. As a woman genuinely interested in the arts and the wife of a *connoisseur* who was a prominent figure of the London art world, Lady Gregory submerged herself in the study of Dante Gabriel Rossetti's life and work. She read both William Sharp and Sir Thomas Hall Caine's recent biographies, the painter's recently published poetry collection, *Ballads and Sonnets*, and the recently republished edition of his *Poems*.[114] She viewed and talked about the paintings with Robert Browning's sister, Sarianna, who reflected at some length on Rossetti's relation to the Brownings and to their family friend Lord Tennyson.[115] Tennyson had spent some time with the Brownings in Ca' Rezzonico, their palace on Venice's Grand Canal. Sir William Gregory, who accompanied his wife to the exhibition, was unimpressed by Rossetti's paintings. She quotes him as saying that he thought Rossetti's female figures were 'strange-lipped, long-jawed, weird, disconsolate women'.[116] Yeats, on the other hand, was deeply moved by Rossetti's pictorial female ideal. Terence Brown explains that Yeats discovered in the pictures a spiritual sensuality, a 'powerful evocation of a life lived for art itself'.[117] Yeats was fascinated by the painter's representation of sensual female beauty; for Yeats, Rossetti was 'drunken with natural beauty' and 'saw the supernatural beauty, the impossible beauty, in its frenzy'.[118] As he confessed in his *Memoirs*, at the time his head was 'full of the mysterious women of Rossetti'.[119] Maud Gonne embodied for him the sensual female ideal that he perceived in Rossetti's paintings. This is not surprising as Gonne deliberately modelled herself on the fashionable late Pre-Raphaelite female ideal that was *en vogue* among London actresses such as Sarah Bernhardt and Ellen Terry.

Yeats wrote that he was 'in all things a Pre-Raphaelite' when he began to move in London art circles and that he thought Gonne was a genuine Pre-Raphaelite beauty when he first saw her on the occasion of her delivering a message to his father from Irish republican John O'Leary. Yeats wrote that '[h]er complexion was luminous, like the apple-blossom through which the light falls' and the poet saw her 'standing that first day by a great heap of such blossom in the window'.[120] Gonne's first appearance reminded Yeats of the beauty of the coming spring, evoking in him a fusion of images by Rossetti, Burne-Jones, Watts, Alma-Tadema—and Botticelli.[121] Coincidentally, Botticelli's *La Primavera* (*Spring*, c. 1477–1478), an allegory of Spring, depicts a lightly clad young woman in a lush garden filled with beautiful flowers and ripening fruits, in the company of a various mythological figures. Walter Pater wrote enthusiastically on Botticelli's art, claiming that in it the charm of poetry and of sentiment was matched by a magical use of lining and colouring.[122] Pater thought that the classical beauty of Botticelli's paintings was 'a more direct inlet into the Greek temper than the works of the Greeks themselves even of the finest period'.[123] A devotee of Pater's teachings and Botticelli's works, Burne-Jones himself travelled around the Apennine Peninsula to view the paintings of the Florentine master. Later, he painted his own version of a celebrated mythological story under the title *Venus Rising from the Sea* (c. 1870), itself based on Botticelli's *The Birth of Venus* (c. 1485). Yeats himself discovered the true beauty of Botticelli's art during his trip to Northern Italy in 1907. Lady Gregory had arranged this trip to be Yeats's *Grand Tour* of fine arts and social governance. Armed with Ruskin's *The Stones of Venice*, he deepened his knowledge of the fine arts and reinforced his awareness of their significant role in social formation. According to the itinerary, Lady Gregory, Yeats, and Robert Gregory travelled through Urbino, Ravenna, Ferrara, Florence, and Venice, where they stayed at the Layards' famous Ca' Capello.[124]

Staying in a palace in which Ruskin had once resided and following in the art critic's footsteps on the cobbled streets of Venice, Yeats began to comprehend the beauty of the city, about which Ruskin had written so passionately and so extensively. Bernadette McCarthy has noted that the poet was overwhelmed by the beauty of the place, somewhere that had inspired many of Turner's watercolours, including those on display at the National Gallery in Dublin, following Henry Vaughan's bequest of his collection of Turner's watercolours to Ireland and Scotland in 1900.[125] Turner's watercolours were first exhibited a year after the bequest was made, in January of 1901.[126] McCarthy argues that as an art student and someone interested in the techniques of pastel and watercolour Yeats paid special attention to Turner's aquatic works of Venice.[127] Yeats discovered in Venice the special atmosphere that inspired the airy, otherworldly quality of Turner's paintings. Turner expressed this ethereal quality through beautiful colour combinations, of which Ruskin wrote at great length in *Modern Painters*. Ruskin thought that Turner's works were 'as perfect as those of Phidias or Leonardo; that is to say, incapable, in their way, of any improvement conceivable by human mind'.[128] Ruskin was particularly taken with the various shades of greens, blues, and golds that Turner used for his Venetian works, claiming that many of his works were indeed 'faultless'.[129] He wrote, for instance, that Turner's *Venice Seen from Near Fusina* (1844) was 'the most perfectly beautiful piece of colour of all that I have seen produced by human hands, by any means, or at any period'.[130] Turner's unique colour combinations and his innovative brush strokes, with which he had applied paint onto the canvas, greatly influenced the French Impressionists as well as Whistler and his Pre-Raphaelite friends. Whistler's *Salute, Sunset (Red and Gold)* (1880) clearly demonstrates the extent of his debt to Turner's painterly imagination. Whistler's painting of brown-golden hues strongly resembles the yellow-golden shades of Turner's *Approach to Venice* (1844). Similarly, Whistler's *Nocturne in Blue and Green* (1870) resembles Turner's watercolours in its composition and its brilliant use of a colour combination of blues and greens. The colour palette of Turner's waterscapes that influenced Whistler was clearly perceptible in the first stage pictures of Yeats's plays from the period between 1903 and 1908. These included the first stage pictures of *The Shadowy Waters*, *On Baile's Strand*, and *The Hour-Glass*.[131]

The Irish Times noted Whistler's influence in the stage pictures of the rewritten version of Yeats's *The Hour-Glass*, produced at the Abbey as part of a double bill with Lady Gregory's *The Deliverer* in January 1911.[132] This was a special production of the plays that premiered the infamous movable screens which Craig had developed for the production of Yeats's plays. Yeats and Craig had been discussing the possibility of producing Yeats's plays with innovative stage designs for a considerable period; there had been increased correspondence between the two men, particularly after William and Frank Fay's withdrawal from the Abbey Theatre in 1908. Yeats's *Plays for an Irish Theatre* (1911), a new edition of his plays that was illustrated with Craig's modernist designs, was testimony of this intensified collaboration. Yeats's intention to restore the supremacy of poetic speech on the painted stage was well matched by Craig's innovative modernist stage designs, as illustrated by the success of *The Hour-Glass* in January 1911. Karen Dorn emphasises how *The Hour-Glass* was *the* Yeats play that Craig had always intended to produce; he wanted to liberate it from the clutch of the *tableau*-like scenic arrangement of earlier productions.[133] The play was finally rescued from the tradition of the Victorian *tableaux* in 1911, and Yeats rewrote the play for an even more daring production in 1912. Before the January 1911 performance, Yeats gave a short talk during which he complimented Craig on his courage in diverging from the realistic scenery that was employed, for instance, by Henry Irving at the Lyceum. Yeats congratulated his friend on his success in 'invent[ing] decorative and ideal scenery for poetic work'.[134] Yeats's enthusiasm was matched by that of contemporary theatre critics. They praised Craig's movable screens, his choice of colours for the scene, and his special use of lighting through which he told the story of the damnation of a Wise Man's soul for denying divine reality. *The Freeman's Journal* pointed out that playwright and designer successfully created a unity between the spoken word, the acting, and the setting—with colours blending it all together to create a perfect 'harmony of mood'.[135]

Craig's vast and abstract architectural setting proved to be less successful in the case of Lady Gregory's religious play *The Deliverer*. For Yeats's *The Hour-Glass*, Craig had created a set of saffron-hued square pillars and undulant screens, which was 'aesthetically harmonious' and 'theatrically attractive'.[136] Yeats himself remarked that the set resembled the interior of some precious pearl; only the blackness of the bell and the hour-glass broke the colour harmony of the scene.[137] For *The Deliverer*, Craig had placed the screens—resembling square pillars—slantwise across the stage to suggest the pillars of an Egyptian temple.[138] Craig's screens—arranged according to a mathematical plan—were the length of the proscenium and were opened and closed from time to time. Amber light coloured the screens from top to side to create the desired effect of an Egyptian setting. Craig's innovative stage design did not work for *The Deliverer* because of the play's intricate symbolism and because of its composition as a 'speaking' narrative *tableau*. Lady Gregory conceived of her play as a political allegory of the fall of the visionary and charismatic statesman Charles Stewart Parnell, an allegory which was enveloped in the biblical story of Moses, the prophet who attempted to free the Jewish people from Egyptian captivity. She included an abundance of references to Catholic Ireland in order to help the audience identify the story of the doomed Irish political leader behind the veil of the biblical story of the Jewish prophet, and she wrote the play in the Kiltartanese dialect to lend further emphasis to the play's connection to Irish history and politics. The process of 'reading the picture' or 'reading the play', that Ruskin was promoting, was greatly hindered by the mysterious and symbolically abstract setting, which looked neither Egyptian nor Irish.[139] *The Irish Times* and *The Freeman's Journal* agreed that the message about the visionary Irish leader, mercilessly let down by his own people, was entirely lost on the vast and abstract stage that Craig had designed for *The Deliverer*. As Holloway put it, the audience was wondering 'what it was about and why all the Egyptians spoke Kiltartan'.[140] Clearly, Lady Gregory's artistic principles were different to those of Yeats, and this left a mark on the production of their plays in January 1911, when Craig's designs made their theatrical *debut* at the Abbey Theatre in Dublin. Yeats was interested in the sensual and sensory kind of late Pre-Raphaelitism, characterised by the works of Rossetti or Burne-Jones, as well as the paintings of those who influenced them, including the Renaissance master Sandro Botticelli and their contemporaries Alma-Tadema and Whistler. Lady Gregory, on the other hand, continued to adhere to the didactic and religious strand of Pre-Raphaelitism, exemplified by the paintings of William Holman Hunt and those of her close friend and President of the Royal Academy Sir John Everett Millais, as well as by the accomplished works of Eyck, Velázquez, Hogarth, and the famous Victorian narrative painters Robert Braithwaite Martineau and William Powell Firth.

Notes

1. Lady Augusta Gregory, *The Collected Plays*, vol. 1 (New York: Oxford University Press, 1970), 262.
2. For the detailed description of the Abbey Theatre, see "New Dublin Theatre: Private View Yesterday—Forthcoming Irish Plays," *The Freeman's Journal*, December 14, 1904.

3. William Henderson, *Newspaper Cuttings*, MS 1731, National Library of Ireland.
4. Christopher Innes, *Edward Gordon Craig* (Cambridge: Cambridge University Press, 1983), 14.
5. Lessing's original wording, 'lebendige Malerei', referred more to the art of the theatre as an actor's painterly activity but the first English translations of the text used the term 'living picture', a phrase that came to be employed widely by art critics during the course of the nineteenth century. For Lessing's original wording, see William Guild Howard, ed., trans., and commentary, *Laokoon: Lessing, Herder and Goethe* (New York: Henry Holt, 1910), 41. The reinterpretation of Horace's dictum 'ut pictura poesis', which concerns the close relationship between a picture and a poem, became a matter of great importance to generations of European art critics after Lessing.
6. Martin Meisel, *Realizations: Narrative, Pictorial, and Theatrical Arts in Nineteenth-Century England* (Princeton, NJ: Princeton University Press, 1983), 44.
7. For the various forms of the *tableau*, see Meisel, *Realizations*, 45–48.
8. George Bernard Shaw, *Our Theatre in the Nineties*, vol. 1 (London: Constable, 1948), 79–87.
9. James W. Flannery, *W. B. Yeats and the Idea of a Theatre* (New Haven: Yale University Press, 1976), 240.
10. Flannery, *W. B. Yeats and the Idea of a Theatre*, 240.
11. Flannery, *W. B. Yeats and the Idea of a Theatre*, 242.
12. For the influence of the rituals of the Hermetic Order of the Golden Dawn, see Flannery, *W. B. Yeats and the Idea of a Theatre*, 239–40.
13. James McNeill Whistler, *The Gentle Art of Making Enemies* (London: Heinemann, 1919), 8.
14. Whistler, *The Gentle Art of Making Enemies*, 147.
15. Richard Ellmann, *Oscar Wilde* (London: Hamilton, 1987), 246–47.
16. Walter Pater, *The Renaissance*, ed. Donald L. Hill (Berkeley: University of California Press, 1980), 140 and 144.
17. Ingo F. Walther, ed., *Masterpieces of Western Art* (Köln: Taschen, 2002), 755.
18. James W. Flannery, "W. B. Yeats, Gordon Craig and the Visual Arts of the Theatre," in *Yeats and the Theatre*, ed. Robert O'Driscoll and Lorna Reynolds (London: Macmillan, 1975), 86.
19. Flannery, "W. B. Yeats, Gordon Craig and the Visual Arts of the Theatre," 87.
20. Flannery, "W. B. Yeats, Gordon Craig and the Visual Arts of the Theatre," 88.

21. W. B. Yeats, *Green Helmet and Other Poems* (Churchtown, Dundrum: Cuala Press, 1910), 13.
22. Elizabeth Bergmann Loiseaux, *Yeats and the Visual Arts* (Syracuse: Syracuse University Press, 2003), 121.
23. For production details, see Plate 12 and 14 in Flannery's *W. B. Yeats and the Idea of a Theatre*.
24. Gregory, *Collected Plays*, vol. 1, 262–63.
25. Brenna Katz Clarke, *The Emergence of the Irish Peasant Play at the Abbey Theatre* (Ann Arbor: UMI Research Press, 1982), 58.
26. Richard L. Stein, *Victoria's Year: English Literature and Culture, 1837–1838* (Oxford: Oxford University Press, 1987), 45.
27. Stein, *Victoria's Year*, 45.
28. Stein, *Victoria's Year*, 46.
29. Stein, *Victoria's Year*, 45.
30. Katz Clarke, *The Emergence of the Irish Peasant Play*, 58.
31. Ann Saddlemyer, sel. and ed., *Theatre Business: The Correspondence of the First Abbey Theatre Directors* (Gerrards Cross: Colin Smythe, 1982), 318.
32. Katz Clarke, *The Emergence of the Irish Peasant Play*, 58. Clarke notes the impact that these original materials had on the actors: 'For the production of *Riders to the Sea* the company imported actual cowskin pampooties or sandals which were worn by the peasants in the Aran Islands. A young man was brought from the islands to advise on all the details of the costumes and to ensure that each piece was authentic [...]. Gabriel Fallon, who played a small part in *Riders to the Sea*, remembers "being amazed because I hadn't visited the west of Ireland, when I went to the wardrobe to get my rig out, those pampooties and things"'. Katz Clarke, *The Emergence of the Irish Peasant Play*, 56.
33. Katz Clarke, *The Emergence of the Irish Peasant Play*, 57.
34. Lady Augusta Gregory, *Sketchbooks, c. 1890–1900*. TX 3033, National Library of Ireland.
35. "Mr. Yeats and Theatre Reform," *The Leader*, May 28, 1903, Henderson, MS 1729, NLI.
36. See Lady Gregory's notes to *Damer's Gold* in Gregory, *Collected Plays*, vol. 1, 261.
37. Diary entry, May 14, 1887. Lady Augusta Gregory, *Typewritten Diaries, 1882–1892*, Lady Augusta Gregory Papers, Albert A. and Henry W. Berg Collection, New York Public Library, New York.
38. Maurice Bourgeois, *John Millington Synge and the Irish Theatre* (London: Constable, 1913), 45. Bourgeois's book was written shortly after the death of his friend, and he had consulted Yeats's 'Synge and the Ireland of His Time' as well as Lady Gregory's *Our Irish Theatre*

when writing up the account of his friend's life and work. Bourgeois, *John Millington Synge*, ix.
39. Bourgeois, *John Millington Synge*, 46.
40. Bourgeois, *John Millington Synge*, 45.
41. Síghle Bhreathnach Lynch, "The Influence of J. M. Synge on the Art of Jack B. Yeats and Paul Henry," in *Back to the Present—Forward to the Past: Irish Writing and History Since 1798*, vol. 1, ed. Patricia Lynch, Joachim Fisher and Brian Coates, 209–18 (Amsterdam: Rodopi, 2006), 215.
42. Bhreathnach Lynch, "The Influence of J. M. Synge," 216.
43. Bhreathnach Lynch, "The Influence of J. M. Synge," 214.
44. Sinéad Garrigan Mattar, *Primitivism, Science, and the Irish Revival* (Oxford: Clarendon, 2004), 154–72.
45. John Millington Synge, *Collected Works*, ed. Alan Price, vol. 2 (Gerrards Cross: Colin Smythe, 1982), 142; Garrigan Mattar, *Primitivism, Science, and the Irish Revival*, 136.
46. Nicholas Grene, *Synge: A Critical Study of the Plays* (London: Macmillan, 1985), 52.
47. Grene, *Synge*, 55.
48. Grene, *Synge*, 53.
49. Robert Hogan and Michael O'Neill, eds., *Joseph Holloway's Abbey Theatre* (Carbondale: South Illinois University Press, 2009), 35.
50. Katz Clarke, *The Emergence of the Irish Peasant Play*, 46 and 52–53.
51. Katz Clarke, *The Emergence of the Irish Peasant Play*, 43 and 46.
52. Katz Clarke, *The Emergence of the Irish Peasant Play*, 46.
53. Katz Clarke, *The Emergence of the Irish Peasant Play*, 54. Benoît-Constant Coquelin and his brother Ernest Alexander Honoré Coquelin co-authored *L'art de dire le monologue*, and were known in the London theatre scene, having worked with Irving, Terry, and Bernhardt. Fay met Coquelin during the Abbey's tour of Britain in 1906. Dawson Byrne, *The Story of Ireland's National Theatre* (New York: Haskell House, 1971), 55.
54. For the reference to Lugné-Poe, see Katz Clarke, *The Emergence of the Irish Peasant Play*, 47.
55. Schuchard writes that Fay sent Yeats a copy of Coquelin's *The Art of the Actor* (*L'art du comédien*) hoping to develop a specific way of acting and delivering monologues for the rural plays. At the time, Yeats was preoccupied with furthering his experiments with the human voice and the psaltery. Ronald Schuchard, *The Last Minstrels: Yeats and the Revival of the Bardic Arts* (Oxford: Oxford University Press, 2008), 119–20. Two of those people who were shaping Yeats's views had published on Coquelin's style of acting: Fay in *The United Irishman*

('M Coquelin in Dublin', July 1899) and Symons in the *Academy* ('Coquelin and Molière', July 1902).
56. Qtd. in Katz Clarke, *The Emergence of the Irish Peasant Play*, 52.
57. Máire Nic Shiubhlaigh, *Splendid Years: Recollections of Maire Nic Shiubhlaigh as Told to Edward Kenny* (Dublin: Duffy, 1955), 55.
58. Katz Clarke quotes Yeats on the matter of dialects on *The Emergence of the Irish Peasant Play*, 43.
59. See Synge's letter to Yeats on December 4, 1906, qtd. in Saddlemyer, *Theatre Business*, 185.
60. William Butler Yeats, John Millington Synge, William Boyle, and Lady Augusta Gregory, *Irish Plays: An Illustrated Programme*, May 26–July 9, 1906, reprinted in Saddlemyer, *Theatre Business*, 316–21, especially 318.
61. See Lady Gregory on Shakespeare's *Hamlet, Coriolanus, Henry V*, and *Richard III* in *Lady Gregory's Diaries, 1892–1902*, ed. James Pethica (Gerrards Cross: Colin Smythe, 1996), 253, 270, 302, and 304.
62. Pethica, *Diaries*, 270.
63. Pethica, *Diaries*, 253.
64. Philip Edwards, *Threshold of a Nation* (Cambridge: Cambridge University Press, 1979), 205–11.
65. Anthony B. Bawson, *Watching Shakespeare* (London: Macmillan, 1988), 5 and 16; J. L. Halio, *A Midsummer Night's Dream. Shakespeare in Production Series* (Manchester: Manchester University Press, 2003), 31–32
66. Benoît-Constant Coquelin worked with Irving, Terry, and Bernhardt at the Lyceum in London. Tree had this to say about the Abbey players after he had seen them in the Court Theatre in London: 'They certainly are [...] charming in their remoteness from ourselves and from any other players that we know [...]. But none of them, in any strict sense of the word, acts. They are exactly the same on the stage as they are (I conceive) off it. [...] they are reproducing just their own selves as they are at ordinary times'. Critical as these comments were, they nonetheless complimented the players for looking natural and effortless on stage, signalling that the long hours spent with voice coaches and speech trainers were more than useful. Tree qtd. in Katz Clarke, *The Emergence of the Irish Peasant Play*, 53.
67. Katherine Newey and Jeffrey Richards, *John Ruskin and the Victorian Theatre* (Basingstoke: Palgrave Macmillan, 2010), 174 and 171. Tree's speeches were part of a more general debate on the use of scenery and stagecraft that had developed in Victorian theatre circles during the late nineteenth century. The debate arose too, in part, from Ruskin's pronouncements on the theatre and its social mission. For Ruskin's

influence on the debate, see Newey and Richards, *John Ruskin and the Victorian Theatre*, 168.
68. Ruskin, "Pre-Raphaelitism," 12.365.
69. Elizabeth Prettejohn, *The Art of the Pre-Raphaelites* (London: Tate Publishing, 2000), 190.
70. Robert Upstone, *The Pre-Raphaelite Dream* (London: Tate Gallery, 2003), 17.
71. Upstone explains that 'the sheep represent Christ's flock, the wound on his hand his future crucifixion, and the set-square hanging on the wall the Trinity. Mary kneels in a pose traditionally used when she is shown at the base of the Cross, and the ladder too relates to the crucifixion, and the dove to the Holy Spirit. Christ's tender kiss is both a benediction and a reference to his own betrayal in the Garden of Gethsemane'. Upstone, *The Pre-Raphaelite Dream*, 17. Upstone further claims here that the reference in the picture is to Tintoretto's *Annunciation*, with which Millais and Hunt were familiar through Ruskin's detailed depiction of the painting in *Modern Painters*.
72. Julia Thomas, *Victorian Narrative Painting* (London: Tate Publishing, 2000), 74.
73. Thomas, *Victorian Narrative Painting*, 74.
74. Thomas, *Victorian Narrative Painting*, 76–79. For a detailed description of the painting, see also Raymond Lister, *Victorian Narrative Painting* (London: Museum Press Ltd., 1966), 54–59.
75. Lady Augusta Gregory, *Coole* (Dublin: Cuala Press, 1931), 14.
76. Lady Augusta Gregory, *Seventy Years, Being the Autobiography of Lady Gregory* (Gerrards Cross: Colin Smythe, 1973), 16.
77. William Michael Rossetti, ed., *Dante Gabriel Rossetti: His Family Letters* (London: Ellis and Elvey, 1895), 189.
78. William Holman Hunt, *Pre-Raphaelitism and the Pre-Raphaelite Brotherhood*, vol. 2 (London, New York: Macmillan, 1905), 124.
79. Hunt, *Pre-Raphaelitism and the Pre-Raphaelite Brotherhood*, 124.
80. Alfred Tennyson, *Poems* (London: Moxon, 1859), 75.
81. Prettejohn, *The Art of the Pre-Raphaelites*, 228; Upstone, *The Pre-Raphaelite Dream*, 94.
82. Information received from the Archives Department of the National Gallery, London.
83. Diary entry, April 16, 1887, Berg.
84. José López-Rey, *Velázquez: The Artist as a Maker; With a Catalogue Raisonné of His Extant Works* (Lausanne-Paris: Bibliothéque des Arts, 1979), 216.
85. López-Rey, *Velázquez*, 208. See also Ana Martín Moreno, *Las Meninas*, trans. Nigel Williams (Madrid: Aldeasa, Museo del Prado, 2003), 8.

86. Moreno intimates that Velázquez's inclusion of the paintings in the background and his addition of the Cross of St. James's were used to emphasise the 'divine origin of the arts'. Moreno, *Las Meninas*, 26.
87. López-Rey, *Velazquez*, 163.
88. Charles de Tolnay, *Teremtő Géniuszok* (Budapest: Gondolat, 1987), 198.
89. Gregory, *Collected Plays*, vol. 2, 133–41.
90. Lady Augusta Gregory, *Cuchulain of Muirthemne: The Story of the Men of the Red Branch of Ulster* (Gerrards Cross: Colin Smythe, 1975), 26–28.
91. William Butler Yeats, *Collected Plays* (London: Macmillan, 1963), 277–78.
92. Julie Anne Stevens, "Political Animals: Somerville and Ross and Percy French on Edwardian Ireland," in *Synge and Edwardian Ireland*, ed. Brian Cliff and Nicholas Grene (Oxford: Oxford University Press, 2012), 107.
93. Edith Somerville and Martin Ross, "The Whiteboys," in *The Irish R.M.* (London: Sphere Books, 1970), 403–21.
94. John Millington Synge, *The Complete Plays* (London: Methuen, 2001), 228.
95. Gregory, *Collected Plays*, vol. 1, 19.
96. Gregory, *Collected Plays*, vol. 1, 20.
97. Cathy Leeney, *Irish Women Playwrights, 1900–1939* (New York: Peter Lang, 2010), 27 and 29–32; Lucy McDiarmid, "The Demotic Lady Gregory," in *High and Low Moderns, Literature and Culture 1889–1939*, ed. Maria DiBattista and Lucy McDiarmid (Oxford: Oxford University Press, 1996), 223–24; and James Pethica, "Lady Gregory's Abbey Theatre Drama: Ireland Real and Ideal," in *The Cambridge Companion to Twentieth-Century Irish Drama*, ed. Shaun Richards (Cambridge: Cambridge University Press, 2004), 66.
98. Gregory, *Collected Plays*, vol. 2, 8.
99. Gregory, *Collected Plays*, vol. 2, 9.
100. *Holy Bible*, New International Version (London: Hodder, 2001). Luke 23:9, 13–15; Mark 15:5; Matthew 27:14, John 19:9.
101. Gregory, *Collected Plays*, vol. 2, 10.
102. Gregory, *Collected Plays*, vol. 3, 21.
103. Mark 10:14–15. See also Matthew 19:13–15 and Luke 18:15–17.
104. Gregory, *Collected Plays*, vol. 3, 24.
105. Gregory, *Collected Plays*, vol. 3, 25–26, Luke 19:30–35.
106. Luke 23:13–25.
107. Mark 6:45–56, especially 6:49, and John 6:16–24.
108. Luke 24:13–35.
109. Mary Bennett, *Artists of the Pre-Raphaelite Circle: The First Generation* (London: Lund Humphries, 1988), 70. Barringer writes that there

is a reinforced connection between Jesus Christ and the sacrificial animal standing on the shore of the Dead Sea. Tim Barringer, *The Pre-Raphaelites* (London: Weidenfeldt, 1998), 130.
110. George P. Landow, *William Holman Hunt and Typological Symbolism* (New Haven: Yale University Press, 1979), 107.
111. The elaborate picture frames the Pre-Raphaelites liked to use served the same purposes as the mirrors or paintings on back walls of painted scenes. They helped the painter defy the spatial limitations of his pictorial art, thereby expanding the remits of his storytelling.
112. Genesis 8:10–11.
113. Diary entries between December 30, 1882 and January 13, 1883, Berg.
114. Entry for January 1, 1883. Lady Augusta Gregory, *Excerpts from Her Readings*, Lady Augusta Gregory Papers, Albert A. and Henry W. Berg Collection, New York Public Library.
115. Diary entry, January 4, 1883, Berg. See also diary entry, January 13, 1883, Berg.
116. Lady Augusta Gregory, ed., *Sir William Gregory* (London: Murray, 1894), 383.
117. Terence Brown, *The Life of W. B. Yeats* (Dublin: Gill and Macmillan, 1999), 13.
118. William Butler Yeats, *Essays and Introductions* (London: Macmillan, 1989), 64.
119. William Butler Yeats, *Memoirs, Autobiography—First Draft, Journal*, ed. Denis Donoghue (London: Macmillan, 1972), 33.
120. Yeats, *Autobiographies*, 123.
121. Yeats, *Autobiographies*, 123.
122. Pater, *The Renaissance*, 54.
123. Pater, *The Renaissance*, 61.
124. Foster, *W. B. Yeats*, vol. 1, 368.
125. Bernadette McCarthy, "W. B. Yeats, John Ruskin, and the 'Lidless Eye'," *Irish University Review* 41, no. 2 (Autumn/Winter 2011): 32.
126. Ruskin was among the first to collect Turner's sketches and watercolours. He proposed a number of measures to preserve the delicate quality of the sketches and watercolours, including the building of a special mahogany case for storing them. Similar to Ruskin, Vaughan too was concerned with the preservation of Turner's work, and insisted that the watercolours be put on display only during the month of January. A. J. Finberg, arr. "Preface," in *The Complete Inventory of the Drawings of the Turner Bequest*, vol. 1 (London: Darling and Son, 1909), vi and ix.
127. McCarthy, "W. B. Yeats, John Ruskin, and the 'Lidless Eye'," 30.
128. John Ruskin, *Modern Painters*, vol. 1, in *The Works of John Ruskin*, ed. E. T. Cook and Alexander Wedderburn, vol. 3 (London: George

Allen, 1903–1912), 248. Further references to Cook and Wedderburn's multivolume work will be as follows: Ruskin, *Title of Individual Work*, volume number.page number. Example here: Ruskin, *Modern Painters*, 3.248.
129. Ruskin, *Modern Painters*, vol. 1, 3.250.
130. Ruskin, *Modern Painters*, vol. 1, 3.250.
131. For the stage pictures of these plays, see James W. Flannery, *W. B. Yeats and the Idea of a Theatre* (New Haven: Yale University Press, 1976), 87–91.
132. "New Scenery System—Lady Gregory's Latest Play," *The Irish Times*, MS 1734, NLI.
133. Karen Dorn, *Players and the Painted Stage: The Theatre of W. B. Yeats* (Sussex: Harvester, 1984), 18 and 20–22. Dorn explains that the early productions of Yeats's plays adhered more closely to the Victorian concept of the 'narrative tableau'. The original stage picture of *The Countess Cathleen*, for instance, included a background tapestry, which dominated the scene and marked the development of both plot and character. Dorn's comments suggest that the pictorial scenic arrangement made popular in paintings like Velázquez's *Las Hilanderas* and *Las Meninas* was simply not working for Yeats's early plays.
134. "The Abbey Theatre—Important Scenic Invention," *The Mail*, Henderson, MS 1734, NLI.
135. "The Deliverer at the Abbey Theatre," *The Freeman's Journal*, Henderson, MS 1734, NLI.
136. Flannery, *W. B. Yeats and the Idea of a Theatre*, 271–72.
137. For Yeats's comments, see Flannery, *W. B. Yeats and the Idea of a Theatre*, 272.
138. "New Scenery System—Lady Gregory's Latest Play," *The Irish Times*, MS 1734, NLI and "The Deliverer at the Abbey Theatre," *The Freeman's Journal*, MS 1734, NLI.
139. For 'reading a picture', see Ruskin, "The Awakening Conscience," 12.335; Kate Flint, *The Victorians and the Visual Imagination* (Cambridge: Cambridge University Press, 2000), 215–16 and 218.
140. Robert Hogan and Michael O'Neill, eds., *Joseph Holloway's Abbey Theatre* (Carbondale: South Illinois University Press, 2009), 148.

The Light of the World: Christianity, Cultural Politics, and Constitutional Reform

CHRISTIANITY AND SOCIAL REFORM

Lady Gregory once compared an artist to a candlestickmaker who 'holds up the light and hands it on from generation to generation, taking it from under the bushel that it may search the dark corners of the house'.[1] This image of the artist as the bearer of light was a reminder of the well-known Victorian painting, *The Light of the World* (1851–1853), by William Holman Hunt. The painting depicts Jesus as he is approaching the door of a house that symbolises the human soul, while he is holding a beautifully ornamented glowing lantern in his left hand. Ruskin himself gave the following interpretation of the famous painting:

> Christ approaches it in the night-time,— Christ, in his everlasting offices of prophet, priest, and king. He wears the white robe, representing the power of the Spirit upon him; the jewelled robe and breastplate, representing the sacerdotal investiture; the rayed crown of gold, inwoven with the crown of thorns; not dead thorns, but now bearing soft leaves, for the healing of the nations.
>
> Now, when Christ enters any human heart, he bears with him a twofold light: first, the light of conscience, which displays past sin, and afterwards the light of peace, the hope of salvation. The lantern, carried in Christ's left hand, is this light of conscience.[2]

Ruskin believed the scene to comprise an intricate symbolism: Jesus was the 'Light of the World' who carried the 'light of conscience' and the 'light of peace', and whose light contributed to the 'healing of the nations'. This reading holds great significance when it comes to the way in which Lady Gregory interpreted an artist's social role and responsibility: throughout her life she was trying to build paths towards peace and reconciliation in Ireland.

As a child, Lady Gregory would attend the Persse family's 'friendly little Killinane [sic] Church', where the services were held by a Wesleyan priest.[3] Rev. John Wesley wrote at great length on the significance of the biblical 'light of the world' imagery for those of the Christian faith, especially in the fourth discourse of his sermon on Jesus's 'Sermon on the Mount' from the Gospel of Matthew.[4] Jesus himself used the luminous imagery to reveal his nature and the purpose of the Christian life: 'I am the light of the world; anyone who follows me will not be walking in the dark but will have the light of life'.[5] These sentiments were later developed in his parable of the lamp:

> No one lights a lamp to cover it with a bowl or put it under a bed. No, it is put on a lamp-stand so that people may see the light when they come in. For nothing is hidden but it will be made clear, nothing secret but it will be made known and brought to light. So take care how you listen: anyone who has will be given more; anyone who has not, will be deprived even of what he thinks he has.[6]

Wesley combined these two parables to form the main argument of his sermon on Christian life. He argued that faith, as given by God, is itself the 'light of the world' and those of the Christian faith are themselves the 'lights of the world'. By their behaviour and by spreading the redemptive message of the Gospels, Christians illuminate the world with God's light.[7] Reiterating Jesus's words from the Gospel of Matthew (5:13–16), Wesley assigned a missionary role to those of the Christian faith:

> 'Let your light so shine before men, that they may see your good works':—So far let a Christian be from ever designing, or desiring to conceal his religion! On the contrary, let it be your desire not to conceal it; not to put the light under a bushel. Let it be your care to place it 'on a candlestick, that it may give light to all that are in the house'. Only take heed, not to seek your own praise herein, not to desire any honour to

yourselves. But let it be your sole aim, that all who see your good works, may 'glorify your Father which is in heaven'.[8]

This message of living one's life in the service of spreading the Gospel message stayed with Lady Gregory throughout her adult life. Her desire to lead a dutiful life was deeply rooted in her Christian faith; it was not merely shaped by her acceptance of the rules of the patriarchal society into which she had been born. The influence of Wesley was an element that Lady Gregory shared with Bernard Shaw. In his 'Preface for Politicians' of 1906 for *John Bull's Other Island*, Shaw mentions that although he was baptised in the Church of Ireland, he was sent to a Wesleyan school.[9] This may account in part for the image of 'the light of the world' that Shaw introduces when he criticises nationalism in Ireland and the folly of the British Government in not introducing Home Rule and thereby bringing the Irish pre-occupation with nationalism (to the detriment of more important issues) to a conclusion.[10]

The idea of Christian service had been instilled in Lady Gregory early in her life. She wrote in *Seventy Years* that after returning from the Sunday School in Kilchriest she and her family would spend the day reading Evangelical literature.[11] Because of the passionate Evangelicalism of her mother and sisters, the bookshelves of the Persse household were filled with volumes of nineteenth-century religious literature for children.[12] Maria Charlesworth's *Ministering Children, A Tale Dedicated to Childhood* taught children the purpose of Christian life. *Doing and Suffering, Memorials of Elizabeth and Frances, Daughters of the Late Rev. E. Birkersteth* told the story of two sisters who bore illness with great humility and who were strengthened in their daily struggles by their deep Christian faith. Mary Martha Sherwood's *The History of Henry Milner* and *The History of the Fairchild Family* recounted nineteenth-century household stories that carried a strong religious message. Both Sherwood's *Stories Explanatory of the Church Catechism*—written for British soldiers stationed in India—and Catherine Marsh's *The Sketch of the Life of Capt. Hedley Vicars, The Christian Soldier* promoted the idea of Christianity serving the maintenance of the British Empire. Despite the fact that the Persse family held the teachings of the Scottish minister Rev. John Cumming in high regard, his anti-Newmanite, anti-Catholic and anti-Irish feelings did not chime with those of the young Augusta. As she remembered, she spent the little time that she had for herself with her nurse Mary Sheridan, who told her stories of old Catholic Ireland.[13]

Ruskin's mother and her passionate Evangelicalism had left a clear mark on the young man, who developed his own kind of orthodox Evangelicalism early on in his life. As Mark Frost emphasises, the art critic's early writings exuded a strong religious message; this included the first volumes of *Modern Painters*. Everything, including nature, argued Ruskin, should be 'read typologically in pursuit of salvation', a message which combined his mother's orthodox Evangelicalism with his own brand of natural theology.[14] Ruskin first began his friendship with the Pre-Raphaelite Brotherhood because he saw their work as expressing his own theory of natural theology, according to which every element in a painting—every plant, flower, or animal—had to be a representation of divine beauty pointing towards the redemptive message of Christ's sacrifice. Ruskin was fascinated with their use of 'symbolic realism' as he saw it expressed in their early works, such as Collins's *Convent Thoughts*. In this work, almost all natural details of the garden function as religious symbols. Ruskin was flattered that the Pre-Raphaelites' 'symbolic realism' was derived from his own ideas as formulated in the first volumes of *Modern Painters*. Mark Frost draws attention to the fact that for about a decade between 1858 and 1868 the art critic turned away from the strict Evangelicalism of his youth, a turn which led to 'extended struggles for self-definition' but which also resulted in Ruskin's developing a 'more tolerant, inclusive faith that could be reconciled to science and mythology'.[15] Between 1858 and 1868 Ruskin became increasingly involved in the art circles of his friend Gabriel Rossetti, who was leaving behind the dogmatic realism of his early youth to develop a new set of aesthetic ideals with the help of Swinburne, Baudelaire, Désiré Nisard, and Théophile Gautier. Rossetti and Swinburne met first during the painting of the Oxford Union murals in the late 1850s. They invited Ruskin into their circles to discover together the writings of those French aesthetes who preached that art and art criticism should be devoid of all forms of didacticism, especially of a religious kind.

During this period Ruskin imagined that a new world would emerge, an 'ideal world constructed out of images drawn from the past, in order to render atmospheres and emotions rather than tell stories'.[16] Ruskin rediscovered the beauty of Venetian art, this time detecting in it a combination of the 'cultivation of every spiritual tendency', which he formerly believed to be the sign of noble art, and the 'power of every animal passion', which he had come to regard as praiseworthy in art only recently.[17] His new volume of *Modern Painters*, published in June 1860, radiated the art critic's new appreciation of the sumptuous aesthetic beauty of Renaissance Venetian art. Ruskin purchased Titian's *The Portrait of Doge Andrea Gritti* in 1864, a portrait which may not have been one of the artist's most sensual pictures, yet which inspired Dante Rossetti to paint *Monna Vanna*, the last of the type of female portraits that he began with *Bocca Baciata* in 1859.[18] Rossetti's *Bocca Baciata* and *Monna Vanna* exemplify the type of sensuous feminine beauty which was admired by many of his contemporaries. Rossetti's former fellow Pre-Raphaelite, Holman Hunt, however, wrote to their friend Thomas Combe that he disapproved of the painting because it was exhibiting a certain kind of 'the animal passion'.[19] Not sharing Hunt's evaluations at this point in time, Ruskin provided Rossetti with the means to publish his translations of Italian troubadour songs that celebrated sumptuous female beauty.[20]

Around this time Ruskin was beginning to fall in love with Rose La Touche, the daughter of a Protestant banker and landlord from Harristown, Co. Kildare, in Ireland.[21] Rose was a devoutly religious young girl, and Ruskin's interest in aestheticism began to fade as his relationship with Rose developed, leading eventually to the ending of his association with Rossetti and Swinburne's art circles in the late 1860s.[22] Under the influence of Rose and the La Touche family, Ruskin was once again seeking the companionship of educationalists and social reformers, some of whom were of strong Evangelical faith. The La Touche family themselves were deeply engaged in educational and social matters in Ireland. They had been involved in the introduction of the National School System, the organisation of the Sunday School Movement, and the work of the Hibernian Society for Establishing Schools and Circulating the Holy Scriptures in Ireland.[23] John David La Touche joined forces with Arthur Guinness and Samuel Bewley to fund the Society for Promoting the Education of the Poor in Ireland. Michael McGinley writes that as descendants of a Huguenot family, who had had to flee France for fear of religious persecution during the seventeenth century, the family promoted religious tolerance and non-denominational education in Ireland.[24] They partook in the introduction of the National School System in the hope that it would improve the system of children's education in Ireland in a non-denominational fashion.[25]

Friends of the La Touche family, the Cowper-Temples were involved in a number of educational projects in England. A firm believer in religious tolerance, William Cowper-Temple put forward an amendment to the Education Act of 1870, which secured the non-denominational nature of the educational project in England and Wales.²⁶ As a reward for his efforts, Prime Minister William Gladstone recommended that Cowper-Temple was to be raised to the peerage in 1880, as Baron Mount Temple of Mount Temple, Co. Sligo.²⁷ Ruskin invited him to become a Trustee of the St George's Guild, the social realisation of Ruskin's old and newly rediscovered aesthetic and social ideals. Cowper-Temple acted as witness when the now renamed St. George's Company acquired the house and land at Walkey in the 1870s, the location where Ruskin intended to undertake his social experiments that involved the teaching of art to labourers.²⁸ Ruskin's renewed interest in social and political matters further manifested itself in his work as Slade Professor of Fine Art at Oxford University and in his later writings such as *Unto This Last*, *Time and Tide*, and, perhaps most importantly, *Fors Clavigera*.²⁹ James Gregory has noted that Ruskin 'brought more Christianity into the series' of *Fors Clavigera*.³⁰ *Fors* was to be the work of a new period in which Ruskin left behind many of the fanciful ideals of his earlier 'French period'. Surrounded by social reformers and educationalists of a Christian faith, Ruskin now promoted the notion that '[r]eligion was meaningless without accepting Christ's calls for a demonstration of faith in good deeds'.³¹ Frost asserts that the St. George's Guild was Ruskin's new experiment in promoting his views on the intertwined nature of social, religious, aesthetic, scientific, and cultural issues.³²

Lady Gregory shared Ruskin's belief that '[r]eligion was meaningless without accepting Christ's calls for a demonstration of faith in good deeds'.³³ Her desire to participate in programmes that aimed at improving the living standards and ameliorating the working conditions of the poor in Ireland was motivated by a strong Christian conviction. Lady Gregory's involvement in her genteel friend's Home Industries Movement and in Plunkett and Russell's Co-operative Movement clearly indicated the seriousness with which she approached matters of social responsibility after Sir William's death in the early 1890s. Lady Gregory's deep sense of responsibility carried over into her work for the Abbey Theatre. Like Ruskin, she also believed that the theatre should be a means to disseminate socially important aesthetic and political ideals. Lady Gregory's perception of the Abbey Theatre's social mission was not dissimilar to Ruskin's own concept of *Fors Clavigera*, his letters to the working people of England which served as a literary platform from which he disseminated his ideas among a readership much wider than that of his Oxford students and fellows. Yeats himself was hoping that one day he would read an Irish version of *Fors Clavigera* and that Standish O'Grady's newspaper, the *All-Ireland Review*, or his own, rather short-lived, theatre magazine *Beltaine*, would be Irish counterparts to Ruskin's work.³⁴ Contrary to Yeats's expectations, however, it was not his friend's newspaper or his own theatre magazine but the Abbey Theatre that came to realise the hopes of the Anglo-Irish literary *élite* of Ireland.

'DOING GOOD' IN THEATRES AND IN MUSEUMS

The Irish Peasant printed an article in December 1905 which resonated with the hopes and dreams of the Abbey Theatre directors, most prominently those of Lady Gregory:

> Apart from the Abbey Theatre there is no regular Irish stage; there is not even a humble Irish touring theatrical company. [...] Many of the Irish plays we have require only the slightest scenery and staging, and could be played very well in unpretending halls and other meeting places. [...] The positive effect of bracing drama on character and thought would soon be surprising.³⁵

So not only does the article call for performances by a touring company in the smaller towns and in the more hidden rural areas of Ireland, it also assumes that theatrical performances have the uncanny ability to influence people's *character*. Mentioning character formation as a 'positive effect' of viewing plays, the article gave voice to the wishes of the leaders of the Co-operative Movement, including those of Anderson, Plunkett, and Russell. The idea that the theatre was to be involved in character formation was also shared by many nineteenth-century theatremakers, many of whom were close friends of Lady Gregory and the late Sir William. She herself believed in the theatre's ability to educate audiences, and the short article in *The Irish Peasant* suggests that her thoughts chimed with the desires of some of those people for whom the educational project was originally conceived.

The sentiments expressed in *The Irish Peasant* may have echoed the wishes of the Abbey Theatre directors, but realising the educational project at hand was not an easy task. Annie Horniman, the theatre's financier, intended to promote her new 'art theatre' principally in Britain. This was to showcase the artistic genius of her *protégé*, W. B. Yeats. Because of this, the Abbey Company embarked on a British tour, which took them to London, Oxford, and Cambridge in 1905, before the tour continued in the theatre halls of Liverpool, Manchester, Birmingham, Leeds, Newcastle, Hull, Glasgow, Edinburgh, and Cardiff during 1906 and 1907.[36] Adrian Frazier has pointed out that the first tour was strategically planned to maximise interest amongst the British aristocracy and social *élite*, while the latter tours were organised to build up interest among the Irish emigrant community of Britain.[37] Both the plays and the touring company were well received in Britain. *The Saturday Herald* commented that '[t]he Scotch season was very successful, each night saw an increasing audience, and a growing appreciation of the plays'.[38] The *Theatre Notes* wrote that Lady Gregory's *Spreading the News* and *Hyacinth Halvey* were 'fascinating, and deliciously funny', while Yeats's *The Shadowy Waters* was considered a 'strange mixture of Shelley and Irish legend, with a suggestion of Wagnerian drama'.[39] '[T]wo of the best farces we have seen for a long while', the *Theatre Notes* commented on Lady Gregory's plays, which 'never degenerate into a noisy succession of impossibilities, with which English farces are usually associated'.[40] *The Saturday Herald* wrote that audiences were 'visibly impressed and stirred' during the performance in Cambridge, with comments made on 'the literary charm of "The Hour Glass", the rollicking humour of "The Jackdaw", the quiet pathos of "The Rising of the Moon", and the painful glamous [sic] of "Riders to the Sea"'.[41] Audiences in Britain may have differed from what the Abbey players were accustomed to back in Ireland but they were certainly receptive of the directors' wishes to restore the old dignity to Ireland, as Lady Gregory and Yeats once put it in their respective versions of the manifesto of the Irish dramatic movement.[42]

The Abbey's touring company embarked on their first tour of Ireland in 1906. Between 1906 and 1908, the company gave performances in all the major playhouses of the country, including the Court Theatre in Galway, the Theatre Royal in Wexford, the Theatre Royal in Waterford, the Theatre Royal in Kilkenny, and the Opera House in Cork. The plays were successful in Ireland but for reasons different to those identified in British newspapers. As *The Evening Herald* commented following the Abbey's performance in Galway in September 1908: 'The Irish players were a great success, and hundreds nightly had to be turned away. A desperate struggle for entrance into the large shed which had been fitted up for a theatre took place at each performance'.[43] Enthusiastic reviews continued to be written on Lady Gregory's one-acters in particular, as a review in *The Irish News and Belfast Morning News* attests: *Spreading the News* and *Hyacinth Halvey* were 'inspired by a natural spontaneous spirit of fun which never fails to meet with a ready response'.[44] The *Manchester Guardian* once pointed out that some elements of the plays only 'hit home' in Ireland, and Ulster's *The Northern Whig* made this quite clear in its review of the Abbey performances: '*Hyacinth Halvey*, a victim who struggles in vain against his eloquent testimonials to character, is a delicate satire on an Irish custom that Sir Horace Plunkett has poked ridicule at with some effect'.[45] Putting aside the comment's note of irony, the connection drawn here—between Lady Gregory's realist play and Plunkett's social co-operative endeavours—points towards the delicately intertwined nature of the work of the Abbey Theatre and that of the Co-operative Movement in Ireland. This co-operation may have been unknown to many members of the audiences for Abbey touring performances in the theatre houses of Britain.

Aiming to promote the work of the Abbey Theatre and in an effort to reach even wider audiences in Ireland, Lady Gregory gave an evening talk on theatre history at the invitation of the Gaelic League at the *Ard Chraobh* in 1908.[46] During the talk she outlined the history of European theatre as it had developed from the times of the ancient Greeks right through to the early twentieth century, touching upon the works of Shakespeare, Molière, Goethe, and Schiller. Lady Gregory was delighted to be present at the *Ard Chraobh*. One of the reviewers present at her talk commented on the event as follows: Lady Gregory's talk 'gave us a sense of the world-culture which some of us seem to lack just now in Ireland'.[47] She was truly pleased with the positive reception of her plays in rural Irish towns and villages, and the fact that her plays had won the approval of the local clergy and the local *cumann* of the Gaelic League.[48] Undoubtedly, she wanted to express her gratitude to these people and organisations by accepting the invitation to speak at the *Ard*. Addressing the *Ard* was important for the success of the Abbey Theatre and the Co-operative Movement; Mathews notes that she was one of the first to realise the link between the work of the Irish Agricultural Organisation Society, the Co-operative Movement, and the Gaelic League.[49]

For someone who intended to spread the news of the co-operative ideal, securing the support of the local clergy was paramount. Liam Kennedy has observed that local Catholic priests presided over many of the co-operative societies throughout the country, exercising a great influence on the development of the Co-operative Movement in Ireland.[50]

According to Kennedy's estimates, roughly half of the co-operative societies had clerical chairmen by the beginning of the twentieth century, and numbers were increasing.[51] The Jesuit priest Fr. Thomas Finlay supported the co-operative endeavour, because in these small societies 'agriculturists [were] their own bankers, lending and borrowing amongst themselves, on terms most favourable to their industry and exempt from all suspicion of usury', and 'the methods by which the usurious money-lender entraps the farmer and the small trader of the rural districts of England, and despoils them when they have been ensnared' could be ended in Ireland by the establishment of the co-operative village banks system.[52] Slowly winning the approval of the local clergy and various national bodies, the Abbey players continued to conquer their Irish audiences. After their tour of the larger towns of Ireland, the company went on to visit the smaller towns of the country, such as Carlow, Maryborough, Tullamore, Kilkenny, Naas, Mullingar, Athlone, Longford, Loughrae, and Doneraile. These visits were designed to bring the news of the theatre and of the co-operative ideal closer to rural people of the country.[53] The success of the Abbey company was indicated in the comments of *The Irish Times*, which remarked on the perfect accordance that the players had with their audience in Doneraile, the place where Plunkett had founded his first co-operative society back in 1889.[54] *The Evening Telegraph* noted that large and enthusiastic audiences greeted the theatre company on their tours of rural Ireland.[55] One of the reasons for this, as Yeats shrewdly put it during his lecture at the Great Galway Exhibition in 1908, was the fact that in Lady Gregory's plays 'country people talk to you in beautiful speech' which had been taken right 'from the lips of the people'.[56] Praising Lady Gregory, one of the locals of the area, Yeats's speech was 'greeted with great applause', the *Connacht Champion* commented.[57]

Ruskin believed that theatres and museums were 'means of noble education' in equal measure; hence, both were, as the Royal Patent of the Abbey Theatre indicated, 'instrumental to the promotion of virtue and instruction of human life'.[58] For Ruskin, both theatres and museums were to fulfil an important role, offering social educational programmes for the middle and working classes as well as programmes for the aesthetic cultivation of all social classes in Victorian Britain and Ireland. For this purpose, Ruskin's objectives for the St. George's Guild included establishing schools, museums, and 'other educational establishments' throughout Britain and Ireland.[59] Ruskin envisaged a series of new museums being set up on both islands for the purpose of general social advancement. St. George's Museum, overlooking the picturesque Rivelin Valley, was to serve as an example for those who were interested in developing educational programmes for the working and middle classes.[60] Sir William Gregory himself shared the view that the middle and working classes should avail themselves of the enriching cultural *milieu* of museums; hence his persistent attitude on the question of keeping the premises of the National Gallery in the city centre of London. Additionally, Sir William argued that public parks should remain open on Sundays to serve the recuperation of all social classes by offering leisurely walks through beautiful parklands and by stimulating aesthetic pleasures through colourful flower displays.

Lady Gregory herself followed in the footsteps of her late husband when she embraced the project of establishing a Municipal Gallery of Modern Art in Dublin. Her nephew Hugh Lane proposed donating his invaluable collection of French paintings to Ireland, should a suitable location be found in Dublin. Following debates about premises and project feasibility, the Municipal Gallery of Modern Art opened its doors to the public in the temporary premises of Clonmell House on 20 January 1908, to Lady Gregory's great delight. She wrote an enthusiastic letter about the new cultural establishment to her friend John Quinn:

> It makes such a difference being able to walk into a beautiful house and spend an hour among beautiful things at will. The working people are flocking to it, and Hugh Lane is to receive the Freedom of the City, the Sinn Féiners and Nationalists contending who should have the honour of first proposing it, and Mahaffy making a speech at the opening.[61]

Walking among beautiful art works in a majestic building would have naturally appealed to her, having partaken in those extended art tours of Continental galleries and museums since the early 1880s. She was delighted too that the new institution would serve the aesthetic cultivation of the middle and working classes, who filled the stalls of the Abbey Theatre in ever increasing numbers.

Disputes began to grow, however, over the permanent housing of Lane's collection. Sir Edwin Lutyens was to design a new museum near the River Liffey, in the centre of Dublin. Facing criticism from both the Irish press and the local authorities, the Dublin Corporation—responsible for the building project—eventually decided to abandon it. Lady Gregory had the following to say about the turn of affairs:

[T]he sharpest opposition was now directed against the employment of Sir E. Lutyens, for no reason save that of alien birth, just as one of the causes that years ago brought to naught Newman's planned Catholic University, was the objection to his having chosen one or two professors who were English. And that reason was but half valid in our case, for Lutyens had an Irish mother.[62]

Her words disguise certain facts: that the specifications demanded for the new museum were too high; that both the local Anglo-Irish aristocracy and political Nationalists opposed the building of a new museum; and that the Dublin Corporation refused to give its name to the art project because there were other, more pressing social and political concerns.[63] Lady Gregory and Yeats were of a different view, believing that the decision was based primarily on political and religious grounds. Their convictions only deepened when Lane was refused the position of Curator of the National Museum in Dublin. Yeats wrote that the decision was an 'entirely theological question', one that entirely disregarded Lane's experience in art matters.[64] Significantly, Lady Gregory quoted the trials and tribulations of Cardinal Newman, a Catholic convert from Protestantism, who had been asked to establish the first Catholic University of Ireland. Newman held the view that the Catholic University should provide the same standard of education as that offered by the Protestant Trinity College in Dublin, his own university in Oxford, and the recently established Queen's Colleges.[65] Therefore, Newman appointed Eugene O'Curry as Professor of Irish History and Archaeology, John O'Hagan as Lecturer in Political Economy, John Pigot as Lecturer in the Law of Real Property, William Kirby Sullivan as Professor of Chemistry, Aubrey De Vere as Lecturer in English Literature, and John Hungerford Pollen as Chair of Fine Arts.

Primate of Ireland Cardinal Paul Cullen opposed the appointment of O'Curry, O'Hagan, Pigot, and Sullivan on the grounds that they had had links with the Young Ireland Movement which staged a country-wide rebellion against British rule in Ireland in 1848.[66] Cardinal Cullen opposed the appointment of Pollen and DeVere, the reason being that they were Protestants. The Roman Catholic Church in Ireland considered the establishment of a Catholic University as one of their most significant achievements to date; it was inevitable that the Cardinal believed that the new institution should only employ professors who were non-political in their outlook and who had been born into Irish

Catholic families. Aside from this, the Cardinal wished education to be based almost entirely on theological grounds; this was to serve the growing power of the Catholic Church in Ireland. Newman's more liberal view of the university stood in stark contrast to this; for him, the teaching of theology went hand in hand with educating students in the fields of science and literature, and for him the worth of professors was based solely on the scholarly merit of their work. For instance, he chose John Hungerford Pollen as Chair of Fine Arts on the basis of his work on the Oxford murals with Rossetti, Morris, and Burne-Jones. Newman's liberal ideals were proving difficult to realise because the Catholic Church hierarchy in Ireland did not welcome his plans to transcend denominational divides for the sake of achieving scholarly standards equal to that of Trinity College or the Queen's Colleges. Newman's proposal to give the laity control over the finances of the university further deepened the divide between himself and Cullen. Newman finally resigned from his post as the first rector of the institution in 1858, following prolonged disagreements between university leadership and the Catholic Church authorities in Ireland.

Plays Political and Historical

Ruskin writes in *Fors Clavigera* that '[v]iolent combativeness for particular sects, as Evan-gelical *[sic]*, Roman Catholic, High Church, Broad Church—or the like, is merely a form of party-egotism, and a defiance of Christ, not confession of Him'.[67] Calling the various denominations 'sects'—with all the connotations of that word—could of itself be perceived as an example of 'violent combativeness'. Significant, however, is the art critic's belief that a certain degree of *rapprochement* between the various Christian denominations was necessary. Lady Gregory herself wholeheartedly embraced the notion that the differences between warring denominations needed to be reconciled in order to find a way forward for a society. One of the books that caught her attention during her travels within the British Empire was the French writer Ernest Renan's *Vie de Jésus* (1863). Renan wrote a biographical account of Jesus's life, carefully placing people and events in the wider social and historical context. The book was unique among its Victorian contemporaries because it paid little attention to the dogmatic debates that had arisen around various aspects of Jesus's life and teachings over the past centuries. Renan's main purpose was to portray the Son of God as the 'Son of

Man'. Lady Gregory wrote in her travel notebook that the unique historical approach adopted by the author allowed Jesus to be regarded as a 'universal saviour'.[68] She found this image of Jesus particularly appealing because it suggested that Jesus had come to save all men and women who believed in his teachings, regardless of their religious denominational affiliations, themselves mere historical constructs. Calling for a *rapprochement* between denominations, the Rev. John Wesley had also preached in his sermon on Jesus's 'Sermon on the Mount', that 'doing good' (as he described the social aspect of Christian teaching), was interlocked with 'peacemaking'. According to Wesley, peacemaking was '[a]nother necessary branch of true Christianity'.[69]

Back in 1898, Lady Gregory had attended a meeting of the Irish Literary Society when those present debated the value and political relevance of the poetry of James Clarence Mangan. Yeats declared at the meeting that '[a]rt should be for its own sake only, that is the sake of the heavenly vision, & "its end should be for peace"'.[70] Yeats might not have followed his own advice in the years to come but it is of considerable significance that Lady Gregory made a note of Yeats's comments in her diary. If the end of art was peace—as Lady Gregory, Yeats, and Coventry Patmore believed at the time—then an artist should become a peacemaker. Lady Gregory held the view that the complex nature of the historical and religious problems in Ireland often hindered the realisation of projects from which Irish society could benefit. If an artist was to be a *candlestickmaker* and a *bearer of peace*—as she firmly believed—then an artist's role was to advance the process of reconciliation between the opposing political and religious factions within Ireland. Lady Gregory's religious one-acter *The Travelling Man* is particularly interesting in this light because the title character of the play transforms into an artist in the instance of building the paradise-like garden with the plates of the child's mother. He is the one who has the knowledge of the new promised land of abundance and beauty; he is the one who breaks the child's dead old stick to replace it with a living branch from a beautiful tree from this new land; and he is the one who raises the child's desire to go to the beautiful place plentiful in all kinds of fruits and flowers. The child's mother, on the other hand, represents those who stood in the way of progress. She dislikes the garden that has been built against her wishes; she clings to a promise given in her past; and she will not accept new teachings or visions. Lady Gregory emphasises this aspect of the story by having the mother echo words from the biblical story of

Jesus's trial, when the Pharisees—steadfastly obedient to the laws of the Old Testament—could not accept Jesus's new teachings and his vision of the Promised Land.[71] In part, what motivated Lady Gregory to write such a play as *The Travelling Man* was her desire to convince opponents of social or educational reforms, or indeed of artistic projects, that the new reforms were liberating rather than coercive. She hoped to make her audiences realise that opposition to reforms might result in the opportunity being squandered of creating a better form of society in Ireland.

Lady Gregory demonstrated in *The Travelling Man* that she had assigned the role of social leadership to the artist who would map out the road of progress for the country. In contrast, Patrick Pearse's *Íosagán* (1910) and *The Singer* (1915) present a strikingly different social message to that in the plays of Lady Gregory. This is of particular importance because in Irish criticism Lady Gregory's work and political thought have been compared to those of Patrick Pearse. *Íosagán* (the Irish-language term for the child Jesus) was first performed in Cullenswood House, Rathmines, in February 1910, around the same time as *The Travelling Man*.[72] Written for children and performed by a cast of St. Enda students, the title character of the play is a young boy who, in travelling the roads and walking the hills, reminds one of the travelling man of Lady Gregory's play. Íosagán's white attire reflects the main colours of Christ's robe in Hunt's painting *The Light of the World*, as does the white flannel shirt of Lady Gregory's protagonist.[73] He too spends his time with children, who symbolise the new generation; adults, who symbolise the old generation, are unable to see or recognise him. There is a glow of light around his head when he enters the scene. In Lady Gregory's play, Christ's return carries the possibility of a new beginning for the young boy's family, despite the play's note of disappointment at the mother's inability to recognise the figure of Jesus in the visitor. Jesus Christ's return in Pearse's play, on the other hand, causes the death of the houseowner. When Íosagán returns to Matthias's house he sees him confess his sins to the priest before falling dead on seeing Íosagán in his abode. The death of the adult in Pearse's play is brought about by Íosagán fulfilling his promise of returning to the person's house. This cataclysmic ending is entirely absent in Lady Gregory's work, suggesting that the spectre of death hanging over Pearse's absorption in Christ's story was alien to the temper of Lady Gregory's Christian allegories.

Written in the autumn of 1915, just months before the Easter Rising of April 1916, Pearse's play *The Singer* tells the story of an artist who stirs Irishmen to fight against their English oppressors. The singer's songs were 'full of terrible love for the people and of great anger against the Gall' and 'were setting people's hearts on fire'.[74] Pearse describes him as a man:

> with the dress and the speech of a mountainy man; shy in himself and very silent, till he stands up to talk to the people. And then he has the voice of a silver trumpet, and words so beautiful that they make the people cry. And there is terrible anger in him, for all that he is shrinking and gentle.[75]

Pearse's play abounds in references to the biblical story of Christ, identifying the singer with the figure of Jesus. The people believe the singer to be 'maybe an angel, or the Son of Mary Himself that has come down on the earth'; his mother was meeting him like 'Mary meeting her Son on the Dolorous Way'; even his dramatic rejection of faith is reminiscent of an event in Christ's life, his Gethsemane experience.[76] In the closing moments of the play, MacDara (the singer as artist), prepares to meet 'the Gall' in a Christ-like fashion:

> One man can free a people as one Man redeemed the world. I will take no pike, I will go into the battle with bare hands. I will stand up before the Gall as Christ hung naked before men on the tree.[77]

MacDara's words identify the parallel between his mission and that of Christ as lying fundamentally in the redeeming quality of blood sacrifice. Seamus Deane, Declan Kiberd, and Séan Farrell Moran have concluded that Pearse's notion of necessary blood sacrifice and inevitable self-sacrifice had its origins in both the biblical story of Christ and the mythical story of Cuchulain.[78] Kiberd considers the final moments of *The Singer* as a dramatic manifestation of this merger.[79] Brian P. Murphy writes that Pearse considered it necessary for Irishmen to 'emulate the sacrifice of Christ and die for their country'.[80] Moran adds to this that, according to Pearse, 'death in service to Ireland could bring personal and national redemption', liberating the people of Ireland as a consequence.[81] The redemptive nature of self-sacrifice was, in fact, an idea prevalent amongst the members of the Irish Republican Brotherhood—Pearse among them—who were drawing up military plans against British rule in Ireland in the early 1910s.[82] In his speech at the Robert Emmet Commemoration in the Aeolian Hall in New York on 9 March 1914,

Pearse praised Emmet, a United Irishman and leader of the 1803 rebellion, for 'dying that his people might live, even as Christ died'.[83] Pearse explained the revolutionary ideas of his fellow-Irishmen who had joined voluntary military organisations—primarily the Irish Republican Brotherhood and the Irish Citizen Army—as follows:

> It is not that we are apostles of hate. Who like us has carried Christ's word of charity about the earth? But the Christ that said 'My peace I leave you, My peace I give you', is the same Christ that said 'I bring not peace, but a sword'.[84]

The Emmet lecture reveals a strong attraction to the idea of living one's life as a messianic, warrior-like individual, as he perceived the figure of Christ. Pearse's view was that there could be no peace in Ireland until the country was liberated from what he saw as the tyrannical governance of the British Empire. While Lady Gregory's visionary Christ-figure was a bearer of good news and the bringer of a living branch, Pearse's Messiah-like Christ-figure was the proud owner of the sword of light, the *claidheamh soluis*.[85] What W. J. McCormack has described as the 'pervasive symbolism of messianic sacrifice and redemption', in its most militant form, was entirely absent from Lady Gregory's dramatic *oeuvre*.[86]

This is significant as Ann Saddlemyer, Lucy McDiarmid, and James Pethica have made compelling cases for the playwright's profound identification with the 'rebel nationalist' cause in Ireland. Saddlemyer has asserted that the playwright was 'single-mindedly a rebel nationalist' since, '[o]f the avowedly nationalistic plays presented by the Abbey Theatre company, Lady Gregory had a hand in most'.[87] Pethica takes up this line of thought, identifying the figure of the rebel in her plays, arguing that its presence points at the dramatist's identification with the Irish rebel cause. Pethica claims that *Cathleen ni Houlihan* signifies the arrival of the disturber figure, followed by the 'artist disturber' in *The Marriage*, the character finally epitomising the figure of Christ—the 'supreme disturber'—in *The Travelling Man*.[88] Pethica has claimed also that the playwright's diary entry from the time of the Irish Civil War suggests '[t]he sustained force of her personal identification with the idea of sacrifice for the "rebel" cause'.[89] Lady Gregory's article 'The Felons of Our Land', published in the *Cornhill Magazine* in 1900, is often quoted to make the case for her political stance as militantly nationalist. Pethica argues that the article is the 'most emphatic celebration of the "rebel" ballad heritage', which 'draws direct analogies between Christ's self-sacrifice' and 'the ennobling sacrifice of those who had been willing to die for their country'.[90] McDiarmid has declared that the playwright's 'literary Fenianism [...] draws on the same traditions and ideology as Pearse's did, and in the 1920s she had the opportunity Pearse never had to grow sentimental and reminiscent'.[91]

Lady Gregory's political and historical plays from the period suggest, however, that the extent of the playwright's identification with the 'rebel cause', or indeed co-opting of this cause to the educational programme of the Abbey Theatre, did not reach the levels estimated by some literary critics. Loosely based on Douglas Hyde's *Rí Seamus* of 1903, *The White Cockade* (1905) recounts the events of the Battle of the Boyne of July 1690. The very direct message of calling for men's self-sacrifice in order to realise the goal of ending foreign rule in Ireland—the message of Pearse's plays—is entirely absent from Lady Gregory's story. While Pearse's plays are tragedies, Lady Gregory's *The White Cockade* is a comedy, allowing her to present the many opposing views and ideals present at the time of the historic battle between the armies of the Catholic aspirant to the English throne, James, and the Protestant aspirant, William of Orange. As with her 'co-operative plays', this history play of hers hit 'impartially all around', to use once again her appraisal of George Moore's *The Bending of the Bough* from 1900.[92] Significantly, the Irish rural community is depicted here as one which is deeply engaged in domestic disputes and idle conversations. This is represented as a hindering force in the realisation of their most important and immediate task of aiding the French army summoned to fight on the side of James, the Catholic aspirant to the English throne. In a state of drunkenness, Matt Kelleher (of an inn-keeping family from Dungannon in Ulster) leads James directly into the hands of William's soldiers.[93] Matt's son Owen has no intention of getting involved in the war; he has no real desire to sacrifice himself for the country or a foreign king; Matt's wife Margaret is only interested in keeping their son out of the war.[94]

Out of these historic circumstances, an aristocrat, Patrick Sarsfield—the Earl of Lucan, of a mixed Catholic and Protestant background—emerges as the hero of the play. Sarsfield is the only person who is willing to fight and dedicate his life to the cause of Ireland. His tragedy, however, is the lack of dedication on the part of the Irish Catholic population to support James's campaign and, furthermore, the split within the military camp of the Jacobite soldiers. Whistling the tune of the satirical song

'Lillibulero', Northerners jeopardise Sarsfield and James's plans to defeat William of Orange's mighty army. Tradition has it that 'Lillibulero'—considered to be a jig with Irish roots that dated back to the English Civil War—was a satire on the sentiments of Irish followers of King James. Before the curtain drops on the scene, the hero Sarsfield is actually ridiculed for going into battle: for sacrificing his life and the lives of his soldiers for a cause already lost.[95] Anna Pilz notes that the Jacobite theme of *The White Cockade* was indeed at odds with the 'Jacobite revival phenomenon' of the nineteenth century in that it severely 'challenge[d] not only political but also romantic Jacobitism', characteristic of the end of the century in particular.[96] Pliz contends, in fact, that in the last moments of the play Lady Gregory discloses 'the faultiness of Jacobite—and nationalist—ideology' and seriously criticises the idea of 'nationalist martyrology' propagated by writers of a far more militant persuasion.[97]

Lady Gregory's next historical play, *The Canavans* (1906), travels back to Shakespeare's age and the Munster Rebellion during the reign of Queen Elizabeth I. Once again the play is a farcical comedy that reflects on the nature of armed rebellion and examines the figure of the militant rebel hero. The play is about two brothers, Peter and Antony Canavan. Peter is a miller who aspires to become the new mayor of the fictional Irish town of Scartana with the help of Queen Elizabeth's men. Antony is an ex-soldier who is treated as a traitor and a thief for having deserted the Queen's army while stationed on the European Continent. Antony deserted for fear of a certain prophecy being fulfilled: that he would die as soon as his name became famous. Because of the many Continental victories of the British army, he was becoming a celebrated figure within the British armed forces (and becoming ever more nervous in consequence). Against Peter's wishes, Antony takes shelter in Peter's mill. The brothers are caught and imprisoned, but Antony's resourceful character helps them escape. In one of the comic moments, Peter declares quite unexpectedly that his resourceful brother is an Irish rebel hero and praises him for being 'the candle of bravery and courage', 'the tower of the western world', and 'the mightiest hero of the Gael'.[98] Peter's praise of himself and of his brother leads to turmoil as enthusiasm for a rebellion begins to grow among the people of Scartana.

At the point of the heroic climax, however, Lady Gregory introduces an anecdote which demystifies the revolutionary scene. At the outbreak of the rebellion, Peter shoots at the commander of the British troops and future Lord Lieutenant of Ireland Lord Essex, who is passing by Peter's house in the company of his troops. Peter fires from the door of his house, then goes inside to hide, fearing return fire. Instead of gunfire, however, he receives an official salute from Lord Essex. This unexpected turn of events happens because, farcically, Peter had forgotten to load his gun, so his shot was perceived by Lord Essex as a welcoming salute that signified Peter's allegiance to the warlord rather than an attempt on his life that Peter intended it to be. Kohfeldt has drawn a parallel between *The Canavans* and *Spreading the News*, arguing that in both plays conclusions are drawn inappropriately and too quickly because of a series of misinterpretations of facts.[99] For sure, a series of misreadings follow the gunshot incident between Peter Canavan, the self-professed rebel hero, and Lord Essex, commander of Queen Elizabeth's army. Misinterpreting Lord Essex's gesture of salute, the people of the small Irish town of Scartana believe that the English warlord was driving his troops away from Peter's house in fear of a mighty enemy. Misinterpreting recent news about the British monarch, the people of Scartana believe Queen Elizabeth to have been assassinated; hence their daring attitude towards Lord Essex. Aware of the history of Ireland, Lady Gregory was cognisant of the fact that rebellions against British rule had failed in the past because they lacked proper organisation and correct evaluation of facts. The gunshot scene at the end of the play subtly reveals her views on the futility of bloodshed during past Irish rebellions. Disorganised as the rebellions had been, they only resulted in unnecessary, yet inevitable, suffering and loss of life.

Following the *Playboy* riots of 1907, during which people of Nationalist and Unionist persuasions confronted one another, Lady Gregory wrote a number of plays that were based around the theme of reconciliation; plays in which characters come to a realisation that they are more similar to one another than they had first assumed. Reworking an earlier piece entitled *The Poorhouse*, *The Workhouse Ward* (1908) is a play about two quarrelling vagabonds stationed in a ward in an Irish workhouse, who realise that they need to reconcile their differences if they are to stay together in the future. *Coats* (1910) tells the story of two quarrelling editors who give up criticising each other when they discover that they have the same intentions regarding a newspaper column in their respective journals. *The Bogie Men* (1912) recounts the story of two chimney sweeps, each of whom realises that the man whom he had disliked since childhood is the same man with whom he had struck up a friendship during their brief conversation. *The Rising of the Moon* (1907) was produced in the immediate aftermath of the *Playboy* riots to calm the heated arguments around Synge's new play, and is often referred to as Lady Gregory's 'most Fenian play'. It is true that she used John 'Leo' Keegan Casey's Fenian ballad of the same title as a basis for the play but she deliberately softened the original sentiment of the song to allow the theme of reconciliation to become central in the performance. Casey was an active Fenian Movement organiser during the 1860s and in 1865 he was imprisoned as part of the British Government's pre-emptive strike to prevent the outbreak of a rebellion in Ireland.[100] Despite this, the Irish Republican Brotherhood was preparing for a rising, hoping that ammunition and armed personnel from the USA would arrive and help the Irish rebel cause. George Denis Zimmerman notes that at the time 'street ballads were once again full of expectation'.[101] Hopeful of the future, Casey's ballad from his collection *A Wreath of Shamrocks* (1866) calls to mind the outbreak of the United Irishmen rebellion of 1798:

> Down by the lonely river, / A dark mass of men were seen,
> Far above the starry banner / Hung our own immortal green.
> Death to every foe and traitor, / Forward on the marching tune,
> And a million pikes were shining / By the rising of the moon.
> ....
> At the risin' of the moon, / At the risin' of the moon,
> For the pikes must be together / At the risin' of the moon.

The rising is recalled in the first part of the ballad, while the last verse of the song fuses lamentation over the fate of those who died in the uprising with renewed calls to stage a new rebellion in Ireland: 'But yet we have in poor old Ireland / Hearts that beat as firm and true / We will follow in their footsteps / By the rising of the moon'.[102]

In a striking contrast to the original sentiment of the song, Lady Gregory did not issue a call for rebellion—as did Casey or as Pearse would have done—but placed the message of reconciliation and unification at the heart of her play. She added a Pre-Raphaelite twist to the tale of the Fenian escapee and the Royal Irish Constabulary officer as she modified the original Fenian rebel ballad into a story of the policeman's 'awakening conscience'. As one of the most famous paintings of the Victorian era and a companion piece to *The Light of the World*, William Holman Hunt's picture *The Awakening Conscience* of 1854 would undoubtedly have been familiar to Lady Gregory, given her and her late husband's position in the London art world. While the subject matter of *The Awakening Conscience* (that early Pre-Raphaelite painting which Ruskin admired so much), is quite different from that of *The Rising of the Moon*, both works are linked in their concentration upon a dawning moment of moral realisation.[103] In Hunt's painting, the woman is drawn away from a man towards the sunlight coming from outside the room through a window; the viewer can observe the sunlight through its reflection in a mirror placed against the rear wall of the room behind the couple. This incoming light represents the moment of the woman's conscience awakening. In *The Rising of the Moon*, the policeman's awakening conscience takes the form of his realisation that not only is the ballad singer whom he meets at the pier the very felon he is seeking to capture, but that he once shared the same feelings for the cause of Ireland. Just as the woman's conscience awakens in Holman Hunt's *The Awakening Conscience* as the light of the sun enters the room from outside, so the policeman's conscience awakens in Lady Gregory's *The Rising of the Moon* as the light of the Moon begins to fall upon the scene of the policeman and the felon, disguised as a ballad singer, at the seaside quay.

Granuaile and *Sean Bhan Bhocht* are two folk songs that help bring about the *rapprochement* between the policeman and the felon in Lady Gregory's play; the female figures in the titles are metaphors for Ireland. *The Rising of the Moon* and *The White Cockade* are also the titles of folk songs that Lady Gregory had borrowed for the titles of these political plays. Nonetheless, instead of using the folk songs to exhort audiences to armed uprising sanctifying the sacrifice of lives, she gives her plays endings that temper the openly military message of the original ballad songs. Judith Hill observes the playwright's acknowledgement of Yeats's influence in the writing of *The Rising of the Moon* but reduces the poet's role in the creative process to that of providing occasional suggestions or criticism.[104] In fact, although first performed only after the *Playboy* riots in 1907, the actual writing of *The Rising of the Moon* coincided with the writing of *Cathleen ni Houlihan* at the start of the 1900s, an early Yeats-Lady Gregory collaboration, the theme of which is incitement to rebellion. The theme of both plays sits far more easily with Yeats's nationalism and his preoccupation with the idea of rebellion at the time than it does with the general tenor of Lady Gregory's plays. The artist-rebel figure Paul Ruttledge of Yeats's play *Where There is Nothing* from 1902—co-authored with George Moore and Douglas Hyde and based loosely on the figure of the socialist rebel William Morris—is a further indication of Yeats's rebel leanings in the early 1900s. Yeats may have suggested the use of the Irish ballad to Lady Gregory as the trigger for the plot of *The Rising of the Moon*, which Lady Gregory went on to alter as she did Yeats's plan for the story of *The Travelling Man*. Yeats wrote to Lady Gregory in November 1902 that the travelling man was 'almost God Pan who was I think in the Renaissance sometimes identified with Christ'.[105] John Kelly and Ronald Schuchard observe that Lady Gregory replied clearly to her friend's suggestion, '[d]emurring from WBY's view [...] that the Christ-figure in *The Travelling Man* was not "the supreme disturber we have thought him" but the proponent of "some near and innocent happiness"'.[106] Lady Gregory and Yeats's ideas for this play were so far apart that he reworked his own idea into a little pagan play entitled *The Black Horse*, while she went on to write her own version of the story in which she formulated her own ideas with regard to the role of the artist in society, depicting Christ as a missionary visionary in *The Travelling Man*.[107]

Home Rule or Home Ruin?

During the 1880s British Prime Minister William Gladstone and Charles Stewart Parnell of the Irish Parliamentary Party proposed a new way of solving 'the Irish question' in the form of Home Rule legislation. At the time of the second Home Rule Bill in the early 1890s, Lady Gregory shared the view of many who believed that the proposed new Home Rule Bill would mean 'Home Ruin' for the people of Ireland. She addressed this matter in her pamphlet *A Phantom's Pilgrimage, or Home Ruin*, published in London in 1893. By the 1910s, however, at the time of the third Home Rule Bill, she had come to view the question of Irish political self-governance from a different perspective. She observed that, without the passing of the new Home Rule legislation in the British Parliament, Ireland and Britain would have to face irrevocable consequences, such was the level of military activity in Ireland. Her new historical-political play *The Wrens*—written for a first performance in London in June 1914 during the third Home Rule debate at Westminster—urged informed members of the audiences in London as well as MPs in the British Parliament to seize the political moment and support the new Government of Ireland Bill proposed by British Prime Minister Herbert H. Asquith.

The reasons behind her rejection of the proposed self-governance bill for Ireland during the 1890s were to a large measure socio-political, as indicated in her pamphlet *A Phantom's Pilgrimage, or Home Ruin*, a piece that imagines Gladstone's return to Ireland on Judgement Day. On the 'day for pronouncing sentence on the soul of the dead', Gladstone, with 'ghostly shirt-collar and skeleton-leaved buttonhole', is granted permission to revisit Ireland for 12 hours in order to see the results of the Home Rule Act.[108] He is excited, exclaiming: 'This [...] represents my best and greatest deed, by which I conferred self-government on an oppressed nation. By this am I content to live or die'.[109] What he finds, however, is enough to condemn his soul, as he hears the curses of the people from all walks of Irish life. The 'trembling emancipated man' is on the brink of starvation and farmers emigrate.[110] A famine victim is living under a heap of stones; a woman 'bare-footed, red-skirted, and bent beneath the weight of a basket of seaweed on her back' sends her curse on those who had given Ireland Home Rule.[111] Towns are no different: streets are dirty and covered in weeds. Factories are closed down; shops and dwelling houses are deserted in streets that are 'silent as the grave'.[112] Schools are closed down due to lack of finance. The situation in the Irish countryside is no different: there is no medical help and there are no ministers to look after those perishing in parishes.[113] Ascendancy culture is in a state of decay; slates are blown off the Big Houses, gardens are full of weeds, and windows are boarded up so that owners could escape the new taxes.[114] Anne Fogarty and Greg Winston have pointed to the conservative politics of the text, typical of the sentiments of the landowning classes of the early 1890s.[115] What is even more significant is Lady Gregory's belief that all segments of Irish society would suffer from the consequences of the abrupt political change that the proposed bill would introduce in Ireland. In *A Phantom's Pilgrimage, or Home Ruin*, Lady Gregory seems to be concerned primarily with the *social* consequences of this change rather than the inevitable modification of the Irish political system itself, a result of Gladstone's proposed solution for the governance of Ireland. This was so, even though she and her late husband were deeply concerned about the possible confiscation of Ascendancy land under the land provisions of the Home Rule Bills, as Judith Hill argues.[116] Interestingly, Lady Gregory warns the reader of her pamphlet that the social degeneration, which in her view would inevitably follow the implementation of the proposed Home Rule Bill, would likely induce a revolutionary atmosphere in Ireland. In a style at times reminiscent of Edmund Burke's famous 1790 pamphlet *Reflections on the Revolution in France*, she writes that the poor angry mob, with 'a murderous gleam' in their eyes, would finally gather outside the Senate House in Dublin to make their case known to those in power.[117]

Lady Gregory developed a less critical stance on Irish self-governance as years passed. During the years of working for the agricultural, the literary, and the cultural movements with social reformers like Plunkett, Balfour, Russell, and Hyde, she developed the formula of 'not working for Home Rule but preparing for it'.[118] She understood this as meaning that the various social and literary movements were working not directly to achieve Home Rule for Ireland—as were the political movement led by John Redmond and the Irish Parliamentary Party—but instead preparing the country should Home Rule become a political reality in the near future. She was convinced that the country needed an extended period of social reform to prepare itself for the political change, and that if the whole of Irish society—from farmers to politicians—was not ready for it, the country would fall into ruin. Her interest in implementing Ruskin's utopian project of social improvement designed for Britain and Ireland stemmed from this deep-rooted conviction. Ruskin had suggested in *Fors Clavigera* that aristocrats were to act as 'shepherd lords' and take direct responsibility for their 'herd', a biblical allegory used extensively in Victorian and Edwardian social and political discourse.[119] This principle of *noblesse oblige*—which wrought Ruskin, Gladstone, and Parnell's political thought—also shaped the political and social thinking of the aristocratic classes of nineteenth and early twentieth-century Ireland and England.

Lady Gregory's interest in Wilfrid Scawen Blunt's political activism is important in this context. Garrigan Mattar has coined the term 'colonial nationalism' to describe Lady Gregory's political views on matters relating to Ireland.[120] Anne Fogarty has argued that this had revealed itself in the playwright's 'contradictory admixture of detachment and passion' towards Irish matters. Garrigan Mattar, Fogarty, and Kiberd have claimed that some of Lady Gregory's political views owed their existence to her sympathy for Blunt's 'rebel nationalism'.[121] Like other genteel women at the time, Lady Gregory was almost instantly attracted to Wilfrid Blunt's Byronic character when they first met in Egypt after the 'revolt of the Colonels', in the winter of 1881–1882. Sympathies for Blunt's nationalist sentiments are certainly there in Lady Gregory's early writings, such as 'Arabi and His Household' (1882) and 'The Felons of Our Land' (1900). Nonetheless, calling these works Lady Gregory's 'earliest recorded anti-imperialist writing', as Lucy McDiarmid does, gives the impression that they were part of a consistent anti-imperialist position in Lady Gregory's writings subsequently, one motivated by her relationship with Blunt.[122]

Such claims, however, are somewhat misleading. 'Arabi and His Household' and 'The Felons of Our Land' are not of a directly propagandist nature, nor do they advocate the idea of rebellion as the only possible solution to social and political grievances within the British Empire. This is in striking contrast to Blunt's views on the matter: he believed at the time that 'there must be bloodshed before things come right' in Egypt.[123] In fact, the overriding sentiment of Lady Gregory's 'Arabi and His Household' is one of concern over the pending execution of a man and the possible outbreak of violence in its aftermath.[124] Lady Gregory's 'The Felons of Our Land' was composed—in the tradition of Samuel Ferguson's writings—as an antiquarian piece, and was published at a time of preparation for the first performances of the Irish Literary Theatre. What Lady Gregory emphasised in 'The Felons' was the fact that in past times leaders of Irish independence movements had come from both Catholic and Protestant backgrounds.[125] Citing the names of Daniel O'Connell, William Phillip Allen, Michael O'Brien, and Michael Larkin, alongside those of Wolfe Tone, John Mitchell, and Lord Edward FitzGerald, Lady Gregory stated that there had been times in Irish history when people from different social backgrounds and religious affiliations stood united under a common aim. As such, 'The Felons' was a call for a uniting of classes and creeds in Irish society to the end of creating a better future for the country as a whole. 'Uniting classes and creeds' was a theme to which she returned in her later writings, especially in support of the non-denominational and peaceful social reform schemes of Horace Plunkett and George Russell's Co-operative Movement.

Lady Gregory's brief affair with Blunt has been identified as a source of inspiration for some of her early history plays, particularly *Kincora*, *Dervorgilla*, and *Grania*. Drawing on arguments first formulated by Elizabeth Coxhead and Mary Lou Kohfeldt, critics Dawn Duncan, Richard Cave, Christopher Murray, and Cathy Leeney have argued for Blunt's lingering presence in these dramatic works, especially in Lady Gregory's representation of the female protagonists Gormleith, Dervorgilla, and Grania.[126] While this claim is true to a certain extent, further claims that there was a direct link between her interest in Egyptian nationalism and a subsequent support for Irish nationalism, and that these dramatic works reveal in Lady Gregory a feminist literary disposition—one that was allied to radical nationalist sentiment—are somewhat dubious.[127] Regrettably, there is a tendency in recent criticism to overlook the thematic variety within Lady Gregory's dramatic work, focussing almost exclusively on *Kincora*, *Dervorgilla*, and *Grania*. Such readings tend to overlook also the variety of Irish female characters that she had created: from Mrs. Tarpey of *Spreading the News* and Mrs. Broderick of *The Jackdaw*, through to Mary Cushin of *The Gaol Gate* and Margaret Kelleher of *The White Cockade*, and on to Queen Gormleith of *Kincora* and Queen Dervorgilla of *Dervorgilla*. Lady Gregory's female characters come from diverse social backgrounds and historical periods, with a wide range of family positions, from that of widowhood to that of unmarried young women. Apart from this, there is a certain lack of understanding in Irish criticism with regard to the allegorical undercurrents in *Kincora*, *Dervorgilla*, and *Grania*. These undercurrents, however, indicate that there was more to the original dramatic situation than has been proposed by twenty-first-century nationalist-feminist readings of these works under the influence of postcolonial perspectives on her drama.

Kincora, for instance, concerns *noblesse oblige* as a guiding principle of the famed Brian Ború, King of Munster. Brian is a self-confessed 'peace maker' who intends to bring peace and reconciliation to Ireland by arranging for King Maelmora of Leinster, High King of Ireland Malachi, and Sitric of the Danes, to sign a 'treaty of pacification'.[128] Brian's new treaty is intended to put an end to territorial wars in Ireland. In Lady Gregory's treatment, Brian is a peaceful and forgiving Christian monarch, who even forgives the treacherous ways of Sitric, son of Olaf of the Danes. Fearing the High King of Ireland's verdict on his act of defiance, however, Sitric calls into Ireland the army of the Danes, aided by the men of Sigurd, Earl of Orkney, and Brodar of the Isle of Man. At the end of the play, Brian is seen with a sword drawn, going into the famous battle at Clontarf, near Dublin, of April 1014.[129] While he would be victorious during battle, he would die soon afterwards, and it is in death that he would find what he calls the 'perfect peace' that he had once been promised in a dream.[130] Like Sarsfield in *The White Cockade* (first performed in the same year as the first version of *Kincora*), King Brian is seen at the end of the play fighting for a cause of unity that is already lost, emphasising once more Lady Gregory's feelings about the tragic loss of human life and the futility of constant rebellion and war.

Similar sentiments are extant in *Dervorgilla*, a play about the old and remorseful Queen of Breffny in the northern region of Ireland. Nearing the end of her life, Queen Dervorgilla asks for forgiveness from God and from the Irish people for the 'sin' of having provoked political turmoil in Ireland. Dervorgilla's story resembles that of Queen Gormleith from *Kincora*, in that Gormleith too repents forsaking her husband and causing the return of foreign fighters to Ireland. Dervorgilla's character is akin to that of Grania from Lady Gregory's mythological play *Grania* (1912) in that Grania too is trapped in an irresolvable interpersonal situation that leads to a 'territorial war'. Grania herself is caught between three men: the King of Foreign, Finn McCumhail of Almhuin, and one of Finn's young warriors, Diarmuid. Diarmuid advances towards her immediately after the King of Foreign suddenly moves to take her for himself. While this action might be read as a rash move of a lovesick young man, as Anthony Roche suggests, a more assured allegorical interpretation would observe, however, that Diarmuid's action is one of defence in loyalty to Finn, protecting Grania from wedding the King of Foreign.[131] At the beginning of the story it is revealed that Grania was first about to wed the King of Foreign, then about to marry Finn, before finally fleeing into the Irish woodlands, followed by Diarmuid. Diarmuid tells Finn that he will follow her to act as her guardian and insists that he will not betray Finn by pursuing a relationship with her. Diarmuid promises to send Finn a loaf of bread on each full moon as a sign of his continuing fidelity to Finn.[132] While it is true that Diarmuid and Grania eventually become husband and wife, it is only after seven years of waiting, during which time—the audience is led to believe—Diarmuid maintained his original promise to Finn about Grania.

Diarmuid's desire to protect Grania from the advances of the King of Foreign conforms to medieval ideas of knighthood and courtly love. The conflict between his love for Finn and his love for Grania demonstrates the depth of Diarmuid's investment in medieval codes of honour, and that of *noblesse oblige*. Murray is correct in drawing attention to the centrality that Lady Gregory granted Grania to the legend when she chose her name alone as the title for her play, in contrast, for instance, to Yeats and Moore's *Diarmuid and Grania* (1901).[133] Nevertheless, *Grania* is as much about the relationship between men as it is about the relationship between men and a woman. Leeney offers an excellent insight into the significance of the character of the King of Foreign, claiming that he 'represents a disturbing erotic energy' that is 'Dionysian, ebullient and dangerous'.[134] The King of Foreign's important offstage presence, however, indicates that there is more depth to Lady Gregory's version of the legend than the simple story of the rivalry between Finn and Diarmuid. In the last moments of the play, fatally wounded during his battle with the King of Foreign, Diarmuid professes his unfaltering allegiance to Finn once again, ignoring completely the terrified and devastated Grania. This moment may indeed carry some of the homoerotic undertones of the original medieval legend; nonetheless, it is significant from a Ruskinian moral point of view that in the last moments of the tragedy Diarmuid struggles to maintain his bond with Finn, despite his words causing disheartening pain to Grania.

Grania herself, however, is not merely a young woman; she is the female personification of the land (of Ireland). According to medieval rituals, writes Michael Byrnes, the king of the land had to wed the goddess of the land in a sacrificial ritual in which he pledged unfaltering allegiance to the goddess, herself the personification of the land.[135] Leeney suggests that Lady Gregory deliberately uses this medieval myth of (female) sovereignty in order to represent the female protagonist as a 'real power that challenges, and penetrates an exclusionary patriarchal structure'.[136] However, this is not self-evident, particularly when the figure of Grania is considered as a sovereignty goddess. If Grania was the sovereignty goddess of the land (or *the* land of Ireland) then Diarmuid himself had become involved in a 'territorial debate' over her between Finn of Almhuin and the King of Foreign. Significantly, *Kincora* and *Dervorgilla* are also built around the theme of such a 'territorial debate'. In *Kincora*, Gormleith first 'belonged' to Malachi, High King of Ireland, then to Brian Ború, future High King of Ireland, while the Danes and the Kings of Foreign gather armies to become sole 'controllers' of both the land (of Ireland) and Queen Gormleith. In *Dervorgilla*, territorial war once raged between O'Rourke, King of Breffny and Diarmuid MacMurrough, King of Leinster, who sent for the King of Foreign to assist him in his fight for his land—and for Dervorgilla as a woman symbolising the sovereignty of the land itself. Dervorgilla herself remembers that 'it was for my sake the wars were stirred up and the Gall brought into Ireland'.[137] A travelling beggar, who had witnessed the destruction of the land in the aftermath of the foreign invasion and had seen the starvation of the people, reminds her that still 'it is pitiful and sharp to-day are the wounds of Ireland'.[138] In Lady Gregory's play, the Irish people reject Dervorgilla's plea for forgiveness for all the blood that had been shed for her sake. They refuse her bountiful gifts when her true identity is finally revealed after one of her servant's death at the hands of English soldiers. As sovereignty figures linked to struggles for territorial authority, Grania, Gormleith, and Dervorgilla stand at odds with the revolutionary appeal of the ultimate sovereignty goddess in *Cathleen ni Houlihan*, the early Yeats-Gregory collaboration that took as its theme the incitement to rebellion in rural Ireland at the time of the United Irishmen uprising in 1798. As mentioned earlier, the subject of *Cathleen ni Houlihan* sat more comfortably with Yeats's political convictions in the early 1900s than those of Lady Gregory, regardless of the extent of her input on the composition of the play.

The intersections between the thought of Lady Gregory and that of John Ruskin illuminate the social and political nature of the attitudes underlying plays like *Kincora*, *Dervorgilla*, and *Grania*. Ruskin himself attended the aesthetic circles of Dante Gabriel Rossetti and his friends Swinburne, Baudelaire, Nisard, and Gautier. Nonetheless, Ruskin did not take to advocating a purely aesthetic way of living, indifferent to questions of morality. Likewise, while Lady Gregory was undoubtedly fascinated by Wilfrid Blunt's rebellious spirit, she did not advocate militant rebellion as the solution to social and political injustices in the late nineteenth and early twentieth century, whether in Egypt or Ireland. Holding a view that opposed nationalist militancy even when she showed sympathy and understanding for what motivated it, Lady Gregory was even at variance with Ruskin himself, who had expressed passionate feelings about the Land War in Ireland. Ruskin once advocated the idea that the land should be taken away from the absentee landlords and redistributed within the rural population of Ireland.[139]

As for Blunt himself, he was a political maverick, an eccentric when it came to formulating political views. Blunt's biographer, Elizabeth Longford, writes that he held radical views on matters relating to the British Empire, conservative views on British home affairs, and was a Home Ruler when it came to issues concerning the political future of Ireland.[140] Blunt had, in fact, campaigned for Home Rule in Ireland under the auspices of the Home Rule Union in the late 1880s. The mission statement of the Home Rule Union stated its objective 'to spread abroad a knowledge of the causes which have brought about the alienation of Ireland from England, and to discover the means whereby the two countries can be united for ever'.[141] This sentiment was far removed from the militant type of rebel nationalism with which Blunt was associated in the early 1880s, and for which his contemporaries, such as John Dillon of the Irish Land League and John O'Leary of the Irish Republican Brotherhood, were condemned by the British Government. Nonetheless, he too, like Parnell, was held in prison for political activities; an imprisonment that was heralded on the pages of the *Journal of the Home Rule Union* as a sacrifice for the cause.[142] Lady Gregory herself had warned Blunt that should he return to Ireland during the Plan of Campaign after Gladstone's fall from power following the defeat of the first Home Rule Bill, he would surely be imprisoned; the warning was dismissed by its addressee.[143]

While Lady Gregory was sceptical of the Home Rule Bills of 1886 and 1893, she was fully supportive of the type of Irish self-governance that the new bill offered at the final stages of the third Home Rule debate at Westminster in 1914. By that time, the efforts of those working for the agricultural and the cultural movement had begun to bear fruit. Plunkett's agricultural organisation helped transform Irish society from land users to land owners who worked in co-operation for the betterment of their living and working conditions in the Irish countryside. Hyde's language revival movement and Gregory's literary and theatrical movements were helping in the widening of Irish people's outlook. They offered models and templates from Ireland's ancient past through the revival and the reworking of ancient myths and legends, while actively working towards a more economically prosperous future for the country. The achievements of many, however, were being put at risk by those who were forging a military campaign against British rule in Ireland during what they saw as calculated and deliberately elongated debates on Ireland's future in the Houses of Parliament in Westminster. Asquith and Redmond successfully put the third Home Rule Bill through the House of Commons in 1912 and in 1913, only to be rejected on both occasions by the House of Lords. The Government of Ireland Bill had its third and final reading at the House of Commons in May 1914, with a substantial majority of the Commons voting in favour of the political solution offered by the new legislation. By this time, new laws had been brought in to regulate the judiciary processes and powers of the House of Lords. Consequently, the second half of the year presented itself as the last possibility to pass the Home Rule Bill in the House of Lords before it was put in front of King George V to accept by Royal Assent. As Donal McCartney, Alvin Jackson, and Alan O'Day point out, the possible defeat of Asquith's bill in the House of Lords, Redmond's recoil from bringing the Irish question to a solution, and the unprecedented resistance of Ulster Protestants to a semi-independent Irish state, seriously suggested the possibility of armed rebellion in Ireland.[144]

With the third Home Rule Bill debated in the Houses of Parliament and menacing clouds of militancy gathering over Ireland, the Abbey Theatre decided to put on a week of performances at the Royal Court Theatre in London with two new plays in the repertoire, Lady Gregory's *The Wrens*, and J. Bernard McCarthy's *The Supplanter*. *The Wrens* was Lady Gregory's last desperate appeal to London to pass the Home Rule Bill in order to prevent militant Irish nationalists taking the question of independence into their own hands, leading to inevitable violence and bloodshed (particularly considering the force of Ulster opposition from 1912). Years later she remembered back to the days of the Easter Rising in 1916 and its consequences for Ireland:

> My mind is filled with the sorrow at the Dublin Tragedy, the death of Pearse and McDonough *[sic]* who ought to have been on our side, the side of intellectual freedom, and I keep wondering whether we could not have brought them into the intellectual movement.[145]

There had been many attempts to forge connections between the 'intellectual movement' of the Abbey Theatre—with its literary and social circle of predominantly Anglo-Irish writers—and the political and cultural nationalist movement of Patrick Pearse and Thomas MacDonagh.[146] Much in keeping with her idea of the Abbey Theatre as a place of reconciliation among the various opposing sections of Irish social and political life, the repertoire of the theatre often included plays and performances of divergent social and political groups. For instance, Pearse and MacDonagh's plays were staged alongside works by Alice Milligan, St. John Ervine, Rutherford Mayne (Samuel John Waddell), and Lewis Purcell (David Parkhill). As well as these, Salvation Army meetings and Gaelic League events were held within the walls of the Abbey Theatre, alongside Irish Volunteers meetings and Christian Science Lectures.[147] Despite the efforts of many who aimed at uniting the opposing sides for the sake of the intellectual movement gathering momentum in Ireland in the 1910s, the Irish Republican Brotherhood and Irish Socialist Republican Party had declared their intention to break Ireland's connection with the British Empire by means of an armed rebellion.[148] As Patrick Buckland has shown, at the same time Protestant Orangemen in the North of Ireland were making serious preparations to defend Ulster by force and fight for the Union of Ireland and Great Britain, if necessary.[149] Therefore, by 1913, the year before *The Wrens* premiered in London, the Irish Republican Brotherhood, the Irish Citizen Army, the Irish Volunteer Force, and the Ulster Volunteer Force had become well-armed military organisations prepared to fight for the causes to which they were dedicated.[150] One of the consequences of the growing spirit of militancy on the island was that the numbers of official British forces increased significantly. They were put on street patrols especially during and after the Great Dublin Lockout of 1913–1914, when there were continuous clashes between the police forces and the armed volunteers, both of whom were trying to keep order at meetings of the Socialist Irish Transport and General Workers' Union.[151]

First performed on 1 June 1914 at the Royal Court Theatre, *The Wrens* was Lady Gregory's last play before the outbreak of the First World War in July 1914. The play recounted the moment of the voting on the Act of Union between Great Britain and Ireland in the House of Commons in Dublin in 1799. James Kelly, Patrick M. Geoghegan, and G. C. Bolton write that, according to historical records, the passing the Act of Union Bill was a lengthy process. On its first reading in the House of Commons in Dublin on 22 January 1799, the Bill was defeated, and it was only in the parliamentary session of 1800 that the Bill was passed both in Dublin and at Westminster.[152] As with the story of the Battle of the Boyne in *The White Cockade*, Lady Gregory decided against representing historical facts in favour of staging the folk-historical version of events that shaped Ireland's subsequent political history. She explained the plot of the play as follows:

> Book History tells us that the Bill was passed on its first reading, on January 22, 1799, by only one vote; and my little play imagines the losing of a vote that would have at least made the numbers equal, through so slight a cause as a quarrel between two strolling vagabonds, that disturbs the attention of a servant from watching the moment to call his master, who would have cast his vote against the Bill.[153]

Lady Gregory adhered to popular belief about the vote; this allowed her to give a poignant and rather sarcastic title for the play as a way of commenting ironically on Irish people's general involvement in national politics.[154] Pilz mentions that the playwright often turned to folk memory in relation to events from Ireland's past because it gave her a certain 'artistic freedom when it came to [matters of] historical accuracy'.[155]

Lady Gregory continued to explore the theme of domestic preoccupations outweighing national sentiment in Ireland in *The Wrens*. As in *The White Cockade* or *The Canavans*, the main characters are preoccupied with their domestic affairs only and are inattentive to the destructive impact their quarrels have on Ireland's political future. William and Margaret Hevenor live in a marriage destroyed by alcoholism. Margaret's main concern is to stop her husband from taking drink and the passing of the Irish Act of Union provides her with a perfect opportunity. William Hevenor is willing to take the oath of temperance because he has heard it from MP Kirwan's servant that the Act of Union Bill will be thrown out in the House of Commons. Therefore he takes the oath until 'the Union bill now within in that house will be thrown out and rejected and beat!'[156] With William having taken the pledge, Margaret's hope is that the Bill will be passed. For this reason, she turns her patriotic song 'And down with the orange and blue! / Out with Castlereagh and Pitt and the Union!' immediately into 'And *up* with the orange and blue!'[157] Margaret belts the song out so loudly that Kirwan's servant cannot hear the ringing of the voting bell and he does not summon his master to cast his vote against the Act of Union. Thus, Margaret—actively, if inadvertently—contributes to the passing of the Act of Union Bill at the House of Commons in Dublin. Margaret Hevenor's preoccupation with finding some sort of financial security for herself makes her character akin to that of Margaret Kelleher of *The White Cockade* and Peter Canavan of *The Canavans*. Margaret resents the fact that her husband spends all his money on alcohol, making it impossible for her to build a home for the family. Lady Gregory had not written about the problem of alcoholism in Ireland before, making it even more significant that she did so in such a politically sensitive play as *The Wrens*. *McDonough's Wife* is the only other play in which she directly addressed the consequences of alcoholism in Ireland. A fiddle-player earning his money from playing at various events, McDonough arrives home only to hear that his wife died the night before.[158] While he was merrily spending his money on drink on his way home, his wife was on her deathbed.[159] It transpires that he has, in fact, spent all his money, shamefully leaving not a single penny for the wake and the funeral.[160] Telling the story of an Irish family ruined by drink, *McDonough's Wife* exposes the problems and choices that

Margaret Hevenor faces in *The Wrens*. Moreover, alcoholism is shown not only as a domestic but also as a national problem in the later play, depicting a situation in which it gets in the way of retaining Irish constitutional independence from the British Crown.

As with *The White Cockade* and *The Canavans*, *The Wrens* shows Irish people concerned only with their own immediate needs and those of their families. Ordinary Irish men and women are depicted as lacking a broader perspective necessary to providing long-term solutions to the many economic and political problems in Ireland. Once again, Lady Gregory depicts Irish people as quarrelsome, this time subtly alluding to the fact that this quarrelling nature of the people might stand in the way of realising what would be best for them and for the country, a theme that she first explored in a collection of letters entitled *Mr. Gregory's Letter-Box* (1898). There the quarrelsome nature of the Irish people was presented as a key factor in hindering the realisation of social-improvement policies initiated by the landed gentry of Ireland and by members of the British political *élite*. She continued to write on the theme in her plays from the *Workhouse Ward* through to *The Image*, *The Coats* and *The Bogie Men*. In *The Wrens*, her last play before the outbreak of the First World War, she returned once again to the theme of domestic disagreements. These disagreements, she argued, seriously affected the political future of Ireland: in the play, the political independence of the country is given up to save a husband. *The Wrens* was staged at a time when Ireland's political independence was once again on the political agenda and it provided the playwright with a unique opportunity to voice her political opinions close to the centre of British political power. As Home Rule had become a real political possibility, the playwright effectively sent the message that the onus was now on the politicians at Westminster to pass the long overdue Home Rule Bill. Should this not happen, or should it not happen *soon enough*, she feared the prospect of violent rebellion and civil war in Ireland. She was keenly aware of the growing danger of the outbreak of an armed rebellion, one that she felt would destroy all the cultural and economic achievements of the past decade, so she issued this last desperate appeal to the decisionmakers in London. In this respect, the 1914 performance of *The Wrens* at the Royal Court Theatre—the theatre house with a deep association with the plays of George Bernard Shaw—sharply recalls the 1911 Coronation performance of a reduced version of Shaw's *John Bull's Other Island* at 10 Downing Street. With Granville-Barker and William Fay acting roles in the performance, this staging was intended to persuade the new monarch, King George V, to accept Prime Minister Henry Asquith's intention to proceed with the introduction of Home Rule for Ireland.

As if to drive home the political message of her play, Lady Gregory accepted the invitation from Prime Minister Asquith for a dinner at 10 Downing Street while the Abbey Theatre Company was in London. This dinner invitation was a strong indication of both Lady Gregory's standing and influence at this crucial moment in Irish political history and the Abbey Theatre's influential role in determining the present and the future policies towards Ireland. Judith Hill emphasises that, at the dinner table, Lady Gregory was seated next to Asquith, who was determined to get the third Home Rule Bill passed through the Houses of Parliament.[161] By now, she had become accustomed to dining with those in political power, having attended dinners with: William Gladstone; Theodore Roosevelt; Queen Victoria; Queen Victoria's granddaughter, Alexandra, Empress Consort of Russia; Alexandra, Queen Consort of the United Kingdom, and her daughter Princess Victoria; and Kaiser Wilhelm II of Germany. Aware also of the need to have the contemporary political *élite* on her side and not to offend any party at this critical moment of Irish history, Lady Gregory deliberately passed no judgement on political leaders or Members of Parliament in her new play. Given the consequences of the Act of Union of 1800 in Ireland, Lady Gregory could have criticised the Dublin MPs for voting in favour of the bill but, at a different time, when weapons were being gathered in Ireland to stage an armed insurrection, she opted for criticising an ordinary Irish MP of the time of Henry Grattan's parliament. Staging her new play in an attempt to encourage the political decision necessary to prevent the outbreak of an armed conflict in Ireland, she stayed true to the motto that was the dearest to her heart, one that she had jotted down in her diary many years previously in Coventry Patmore's famous words: the end of art should be for peace.[162]

Notes

1. Lady Augusta Gregory, ed., *Ideals in Ireland* (London: Unicorn, 1901), 10.
2. John Ruskin, "The Light of the World," in *The Works of John Ruskin*, ed. E. T. Cook and Alexander Wedderburn, vol. 12 (London: George Allen, 1903–1912), 329–30.

Further references to Cook and Wedderburn's multivolume work will be as follows: Ruskin, *Title of Individual Work*, volume number.page number. Example here: Ruskin, "The Light of the World," 12.329–30.

3. Lady Augusta Gregory, *Seventy Years, Being the Autobiography of Lady Gregory* (Gerrards Cross: Colin Smythe, 1973), 11.
4. Burwash, Nathaniel, ed., *Wesley's Doctrinal Standards. Part 1: Sermons* (Toronto: Briggs, 1881), 236–46.
5. John 8:12, *Holy Bible*, New International Version (London: Hodder, 2001).
6. Luke 8:16–18.
7. Burwash, *Wesley's Doctrinal Standards*, 236–46.
8. Burwash, *Wesley's Doctrinal Standards*, 246.
9. George Bernard Shaw, "Preface for Politicians," in *John Bull's Other Island* (London: Penguin, 1984), 16.
10. Shaw, "Preface," 31.
11. Gregory, *Seventy Years*, 12–13.
12. Gregory, *Seventy Years*, 15; specific books mentioned on 12.
13. Gregory, *Seventy Years*, 3.
14. Mark Frost, *The Lost Companions and John Ruskin's Guild of St. George* (London: Anthem, 2014), 30. Frost sees this idea as having evolved from the art critic's early interest in the works of William Wordsworth and the Romantic English poet's admiration of Nature.
15. Frost, *The Lost Companions*, 35. Frost here is referring to Ruskin's increasing interest in the history and mythology of the ancient Greeks.
16. Robert Hewison, Ian Warrell, and Stephen Wildman, *Ruskin, Turner and the Pre-Rapahelites* (London: Tate Gallery, 2000), 231.
17. Alastair Grieve, "Rossetti and the Scandal of Art for Art's Sake in the 1860s," in *After the Pre-Raphaelites*, ed. Elizabeth Prettejohn (Manchester: Manchester University Press, 1999), 22.
18. Grieve, "Rossetti and the Scandal of the Art for Art's Sake in the 1860s," 29.
19. Grieve, "Rossetti and the Scandal of the Art for Art's Sake in the 1860s," 22.
20. Grieve, "Rossetti and the Scandal of the Art for Art's Sake in the 1860s," 29.
21. David Digues La Touche, the founding father of the dynasty in Ireland, came to Ireland in General Caillemote's Regiment, and fought for William against James at the Battle of the Boyne in 1690. Following the victory of the Protestant William's army, he settled in Ireland fearing religious persecution in an increasingly Roman Catholic France. Michael McGinley, *The La Touche Family in Ireland* (Greystones, Co. Wicklow: The La Touche Legacy Committee, 2004), 12 and 132–33.

22. Van Akin Burd, ed., *John Ruskin and Rose La Touche: Her Unpublished Diaries of 1861 and 1867* (Oxford: Clarendon, 1979); McGinley, *The La Touche Family*, 247–67.
23. McGinley, *The La Touche Family*, 159 and 164–65.
24. For the promotion of religious tolerance, see McGinley, *The La Touche Family*, 159.
25. McGinley, *The La Touche Family*, 159. The introduction of the National School System, its non-denominational nature and its role in social improvement were much debated issues both in Britain and in Ireland. For further discussion of the topic, see F. S. Lyons, *Ireland since the Famine* (London: Collins/Fontana, 1982), 82–83.
26. James Gregory, *Reformers, Patrons and Philanthropists: The Cowper-Temples and High Politics in Victorian England* (London: Tauris, 2010), 1.
27. Gregory, *Reformers, Patrons and Philanthropists*, 149.
28. Frost, *The Lost Companions*, 115; Gregory, *Reformers, Patrons and Philanthropists*, 123.
29. There were many reasons why Ruskin accepted the prestigious Slade Professorship of Fine Art at Oxford University. Besides the financial benefits of such a post, he was taken with the idea that the post would enable him to disseminate his aesthetic and social ideals among the new generations of the British and Anglo-Irish social *élite* who were to determine the social and political future of the United Kingdom. Added to this, he hoped that the prestigious position would soften the hearts of Rose La Touche's parents, who vigorously opposed the thought of a marriage between the art critic and their young daughter.
30. Gregory, *Reformers, Patrons and Philanthropists*, 131.
31. Frost, *The Lost Companions*, 36.
32. Frost, *The Lost Companions*, 36.
33. Frost, *The Lost Companions*, 36.
34. For O'Grady's *All-Ireland Review*, see Michael McAteer, *Standish O'Grady, AE and Yeats: History, Politics, Culture* (Dublin: Irish Academic Press, 2002), 149. The journal did publish articles relating to significant places and key events, such as the National University of Ireland, the Wyndham Land Act, the Landlord's Convention, and the Abbey Theatre. For Yeats on *Beltaine*, see W. B. Yeats, *The Collected Letters of W. B. Yeats; Volume Three: 1901–1904*, ed. John Kelly and Ronald Schuchard (Oxford: Clarendon, 1994), 75. Bringing to light the significance that Yeats had attributed to his own *Fors* project, McAteer points out that the poet-playwright incessantly referred to his late essay *On the Boiler* (1938) as Ruskin's *Fors Clavigera*. Michael McAteer, *Yeats and European Drama* (Cambridge: Cambridge University Press, 2010), 183.

35. "Plays for the People—Why Not an Irish Touring Company?" *Irish Peasant*, December 9, 1905, William Henderson, *Newspaper Cuttings*, MS 1730, National Library of Ireland.
36. For Horniman, see Adrian Frazier, *Behind the Scenes: Yeats, Horniman, and the Struggle for the Abbey Theatre* (Berkeley: University of California Press, 1990), 169–70.
37. Frazier, *Behind the Scenes*, 169.
38. "An Irish Theatre on Tour at Cambridge," *The Saturday Herald*, May 25, 1907, Henderson, MS 1730, NLI.
39. *Theatre Notes*, Henderson, MS 1730, NLI.
40. *Theatre Notes*, Henderson, MS 1730, NLI.
41. "An Irish Theatre on Tour at Cambridge," *The Saturday Herald*, May 25, 1907, Henderson, MS 1730, NLI.
42. Lady Augusta Gregory, *Our Irish Theatre: A Chapter of Autobiography* (Gerrards Cross: Colin Smythe, 1972), 20.
43. *The Evening Herald*, September 21, 1908, Henderson, MS 1731, NLI.
44. *The Irish News and Belfast Morning News*, December 4, 1908, Henderson, MS 1731, NLI.
45. *The Northern Whig*, December 4, 1908, Henderson, MS 1731, NLI.
46. "Lady Gregory on Drama—Stimulating Evening at the *Ard Chraobh*," no day given, 1908, Henderson, MS 1731, NLI.
47. "Lady Gregory on Drama—Stimulating Evening at the *Ard Chraobh*," Henderson, MS 1731, NLI.
48. Gregory, *Our Irish Theatre*, 101; "Lady Gregory on Drama—Stimulating Evening at the *Ard Chraobh*," Henderson, MS 1731, NLI.
49. P. J. Mathews, *Revival: The Abbey Theatre, Sinn Féin, the Gaelic League and the Co-operative Movement* (Cork: Cork University Press, 2003), 11.
50. Liam Kennedy, *Colonialism, Religion and Nationalism in Ireland* (Belfast: Queen's University of Belfast, 1996), 113 and 127.
51. Kennedy, *Colonialism, Religion and Nationalism in Ireland*, 113; Horace Plunkett, *Ireland in the New Century* (London: Murray, 1904), 119; and Rev. M. O'Riordan, *Catholicity and Progress in Ireland* (London: Kegan Paul, 1906), 208.
52. Rev. T. A. Finlay, S. J., "The Usurer in Ireland," *The New Ireland Review* (July 1894): 315 and 304–5.
53. Robert Hogan, Richard Burnham, and Daniel P. Poteet, eds., *The Abbey Theatre: The Rise of the Realists, 1910–1915* (Dublin: Dolmen, 1979), 198.
54. Hogan, Burnham, and Poteet, *The Abbey Theatre*, 198
55. Hogan, Burnham, and Poteet, *The Abbey Theatre*, 200; on this, see also 198.
56. Striving for recognition in Ireland, Yeats gave a very emotional speech at the Great Exhibition in Galway on Friday, September 18, 1908:

'Connacht is Ireland; Dublin is half England—shabby England perhaps we should call it. [...] If we are accepted in Connacht we have been accepted in Ireland'. *Connacht Champion*, September 26, 1908, Henderson, MS 1731, NLI.

57. *Connacht Champion*, September 26, 1908, Henderson, MS 1731, NLI.
58. Gregory, *Our Irish Theatre*, 35.
59. Ruskin, *The Guild and Museum of St. George*, 30.5.
60. Ruskin himself took part in educational programmes offered to the working classes in England. He taught drawing lessons at the Working Men's College set up by the Christian Socialist Movement in 1854. Edward Norman, *The Victorian Christian Socialists* (Cambridge: Cambridge University Press, 1987), 132.
61. Quoted in Judith Hill, *Lady Gregory: An Irish Life* (Stroud: Sutton, 2005), 215; for more on Hugh Lane, see 214–15.
62. Lady Augusta Gregory, *Hugh Lane* (Gerrards Cross: Colin Smythe, 1973), 128–29.
63. Mary Lou Kohfeldt, *Lady Gregory, the Woman Behind the Irish Literary Renaissance* (London: Deutsch, 1984), 240; Hill, *Lady Gregory*, 267–68.
64. Gregory, *Hugh Lane*, 83–85 and 87.
65. For Newman and the establishment of the Catholic University, see Charles Stephen Dessain, *John Henry Newman* (London: Nelson, 1966), 88–108; Sheridan Gilley, *Newman and His Age* (London: Darton, 1990), 275–308; Brian Martin, *John Henry Newman: His Life and Work* (London: Chatto and Windus, 1982), 96–112; Robert Sencourt, *The Life of Newman* (London: Dacre, 1948), 156–66; and Wilfrid Ward, *The Life of John Henry Cardinal Newman*, vol. 1 (London: Longmans, 1912), 305–416.
66. For the Cullen-Newman disagreement over the appointments, see Dessain, *John Henry Newman*, 106; Gilley, *Newman and His Age*, 280–81; and Ward, *The Life of John Henry Cardinal Newman*, vol. 1, 382.
67. Ruskin, *Fors Calvigera*, 29.337.
68. Lady Augusta Gregory, *Excerpts from her readings*, Lady Augusta Gregory Papers, Albert A. and Henry W. Berg Collection, New York Public Library.
69. Burwash, *Wesley's Doctrinal Standards*, 234.
70. James Pethica, ed., *Lady Gregory's Diaries, 1892–1902* (Gerrards Cross: Colin Smythe, 1996), 172.
71. Lady Augusta Gregory, *The Collected Plays*, vol. 3 (New York: Oxford University Press, 1970), 27–28; Luke 23:13–25.
72. Séamas Ó Buchalla, coll. and ed., *Literary Writings of Patrick Pearse* (Dublin: Mercier, 1979), 64.

73. Janice Norwood draws attention to the fact that the influence of Holman Hunt's *The Light of the World* on contemporary theatrical representation was not insignificant; in particular, she refers to the 1896 production of Wilson Barrett's *The Sign of the Cross* staged at the Lyric Theatre in London. Janice Norwood, "The Britannia Theatre: Visual Culture and the Repertoire of a Popular Theatre," in *Ruskin, the Theatre and Victorian Visual Culture*, ed. Anselm Heinrich, Katherine Newey, and Jeffrey Richards (Basingstoke: Palgrave Macmillan, 2009), 145.
74. Pádraic H. Pearse, *The Singer and Other Plays* (Dublin: Talbot, 1960), 21.
75. Pearse, *The Singer and Other Plays*, 16–17.
76. Pearse, *The Singer and Other Plays*, 17 and 24; for the Gethsemane experience, see Seán Farrell Moran, *Patrick Pearse and the Politics of Redemption* (Washington, DC: Catholic University of America Press, 1994), 159.
77. Pearse, *The Singer and Other Plays*, 44.
78. Seamus Deane, *Celtic Revivals: Essays in Modern Irish Literature, 1880–1980* (London: Faber, 1985), 68; Declan Kiberd, *Irish Classics* (Cambridge, MA: Harvard University Press, 2001), 416; and Farrell Moran, *Patrick Pearse and the Politics of Redemption*, 194.
79. Kiberd, *Irish Classics*, 416.
80. Brian P. Murphy, *Patrick Pearse and the Lost Republican Ideal* (Dublin: Duffy, 1991), 48.
81. Farrell Moran, *Patrick Pearse and the Politics of Redemption*, 2.
82. Murphy, *Patrick Pearse and the Lost Republican Ideal*, 49. Discussing Pearse's dissatisfaction with the Gaelic League's preparation for an armed campaign and the numerical weakness of the military group of the Irish Republican Brotherhood, Murphy asserts the following: 'Pearse realised that their forces [of those who wanted an armed revolution] were so small that they could not succeed. His writing, therefore, in the months before the Rising, attempted to justify the sacrifice of blood to which he and his comrades were committed'. Murphy, *Patrick Pearse and the Lost Republican Ideal*, 47–48.
83. Pádraic H. Pearse, *Political Writings and Speeches* (Dublin: Talbot, 1966), 71.
84. Pearse, *Political Writings and Speeches*, 77.
85. For the "Sword of Light," see Kiberd, *Irish Classics*, 415.
86. W. J. McCormack, *From Burke to Beckett: Ascendancy Tradition and Betrayal in Literary History* (Cork: Cork University Press, 1994), 226.
87. Ann Saddlemyer, "Augusta Gregory, Irish Nationalist: 'After All, What Is Wanted but a Hag and a Voice?'" in *Myth and Reality in Irish Literature*, ed. Joseph Ronsley (Waterloo, ON: Wilfrid Laurier University Press, 1977), 29–30. See also Ann Saddlemyer, *In Defence of Lady Gregory, Playwright* (Dublin: Dolmen, 1966), 9 and 87.

88. For *Cathleen ni Houlihan* and *The Travelling Man*, see James Pethica, "A Young Man's Ghost: Lady Gregory and J. M. Synge," *Irish University Review* 34, no. 1 (Spring/Summer 2004): 5 and 9. For *The Marriage*, see James Pethica, "Lady Gregory's Abbey Theatre Drama: Ireland Real and Ideal," in *The Cambridge Companion to Twentieth-Century Irish Drama*, ed. Shaun Richards (Cambridge: Cambridge University Press, 2004), 67.
89. James Pethica, "'Our Kathleen': Yeats's Collaboration with Lady Gregory in the Writing of *Cathleen ni Houlihan*," in *Yeats and Women*, ed. Deidre Toomey (Basingstoke: Macmillan, 1997), 216.
90. Pethica, "Lady Gregory's Abbey Theatre Drama," 66. Here Pethica even puts the onus on Lady Gregory for Yeats's growing interest in nationalist ideology, claiming that in 'Felons of Our Land' she 'effectively challenges him to explore the meaning of patriotism more frontally in his work'.
91. McDiarmid, "The Demotic Lady Gregory," 226.
92. Gregory, *Our Irish Theatre*, 28.
93. Lady Augusta Gregory, *The Collected Plays*, vol. 2 (New York: Oxford University Press, 1970), 225–26 and 238.
94. Gregory, *Collected Plays*, vol. 2, 220–24.
95. Gregory, *Collected Plays*, vol. 2, 254.
96. Anna Pilz, "'A Bad Master': Religion, Jacobitism, and the Politics of Representation in Lady Gregory's *The White Cockade*," in *Irish Women's Writing, 1878–1922*, ed. Anna Pilz and Whitney Standlee (Manchester: Manchester University Press, 2016), 140 and 148. Pilz considers *The White Cockade* in relation to the Jacobite revival of the late nineteenth century in particular, foregrounding the play's shortcomings as a piece of militant nationalist propaganda.
97. Pilz, "'A Bad Master'," 147–48.
98. Gregory, *Collected Plays*, vol. 2, 214.
99. Kohfeldt, *Lady Gregory*, 191.
100. Georges Denis Zimmermann, *Songs of Irish Rebellion: Irish Political Street Ballads and Rebel Songs, 1780–1900* (Dublin: Four Courts Press, 2002), 48.
101. Zimmermann, *Songs of Irish Rebellion*, 48.
102. Zimmermann, *Songs of Irish Rebellion*, 260.
103. Ruskin referred to this painting many times during his long career as art critic; in a letter to the *Times* on May 25, 1854 he wrote that the picture 'subdue[d] the severities of judgment into the sanctity of compassion'. Ruskin, 12.333–35, specifically 335.
104. Hill, *Lady Gregory*, 173.
105. Yeats, *Collected Letters*, vol. 3, 252.
106. Yeats, *Collected Letters*, vol. 3, 264.

107. Yeats, *Collected Letters*, vol. 3, 357.
108. Lady Augusta Gregory, *A Phantom's Pilgrimage, or Home Ruin* (London: Ridgeway, 1893), 1–2.
109. Gregory, *A Phantom's Pilgrimage*, 3.
110. Gregory, *A Phantom's Pilgrimage*, 5.
111. Gregory, *A Phantom's Pilgrimage*, 7.
112. Gregory, *A Phantom's Pilgrimage*, 8 and 10.
113. Gregory, *A Phantom's Pilgrimage*, 15.
114. Gregory, *A Phantom's Pilgrimage*, 13.
115. Anne Fogarty, "'A Woman of the House': Gender and Nationalism in the Writings of Augusta Gregory," in *Border Crossings: Irish Women Writers and National Identities*, ed. Kathryn Kirkpatrick (Tuscaloosa: University of Alabama Press, 2000), 110; Greg Winston, "Redefining Coole: Lady Gregory, Class Politics and the Land War," *Colby Quarterly* 37, no. 3 (2001): 216.
116. Hill, *Lady Gregory*, 70.
117. Gregory, *A Phantom's Pilgrimage*, 11–12.
118. Saddlemyer has cited a manuscript article in which Lady Gregory wrote: 'my formula has been "not working for Home Rule but preparing for it"'. Qtd. in Saddlemyer, "Augusta Gregory, Irish Nationalist," 34. Lady Gregory's words here repeated her earlier comments regarding the aims of the literary movement, which she voiced after the first plays of Moore, Martyn, and Yeats had been criticised in the contemporary press. Qtd. in Hill, *Lady Gregory*, 144. Lady Gregory jotted down the very same words regarding Home Rule in her diary in February 1900 and repeated them again in her biography of her nephew Hugh Lane decades later. Pethica, *Diaries*, 259; Gregory, *Hugh Lane*, 45.
119. Ruskin, *Fors Clavigera*, 27.161.
120. Sinéad Garrigan Mattar, "'Wage for Each People Her Hand Has Destroyed': Lady Gregory's Colonial Nationalism," *Irish University Review* 34, no. 1 (Spring/Summer 2004): 49–66.
121. Garrigan Mattar, "'Wage for Each People Her Hand Has Destroyed'," 49; Fogarty, "'A Woman of the House'," 110; Kiberd, *Inventing Ireland*, 83–95.
122. Lucy McDiarmid, *Poets and the Peacock Dinner: The Literary History of a Meal* (Oxford: Oxford University Press, 2016), 73.
123. Qtd. in Kohfeldt, *Lady Gregory*, 49.
124. Lady Augusta Gregory, "Arabi and His Household" (London: Kegan Paul, 1882). For Arabi's imprisonment and the pending execution, see Elizabeth Longford, "Lady Gregory and Wilfrid Scawen Blunt," in *Lady Gregory, Fifty Years After*, ed. Ann Saddlemyer and Colin Smythe (Gerrards Cross: Colin Smythe, 1987), 91.

125. Lady Augusta Gregory, "The Felons of Our Land," *Cornhill Magazine* (1900): 622–34.
126. Coxhead and Kohfeldt mention that the subject matter of *Grania* was biographical; Kohfeldt asserts that Lady Gregory attempted to 'explore' her 'own personality' in *Grania*. Richard Cave claims that *Grania* focussed on the figure of the woman who was torn between 'her private longing' and 'the demands of her public status'. Widening the circle, Murray and Leeney write about Lady Gregory's interrogation of the place of woman in Irish society, bringing the issue of Irish nationalism into a connection with these early plays of Lady Gregory. Leeney claims more overtly that *Kincora* and *Grania* interrogate 'the place of women in the creation of national discourses, and nationalist culture', a comment of particular significance for Leeney as she sees the Abbey Theatre as integral to the creation of an Irish 'national identity'. Dawn Duncan has drawn attention to Grania's 'journey of [self-] discovery', citing Edward A. Kopper's thoughts on the playwright being 'a champion of woman's rights in a male-dominated society'. Some of these ideas are rather problematic, especially those that connect Lady Gregory's personal experiences in Egypt to the nationalist discourse in Ireland at the beginning of the twentieth century. Nonetheless, these interpretations are useful insofar as they duly acknowledge Lady Gregory's unique literary voice. Coxhead, *Lady Gregory*, 146–47; Kohfeldt, *Lady Gregory*, 213; Richard Cave, "Revaluations: Representations of Women in the Tragedies of Gregory and Yeats," *Irish University Review* 34, no. 1 (Spring/Summer 2004): 130; Christopher Murray, *Twentieth-Century Irish Drama: Mirror up to Nation* (Manchester: Manchester University Press, 1997), 58; Cathy Leeney, *Irish Women Playwrights, 1900–1939: Gender and Violence on Stage* (New York: Peter Lang, 2010), 56 and 52; Dawn Duncan, "Lady Gregory and the Feminine Journey: *The Gaol Gate*, *Grania*, and *The Story Brought by Brigit*," *Irish University Review* 34, no. 1 (Spring/Summer 2004): 137, Kopper is qtd. on 139; and Edward A. Kopper, *Lady Isabella Persse Gregory* (Boston: Twayne, 1976), 48.
127. See, for instance, the critical reading in Paul Murphy, "Woman as Fantasy Object in Lady Gregory's Historical Tragedies," in *Women in Irish Drama: A Century of Authorship and Representation*, ed. Melissa Sihra (Basingstoke: Palgrave Macmillan, 2007), 39.
128. Gregory, *Collected Plays*, vol. 2, 55. References are to Lady Gregory's second version of *Kincora*.
129. Gregory, *Collected Plays*, vol. 2, 92.
130. Gregory, *Collected Plays*, vol. 2, 85 and 92.
131. Anthony Roche, *The Irish Dramatic Revival, 1899–1939* (London: Bloomsbury Methuen, 2015), 117.

132. Gregory, *Collected Plays*, vol. 2, 22.
133. Murray, *Twentieth-century Irish Drama*, 59.
134. Leeney, *Irish Women Playwrights*, 55.
135. Michael Byrnes, "Feis," in *Medieval Ireland: An Encyclopedia* (Routledge Revivals), ed. Seán Duffy (New York: Routledge, 2005), 165.
136. Leeney, *Irish Women Playwrights*, 44.
137. Gregory, *Collected Plays*, vol. 2, 99.
138. Gregory, *Collected Plays*, vol. 2, 103.
139. Ruskin, *Fors Clavigera*, 29.403; Ruskin, "Letter," 34.544.
140. Elizabeth Longford, *A Pilgrimage of Passion: The Life of Wilfrid Scawen Blunt* (London: Tauris Parke, 2007), 217.
141. "The Work of the Home Rule Union," *Journal of the Home Rule Union* 1, no. 1 (March 1888): 2.
142. "The Work of the Home Rule Union," 1–3.
143. Hill, *Lady Gregory*, 71–72.
144. Donal McCartney, "From Parnell to Pearse," in *The Course of Irish History*, ed. T. W. Moody and F. X. Martin (Dublin: Mercier, 1994), 294–312, 306. Alvin Jackson writes of "Potential Civil War in Ulster, and the Reality of Bloodshed on the Streets of Dublin," in *Home Rule: An Irish History* (Oxford: Oxford University Press, 2003), 137. Alan O'Day adds that 'Carson, Craig and Law ensured that Ulster's case would be heard, that the fight would be carried into the public arena in ways exceeding the polite norms of the Establishment political mores'. Alan O'Day, *Irish Home Rule, 1867–1921* (Manchester: Manchester University Press, 1998), 246. For further discussion of the Home Rule crisis, see Gabriel Doherty, ed., *The Home Rule Crisis, 1912–1914* (Cork: Mercier, 2014).
145. Gregory, *Seventy Years*, 544.
146. Gregory, *Seventy Years*, 548. Quoting Pearse, she writes here about the 'comradeship between the Gaelic League and the Irish National theatre and the Anglo-Irish writers', a comradeship which was intended to be promoted both by herself and Pearse: 'After all, we are all allies'.
147. *Joseph Holloway's Copybook*, Joseph Holloway Papers, MS 4439, National Library of Ireland.
148. Rumpf and Hepburn remark on the belief that republicans and socialists shared, namely, that armed uprising was necessary in the event of a European war. Nevertheless, this did not annul the differences between Arthur Griffith's Sinn Féin and James Connolly's Irish Socialist Republican Party. Griffith heavily criticised the 1913 Dublin Lockout, organised by the trade unions, because it jeopardised the future growth of the Irish capitalists on whom, he believed, rested the future economic

success of Ireland. E. Rumpf and A. C. Hepburn, *Nationalism and Socialism in Twentieth-Century Ireland* (Liverpool: Liverpool University Press, 1977), 13. Adrian Pimley also remarks on the difference between Connolly's socialist republic and what he calls Griffith's 'bourgeois republic'. Adrian Pimley, "The Working-Class Movement and the Irish Revolution, 1896–1923," in *The Revolution in Ireland, 1879–1923*, ed. D. G. Boyce (Dublin: Gill and Macmillan, 1988), 193–216, more specifically on 200.
149. For more on Unionist preparation against Home Rule, see Patrick Buckland, "Irish Unionism and the New Ireland," in *The Revolution in Ireland, 1879–1923*, ed. D. G. Boyce (Dublin: Gill and Macmillan, 1988), 71–90; more on the establishment of the Ulster Volunteer Force on 77.
150. For the growing spirit of militancy, see McCartney, 298–303.
151. Pimley, "The Working-Class Movement and the Irish Revolution, 1896–1923," 204.
152. James Kelly, "The Act of Union: Its Origins and Background," in *Acts of Union: The Causes, Contexts and Consequences of the Act of Union*, ed. Dáire Keogh and Kevin Whelan (Dublin: Four Courts, 2001), 48 and 50; Patrick M. Geoghegan, "The Irish House of Commons, 1799–1800," in *The Irish Act of Union, 1800: Bicentennial Essays*, ed. Michael Brown, Patrick M. Geoghegan, and James Kelly (Dublin: Irish Academic Press, 2003), 137–38; Patrick M. Geoghegan, *The Irish Act of Union: A Study in High Politics, 1798–1801* (Dublin: Gill and Macmillan, 1999), 63; and G. C. Bolton, *The Passing of the Irish Act of Union* (Oxford: Oxford University Press, 1966), 113. During the Union campaign between February and December 1799, 'the three 'C's' had been adopted to guarantee victory: compensation, catholic emancipation, and corruption'. Patrick M. Geoghegan, "The Making of the Union," in *Acts of Union: The Causes, Contexts and Consequences of the Act of Union*, ed. Dáire Keogh and Kevin Whelan (Dublin: Four Courts, 2001), 34–45, especially 40.
153. Lady Augusta Gregory, *The Collected Plays*, vol. 1 (New York: Oxford University Press, 1970), 265.
154. Lady Gregory put together *The Kiltartan History Book*, a new project of hers in antiquarian studies, which was a collection of folk tales on Irish history. She dedicated the collection to the students of the Catholic University. Robert Gregory was responsible for illustrating the book, including pictures of Daniel O'Connell, William of Orange, Napoleon, and William Gladstone. These curiously reveal Robert's imperial and his mother's reconciliatory politics at the same time.
155. Pilz, "'A Bad Master'," 138.

156. Gregory, *Collected Plays*, vol. 1, 186.
157. Gregory, *Collected Plays*, vol. 1, 188–89.
158. Gregory, *Collected Plays*, vol. 2, 115.
159. Gregory, *Collected Plays*, vol. 2, 120.
160. Gregory, *Collected Plays*, vol. 2, 120. However, Lady Gregory does not leave her character in shame: at the end of the play, McDonough is seen paying the keening women and those who carry his wife's coffin with his music.
161. Hill, *Lady Gregory*, 275.
162. Pethica, *Diaries*, 172.

Conclusion

Lady Gregory's world changed with the outbreak of the First World War in the summer of 1914. With a European War on the horizon, the enactment of the Home Rule Bill was postponed—the Suspensory Act was passed by Royal Assent in the autumn of 1914. After some deliberation, Lady Gregory's son Robert joined the 4th Battalion of the Connaught Rangers in 1915, before joining the Royal Flying Corps in support of the British war effort on the European Continent.[1] He was deployed as a flying officer to the Somme and Ypres battlefields in France during 1916. He impressed as a scout pilot and was made Flight Commander, continuing his valued service in Belgium. He was decorated with the *Légion d'Honneur* and the Military Cross for bravery in 1917. After a short visit to Coole Park, Robert was ordered back to the front, this time to Northern Italy, following the Italian Government's request that Britain should help the Italian army fight against the forces of the Austro-Hungarian Monarchy that were stationed in the territory. Shortly after, Robert's squadron was deployed near Venice where they carried out aerial combat missions and patrols of enemy lines. It was there, in that part of Italy of which his mother was so fond, that Robert lost his life in action on 23 January 1918. Three of Lady Gregory's nephews—Robert's first cousins—had died during the Great War: Rudolph Persse at Ypres and Geoffrey Persse at Gallipoli, both in 1915. Still riven with grief, Lady Gregory dedicated the last chapter of her autobiography, *Seventy Years*, to her son's life and legacy.[2] Quoting from letters of condolences, Lady Gregory depicted her son as an intelligent and courageous man, with a great sense of duty towards the country he served and towards the men who were under his command.

Her third nephew, Hugh Lane, died when the British-registered ocean liner *Lusitania* was sunk by German submarines off the coast of Co. Cork in 1915.[3] Not long before this, Lane had been appointed the new director of the National Gallery in Dublin, an appointment which restored his faith in the Dublin art world and repaired his waning relations with those in political power in Ireland. Following his appointment, Lane wrote a new codicil regarding his fine collection of European masterworks, bequeathing all the pictures to Dublin and naming his aunt, Lady Gregory, as Trustee of the collection. This codicil, however, was unwitnessed, which meant that the National Gallery of London could still consider itself the rightful inheritor of the paintings because the museum had in its possession Lane's earlier, witnessed, will. He had written and signed this will two years previously during the disputes between architects, aristocrats, and politicians over the housing of the collection in Dublin. Named as trustee of her nephew's picture collection in the later codicil, Lady Gregory felt obliged to fight for the paintings, a fight that took up much of her time and energies during the war years. As part of a campaign to secure the paintings for Dublin, she wrote up the biography of her nephew, later published by John Murray. She presented Hugh Lane as a serious patron of arts who had promoted those of artistic talent in Ireland with great enthusiasm. Lady Gregory wrote that he had organised an exhibition of Irish painting at the Guildhall in London, which, according to her estimates, was viewed by around 70,000 people during the eight weeks on display.[4] While organising this Irish Exhibition, Lane was also helping W. B. Yeats's father set up a studio at St. Stephen's Green, where he was to paint those whom Lady Gregory called her 'best countrymen': the likes of Hyde, Martyn, Plunkett, Synge, Russell, and O'Grady.[5] Lane had also facilitated the transfer of the G. F. Watts exhibition from London to Dublin in order to expose young artists to the best in contemporary art. The Watts exhibition, at which both Russell and Yeats's father gave lectures, was immensely popular with those moving in the world of art and literature in Dublin.[6]

Lady Gregory proudly recorded Watts's views of her *Cuchulain of Muirthemne*, Watt having declared that her 'wonderful Cuchulain' 'had been quite the book to us of this last year'.[7] As with her earlier writings, matters relating to the arts and social reform blend beautifully in her account of her nephew's life and achievements: O'Grady, Plunkett, and Lane are depicted as men who were involved in projects of different natures but who were working for a common goal. Lady Gregory made it very clear in the book that Lane's art collection was needed in Ireland in order to realise these goals: those of the co-operative improvement of Irish society and the aesthetic cultivation of Irish people, goals that Ruskin had earlier set before his countrymen in Britain and Ireland during the Victorian era. She set for herself the task of securing the Lane pictures, even if it involved an elongated dispute in the British Houses of Parliament. Her husband Sir William had done this before, fighting many parliamentary battles to secure valuable paintings or collection of paintings for the British viewing public. There was no reason to assume that Lady Gregory could not achieve some of the successes of earlier decades, this time for the sake of the social educational programme which had been developing recently in Ireland. To this end, she had secured the support of the Dublin Corporation, the Lord Mayor of Dublin, and the Learned and Educational Societies of Dublin (these included the Board of Education, the National University of Ireland, the Royal Hibernian Academy, and the Royal Society of Antiquarians).[8] These organisations, wrote Lady Gregory, had 'appealed to Parliament to pass a Bill legalising the codicil, as it had already done in the case of wills signed without a witness by soldiers who lost their lives in the War'.[9] The result was not what those involved in the project were hoping for, as Lane's pictures remained in London. Nonetheless, her participation in meetings and debates allowed Lady Gregory to relieve her mind of the anxieties over Robert's involvement in the European theatres of war.

With Robert's death in January 1918, Lady Gregory's residence in Coole Park and the future of the family demesne became uncertain. Robert had written a brief will, in haste, on his way to the French frontline, a will in which he had left the house and the demesne to his wife Margaret.[10] Ironically, Lady Gregory's acceptance of the legitimacy of unwitnessed wills of those who been killed during the Great War—which she had used as a claim in her fight for her nephew's pictures—turned against her when she tried to retain the family demesne in Coole Park. Prior to his engagement in the British war effort, Robert had been handling the affairs of the estate, which included the selling of both the land and the house to the Congested Districts Board.[11] Lady Gregory had accepted the need to sell some of the land to help tenants, especially land that she had bought as a shooting ground for Robert and his Oxford University friends during the hunting season in Ireland. The Congested

Districts Board's first offer, which included buying the house, was declined because Lady Gregory was not ready to part with the house in which many of the greatest names of the Irish cultural and literary revival had gathered to share their views on the future of Ireland. The family considered the Board's next offer to buy the land but not the house, issued in the winter of 1914, but the amount offered would not have covered the costs of keeping the house, so eventually the new offer was turned down. Margaret, who was left in charge of the land and the house after Robert's death, felt little duty or desire to keep the Coole estate, regarding it an unnecessary financial burden on the family. Margaret was also worried about the safety of the family; during the Anglo-Irish War the family experienced atrocities both from the Irish Republican Army and the Black and Tans. After long deliberation, the land was sold in 1920, the woods in 1921 and the house in 1927. Lady Gregory tried to hinder the selling of the house. She even offered to buy it herself but her income from writing and lecturing could not cover the upkeep of her beloved home. Finally, the house, with its great collection of art works and the invaluable collection of its library, was sold to the Government of the Irish Free State in 1927. Lady Gregory feared for the future of her home and sat down to compose *Coole*, published in 1931, in which she bade farewell to the Coole estate and paid homage to the artistic legacy of the old house. She was right to be fearful as eight years after her death the house was demolished; its bricks were sold to former tenants as house building material. The history of the house came to resemble her parable about artists as candlestickmakers, a parable she had borrowed from Jesus's words from the Bible, which had been used in public discourse by Ruskin, Wesley, and the Pre-Raphaelites. The bricks of her house became building blocks of other people's homes in much the same manner as her own life as an artist had become a building block on which future generations of artists could build their lives and trade.

Yeats, for whom Coole Park had meant so much, supported Lady Gregory in her efforts to retain the house and demesne in the family; if not for Robert, then for Richard's sake. In a way, Yeats was more at home in the house than Robert had ever been, taking the Master's Bedroom even when Robert was at home on leave from school or during his exam periods, a habit which generated some family argument within the Gregory household in the early days of the Irish Literary Revival. Yeats, however, was unable to lend Lady Gregory the support that she needed during the discussions with Margaret over the future of Coole

Park because he was getting married around the same time, starting a new life for himself and his wife, Georgie Hyde-Lees, whom he married in 1917. Although he took Thoor Ballylee, near Coole Park, for his abode in Ireland—almost certainly a gesture of friendship towards a lifelong friend and companion—Yeats spent most of his time in England, amongst others in the circles of Ezra Pound at Stone Cottage, effectively leaving Lady Gregory to handle the affairs of the Abbey Theatre alone.[12] At the Abbey, the Ruskinian echoes of the early period of the Irish Literary Revival were being drowned out by the battle cries of wars in and outside Ireland. The Ruskinian principles of education and entertainment, which the first directors applied to most of the affairs of the Abbey Theatre, were being put to a test by historic circumstances which were, Lady Gregory wrote in *Seventy Years*, 'far sadder' than previous ones because now 'brother [was] against brother, friend [was] against friend'.[13] Struggling against historic circumstances while working to preserve her home and retaining her nephew's paintings, Lady Gregory wrote a long letter to George Bernard Shaw on 15 September 1915:

> I am not very light-hearted, for Robert is carrying out his desire of this time last year, and is going to the war. [...] Then the matter of Hugh's pictures gives me a good deal of work, but so far as the Corporation providing a building I am full of hope; [...]. I am hoping also that the best pictures from Lindsey House will be brought over to our N.[ational] G.[allery] and not sold for its benefit. Dublin should be a great Art Centre then. I am very anxious still about a successor to Hugh at the National Gallery. [...] As to the Abbey, [...] I felt that if we can keep it alive till the end of the war and the beginning of Home Rule, we can give it over to the nation, buildings, company and stock in trade. We should give it into the hands of the trustees, more or less Nationalist, anyhow those who are anxious to help the new government on, and let them do their best with it. Yeats approves of this idea and so does Bailey, and that makes us very anxious to keep or get it solvent, and not let the Company scatter.[14]

According to Lady Gregory, the plan was to keep the Abbey Theatre in its original form until the enactment of the long overdue Government of Ireland Act, postponed by the Suspensory Act of 1914. What she called a 'horrible and interminable' war, however, continued and she soon realised that keeping the theatre solvent and its company together during the war years and during the revolutionary period that followed was more difficult than she had imagined.[15] John Ervine, J. Augustus Keogh, and Fred

O'Donovan followed one another in quick succession as theatre directors, none of them able to solve the financial and the repertory problems. Even Ezra Pound (perhaps especially Ezra Pound), whom Yeats suggested for the managerial role of the theatre, could not have solved the institution's increasing number of problems, including the departure of a group of young players who were unsatisfied both with the daily running and the general politics of the theatre during the war years.[16]

Lady Gregory and Yeats had been advocates of reconciliatory politics since the early days but the Easter Rising of 1916, as well as the revolutionary period that followed the end of the Great War, created historical circumstances in which the politics of reconciliation—as Lady Gregory had first conceived it, based on her understanding of Ruskin's social policies—could not be maintained as the core principles of the Abbey Theatre. As Lauren Arrington observes, pressure was mounting in the new historical scenario that the Abbey Theatre, as Ireland's National Theatre, should shape its politics along the sentiments of the advanced nationalist majority of Irish society, dramatically increasing in number and militant display during the war years.[17] Shaping its politics according to the sentiments of the majority, however, would have meant for the Abbey Theatre giving up its early principles of political neutrality, an unwelcome development in Lady Gregory's eyes.[18] As an advocate of progressive social reform, Lady Gregory was sceptical about the possible outcome of a militant uprising in Ireland. This was so despite the fact that her own work for the literary and language movement was immensely influential for those who became the leaders of the Easter Rising in 1916. Pearse, Connolly, MacDonagh (three of the seven signatories of the Proclamation of the Irish Republic, read out by Pearse in front of the General Post Office on Easter Monday, 24 April 1916) had grown up on the legends of Finn McCumhail and Cuchulain of the Red Branch Knights of Ulster, gathered by Samuel Ferguson, Standish O'Grady, and Lady Gregory during the early period of the Irish Literary Revival. Pearse and MacDonagh even went as far as adapting the warrior ethos of the ancient Celtic legends of Finn and Cuchulain to the educational programme of St. Enda's School and to the military programme of the Irish Volunteers and of the Irish Republican Brotherhood.[19] Yeats himself feared for the future of the literary movement in the aftermath of the Easter Rising and its brutal suppression by the British government: 'now everybody in Ireland will turn against idealist politics and even our theatre and our literature'.[20] These were his private sentiments at the time even though he later immortalised MacDonagh, Connolly, MacBride, and Pearse (whom he called earlier a 'dangerous man' for having 'the vertigo of self-sacrifice') in his poems 'Easter 1916', 'Sixteen Dead Men', and 'The Rose Tree'.[21] At the time, however, Yeats was disturbed by the fact that by executing the leaders of the Easter Rising, the British government had 'allowed them to make their own ballads'.[22] By this Yeats had in mind the notion of Pearse, MacDonagh, and Connolly joining the pantheon of Irish martyrs and rebel heroes, men whose memories would be kept alive in many a ballad song, alongside those of their own rebel heroes: the United Irishmen, Wolfe Tone, and Robert Emmet. These memories Yeats himself had cherished once, being the President of the '98 Centennial Committee for Great Britain and France, established to commemorate the centenary of the United Irishmen republican uprising of 1798. Lady Gregory replied to Yeats's anxious sentiments at the time with the following words: 'all is unrest and is discontent, there is nowhere for the imagination to rest; but there must be some spiritual building possible just as after Parnell's fall, but perhaps more intense'.[23]

Spiritual building might have been possible at some point during the years that followed the Rising but the actual rebuilding of the country had little chance of being realised. After the Great War Lady Gregory had to witness the destruction of many of the achievements of the various progressive social reform movements of the early twentieth century and of the homes of those who were the driving forces behind these social reform movements in Ireland. The Irish War of Independence of 1919–1921 and the Civil War of 1922–1923, which followed the signing of the Anglo-Irish Treaty in December 1921, destroyed many of the achievements of the Co-operative Movement in particular. During the Anglo-Irish War, the British army attacked, looted, and burnt down many co-operative mills and creameries. Shocked by the extent of the destruction of both the objects themselves and the people who had owned them, George Russell, chief ideologist of the Co-operative Movement, issued an appeal to the British people to demand investigations into the matter. In *A Plea for Justice: Being a Demand for a Public Enquiry into the Attacks on Co-operative Societies in Ireland*, Russell provided a long list of damages suffered by small co-operative establishments, a list which clearly demonstrated the extent of the destruction caused by the British armed forces. Russell went further when writing the following:

We charge certain unknown agents of the Crown with indiscriminate wrecking and burning of our societies. The Chief Secretary retorts by saying that they are centres of revolutionary propaganda.[24]

The British army were, in fact, demolishing the buildings of the co-operative societies because the buildings were regarded as hiding places for the ammunition of the Irish Republican Army engaged in a guerrilla war against the British army's Auxiliaries. Lady Gregory detested the reprisals carried out by the Black and Tans, as they came to be called, for Irish Republican Army ambushes of their garrisons, in much the same way as she abhorred what Innes calls the 'harsh and repressive measures of the Free State Government'.[25] Lady Gregory thought the wrecking of the co-operative mills and creameries a serious, and quite possibly a final blow to achieving a peaceful social transition in Ireland, a goal for which she had been working during the first decade of the twentieth century alongside those friends of hers who shared her Ruskinian ideals.

Ruskin's social ideals of improving the living and working conditions of all social classes while keeping intact the existing social order, in which the aristocracy were to act as guardians of peace and custodians of knowledge, were quickly vanishing during the revolutionary period. The co-operative establishments were not the only targets of violent raids and ambushes in Ireland. As Lady Gregory herself experienced, the ancestral homes of the Anglo-Irish aristocracy were being burned and looted by the Irish Republican Army, because they were considered to be symbols of the established social order, regardless of the extent of the owner's social engagement. The family homes of Horace Plunkett and George Moore had been attacked and burned, leaving Lady Gregory fearing for her own life at Coole Park. Although her home had been attacked once, she was pleased to note that the good relations that she had built with her tenants and with the Catholic farmers living in her neighbourhood protected her home during the period of revolutionary turmoil. Detesting the pervasive violence in the country during the revolutionary period, she had offered to establish a new party, 'Glan molais', or 'Without malice'.[26] Once again, this was to promote ideals of progressive social and political reform, suggesting that, even amidst the political turmoil Ireland was experiencing at the time, she still believed in the possibility of changing the course of Ireland's violent history by predominantly peaceful means.

Notes

1. Judith Hill, *Lady Gregory: An Irish Life* (Stroud: Sutton, 2005), 283 and 285. For Robert's military career, see Hill, *Lady Gregory*, 283–98.
2. Lady Augusta Gregory, *Seventy Years, Being the Autobiography of Lady Gregory* (Gerrards Cross: Colin Smythe, 1973), 550–59.
3. Hill, *Lady Gregory*, 281.
4. Lady Augusta Gregory, *Hugh Lane* (Gerrards Cross: Colin Smythe, 1973), 49. Lady Gregory wrote here: 'Ireland had already, for a little time, been joined in men's mind with literature and drama as well as with the old political story, and now we found ourselves questioned with a new interest about our painters'.
5. Gregory, *Hugh Lane*, 35–36. Lane also commissioned John B. Yeats to paint portraits of Wyndham and Redmond. Gregory, *Hugh Lane*, 34.
6. Gregory, *Hugh Lane*, 79.
7. Gregory, *Hugh Lane*, 79–80.
8. Gregory, *Hugh Lane*, 230–31.
9. Gregory, *Hugh Lane*, 234.
10. Quoted in Foster, R. F. *W. B. Yeats, A Life: The Arch-Poet*, vol. 2 (Oxford: Oxford University Press, 2003), 692. Of course, Lady Gregory had the right to live in the house during her lifetime because of her husband's will dating back to 1892.
11. For the selling of Coole Park, see Hill, *Lady Gregory*, 239–40, 276, 315, 321, 345–47 and Foster, vol. 2, 173, 335, 350.
12. For Lady Gregory and Yeats's declining interest in the affairs of the Abbey Theatre, see Mary Lou Kohfeldt, *Lady Gregory, the Woman Behind the Irish Literary Renaissance* (London: Deutsch, 1984), 252.
13. Gregory, *Seventy Years*, 545.
14. Dan H. Laurence and Nicholas Grene, eds., *Shaw, Lady Gregory and the Abbey* (Gerrards Cross: Colin Smythe, 1993), 97–99. Similar sentiments in a letter from her to Yeats on July 8, 1916: 'We can't let the Abbey die on the verge of Home Rule, or let it die at all after all the work we have put into it'. Qtd. in Hill, *Lady Gregory*, 391.
15. Qtd. Hill, *Lady Gregory*, 295.
16. For Ezra Pound, see Foster, vol. 2, 53; Hill, *Lady Gregory*, 391.
17. Lauren Arrington, *W. B. Yeats, the Abbey Theatre, Censorship, and the Irish State* (Oxford: Oxford University Press, 2010), 20–21.
18. Arrington, *W. B. Yeats*, 23.
19. Elaine Sisson, *Pearse's Patriots* (Cork: Cork University Press, 2005), 78–98; Joost Augusteijn, *Patrick Pearse: The Making of a Revolutionary* (Basingstoke: Palgrave Macmillan, 2010), 146–215. Augusteijn writes about the importance of 'character formation' in the educational

programme of St. Enda's. This was to be achieved with the help of the formative power of the arts, especially literature and theatre.
20. Qtd. in Gregory, *Seventy Years*, 549.
21. For more on the composition of these poems and their publication history, see Tom Paulin, *Minotaur: Poetry and the Nation State* (London: Faber and Faber, 1992), 133–50. Yeats is quoted here writing to Clement Shorter: 'Please be very careful with the Rebellion poem: Lady Gregory asked me not to send it you until we had finished our dispute with the authorities about the Lane pictures. She was afraid of it getting about and damaging us and she is not timid'. Paulin, *Minotaur*, 138.
22. Yeats qtd. in Gregory, *Seventy Years*, 547.
23. Gregory, *Seventy Years*, 548.
24. George Russell, *A Plea for Justice: Being a Demand for a Public Enquiry into the Attacks on Co-operative Societies in Ireland* (Dublin: Irish Homestead Ltd, 1921), 4.
25. C. L. Innes, *Woman and Nation in Irish Literature and Society* (London: Harvester Wheatsheaf, 1993), 161.
26. Innes, *Woman and Nation in Irish Literature and Society*, 161.

Bibliography

Primary Sources

Unpublished

Gregory, Lady Augusta. *Excerpts from her readings*, Lady Augusta Gregory Papers, Albert A. and Henry W. Berg Collection, New York Public Library.

———. *Holograph Diary, 1880–1882*. Gregory Family Papers, Special Collections and Archives Division, Robert W. Woodruff Library, Emory University.

———. *Typewritten Diaries, 1882–1892*. Lady Augusta Gregory Papers, Albert A. and Henry W. Berg Collection, New York Public Library.

———. *Sketchbooks*, 3032 TX—3039 TX, National Library of Ireland.

Henderson, William. *Newspaper Cuttings*, MS 1729—MS 1732 National Library of Ireland.

Joseph Holloway's Copybook, Joseph Holloway Papers, MS 4439, National Library of Ireland.

Published

Gregory, Lady Augusta. *A Phantom's Pilgrimage, or Home Ruin*. London: Ridgeway, 1893.

———. "Arabi and His Household." London: Kegan Paul, 1882.

———. *Coole*. Dublin: Cuala Press, 1931.

———. *Cuchulain of Muirthemne: The Story of the Men of the Red Branch of Ulster*. Gerrards Cross: Colin Smythe, 1975.

———. *Gods and Fighting Men*. Gerrards Cross: Colin Smythe, 1970.
———. "Ireland, Real and Ideal." *The Nineteenth Century* 44 (November 1898): 762–82.
———. "Letter." *An Claidheamh Soluis*, December 2, 1899, 605.
———. *Our Irish Theatre: A Chapter of Autobiography*. Gerrards Cross: Colin Smythe, 1972.
———. "Raftery's Grave." *An Claidheamh Soluis*, September 8, 1900, 406.
———. *Seventy Years, Being the Autobiography of Lady Gregory*. Gerrards Cross: Colin Smythe, 1974.
———. *Sir Hugh Lane: His Life and Legacy*. Gerrards Cross: Colin Smythe, 1973.
———. *The Collected Plays*. 4 vols. Edited by Ann Saddlemyer. New York: Oxford University Press, 1970.
———. "The Felons of Our Land." *Cornhill Magazine*, 1900, 625–34.
———. *The Kiltartan History Book*. Dublin: Maunsel, 1909.
———. *The Kiltartan Molière*. Dublin: Maunsel, 1910.
———. "The Poet Raftery." *The Argosy*, January 1901, 44–58.
———, ed. *Ideals in Ireland*. London: Unicorn, 1901.
———, ed. *Mr. Gregory's Letter-Box, 1813–1830*. London: Smith and Elder, 1898.
———, ed. *Sir William Gregory*. London: Murray, 1894.
Gregory, Sir William. *Arundel Society*. Pamphlet, May 1887. Reprinted from *The Nineteenth Century*, April 1884. Gregory Family Papers, Special Collections and Archives Division, Robert W. Woodruff Library, Emory University.
Pethica, James, ed. *Lady Gregory's Diaries, 1892–1902*. Gerrards Cross: Colin Smythe, 1996.

Secondary Sources

Alexander, Edward. *Matthew Arnold, John Ruskin and the Modern Temper*. Columbus, OH: Ohio State University Press, 1973.
Anderson, R. A. *With Horace Plunkett in Ireland*. London: Macmillan, 1935.
Andrews, Richard. "Molière, *Commedia dell'arte*, and the Question of Influence in Early Modern European Theatre." *The Modern Language Review* 100, no. 2 (2005): 444–60.
Archer, William, and Harley Granville-Barker. *Schemes and Estimates for a National Theatre*. New York: Duffield, 1908.
Arensberg, Conrad M., and Solon T. Kinball. *Family and Community in Ireland*. Cambridge, MA: Harvard University Press, 1968.
Arrington, Lauren. *W. B. Yeats, the Abbey Theatre, Censorship, and the Irish State*. Oxford: Oxford University Press, 2010.
Atwood, Sarah. *Ruskin's Educational Ideals*. Farnham: Ashgate, 2011.

Augusteijn, Joost. *Patrick Pearse: The Making of a Revolutionary*. Basingstoke: Palgrave Macmillan, 2010.
Barringer, Tim. *The Pre-Raphaelites*. London: Weidenfeldt, 1998.
Bawson, Anthony B. *Watching Shakespeare*. London: Macmillan, 1988.
Bennett, Mary. *Artists of the Pre-Raphaelite Circle: The First Generation*. London: Lund Humphries, 1988.
Bergmann Loiseaux, Elizabeth. *Yeats and the Visual Arts*. Syracuse: Syracuse University Press, 2003.
Berrige, G. R. *British Diplomacy in Turkey, 1853 to the Present: A Study in the Evolution of the Resident Embassy*. Leiden: Martinus Nijhoff, 2009.
Bhreathnach Lynch, Síghle. "The Influence of J. M. Synge on the Art of Jack B. Yeats and Paul Henry." In *Back to the Present—Forward to the Past: Irish Writing and History since 1798*, vol. 1, edited by Patricia Lynch, Joachim Fisher, and Brian Coates, 209–18. Amsterdam: Rodopi, 2006.
Birch, Dinah. "Ruskin's Revised Eighteenth Century." In *The Victorians and the Eighteenth Century: Reassessing the Tradition*, edited by Francis O'Gorman and Katherine Turner, 163–81. Aldershot: Ashgate, 2004.
Bolger, Patrick. *The Irish Co-operative Movement*. Dublin: Cahill, 1977.
Bolton, G. C. *The Passing of the Irish Act of Union*. Oxford: Oxford University Press, 1966.
Booth, Michael R. *Victorian Spectacular Theatre, 1850–1910*. London: Routledge, 1981.
Bourgeois, Maurice. *John Millington Synge and the Irish Theatre*. London: Constable, 1913.
Bowen, Desmond. *Souperism: Myth or Reality*. Cork: Mercier, 1970.
———. *The Protestant Crusade in Ireland, 1800–70*. Dublin: Macmillan, 1978.
Boylan, Thomas, and Timothy P. Foley. *Political Economy and Colonial Ireland*. London: Routledge, 1992.
Broughall, Quentin. "A Careful Hellenism and a Reckless Roman-ness: the Gladstone-Disraeli Rivalry in the Context of Classics." In *Gladstone: Ireland and Beyond*, edited by Mary E. Daly and K. Theodore Hoppen, 142–56. Dublin: Four Courts Press, 2011.
Brown, Karen E. *The Yeats Circle: Verbal and Visual Relations in Ireland, 1880–1939*. Farnham: Ashgate, 2011.
Brown, Terence. *The Life of W. B. Yeats*. Dublin: Gill and Macmillan, 1999.
Buckland, Patrick. "Irish Unionism and the New Ireland." In *The Revolution in Ireland, 1879–1923*, edited by D. G. Boyce, 71–90. Dublin: Gill and Macmillan, 1988.
Burd, Van Akin, ed. *John Ruskin and Rose La Touche: Her Unpublished Diaries of 1861 and 1867*. Oxford: Clarendon, 1979.
Burwash, Nathaniel, ed. *Wesley's Doctrinal Standards. Part 1: Sermons*. Toronto: Briggs, 1881.

Byrne, Dawson. *The Story of Ireland's National Theatre*. New York: Haskell House, 1971.
Carr, Comyns. *Some Eminent Victorians*. London: Duckworth, 1908.
Cataldi, Melita. "Lady Gregory's Sketchbooks." In *Roots and Beginnings*, edited by Pietro Deandrea and Viktoria Tchernikova, 303–16. Venezia: Cafoscarina, 2003.
Catalogue of Printed Books formerly in the Library at Coole, the Property of the Lady Gregory Estate——Sotheby Auction Catalogue for 20 and 21 March 1972. London: Sotheby and Co., 1972.
Cave, Richard. "Revaluations: Representations of Women in the Tragedies of Gregory and Yeats." *Irish University Review* 34, no. 1 (Spring/Summer 2004): 122–32.
Chapman, Don. *Oxford Playhouses: High and Low Drama in a University City*. Hatfield: University of Hertfordshire Press, 2008.
Cole, G. D. H. *A Century of Co-operation*. London: Allen and Unwin, 1944.
Coxhead, Elizabeth. *Lady Gregory: A Literary Portrait*. London: Macmillan, 1961.
Deane, Seamus. *Celtic Revivals: Essays in Modern Irish Literature, 1880–1980*. London: Faber, 1985.
Denman, Peter. *Samuel Ferguson: The Literary Achievement*. Gerrards Cross: Colin Smythe, 1990.
Denvir, Bernard. *The Late Victorians: Art, Design and Society 1852–1910*. London: Longmans, 1986.
De Petris, Carla. "Lady Gregory and Italy: A Lasting and Profitable Relationship." *Irish University Review* 34, no. 1 (Spring/Summer 2004): 37–48.
Dessain, Charles Stephen. *John Henry Newman*. London: Nelson, 1966.
Dobson, Michael. *Shakespeare and Amateur Performance: A Cultural History*. Cambridge: Cambridge University Press, 2011.
Doherty, Gabriel, ed. *The Home Rule Crisis, 1912–1914*. Cork: Mercier, 2014.
Donovan, Katie. "Let Us Now Praise Famous Women." In *Lady Gregory Autumn Gatherings, Reflections at Coole*, edited by Seán Tobin and assoc. ed. Lois Tobin, 111–7. Galway: Lady Gregory Autumn Gathering, 2000.
Dorn, Karen. *Players and the Painted Stage: The Theatre of W. B. Yeats*. Brighton, Sussex: Harvester, 1984.
Duncan, Dawn. "Lady Gregory and the Feminine Journey: *The Gaol Gate, Grania*, and *The Story Brought by Brigit*." *Irish University Review* 34, no. 1 (Spring/Summer 2004): 133–43.
Eagles, Stuart. *After Ruskin: The Social and Political Legacies of a Victorian Prophet, 1870–1920*. Oxford: Oxford University Press, 2011.

Edwards, Philip. *Threshold of a Nation*. Cambridge: Cambridge University Press, 1979.
Eliot, George. *Middlemarch*. Oxford: Oxford University Press, 1998.
Ellmann, Richard. *Oscar Wilde*. London: Hamilton, 1987.
Evangelista, Stefano. *British Aestheticism and Ancient Greece: Hellenism, Reception and Gods in Exile*. Basingstoke: Palgrave Macmillan, 2009.
Fahy, Sister Mary de Lourdes. "Lady Gregory—A Local Habitation and a Name." In *Lady Gregory Autumn Gatherings, Reflections at Coole*, edited by Seán Tobin and assoc. ed. Lois Tobin, 5–10. Galway: Lady Gregory Autumn Gathering, 2000.
Farrell Moran, Seán. *Patrick Pearse and the Politics of Redemption*. Washington, DC: Catholic University of America Press, 1994.
Finberg, A. J., arr. "Preface." In *The Complete Inventory of the Drawings of the Turner Bequest*, vol. 1, v–xviii. London: Darling and Son, 1909.
Finlay, Rev. T. A., S. J. "The Usurer in Ireland." *The New Ireland Review* 1 (July 1894): 304–16.
Flannery, James W. *W. B. Yeats and the Idea of a Theatre*. New Haven: Yale University Press, 1976.
———. "W. B. Yeats, Gordon Craig and the Visual Arts of the Theatre." In *Yeats and the Theatre*, edited by Robert O'Driscoll and Lorna Reynolds, 82–108. London: Macmillan, 1975.
Flint, Kate. *The Victorians and the Victorian Imagination*. Cambridge: Cambridge University Press, 2000.
Fogarty, Anne. "'A Woman of the House': Gender and Nationalism in the Writings of Augusta Gregory." In *Border Crossings: Irish Women Writers and National Identities*, edited by Kathryn Kirkpatrick, 100–22. Tuscaloosa: University of Alabama Press, 2000.
Foster, R. F. *W. B. Yeats, A Life: The Apprentice Mage*, vol. 1. Oxford: Oxford University Press, 1998.
———. *W. B. Yeats, A Life: The Arch-Poet*, vol. 2. Oxford: Oxford University Press, 2003.
———. *The Irish Story*. London: Penguin, 2002.
———. *Vivid Faces: The Revolutionary Generation in Ireland, 1890–1923*. New York: Norton and Company, 2015.
Fraser, Hilary. *Women Writing Art History in the Nineteenth Century: Looking Like a Woman*. Cambridge: Cambridge University Press, 2014.
Frazier, Adrian. *Behind the Scenes: Yeats, Horniman, and the Struggle for the Abbey Theatre*. Berkeley: University of California Press, 1990.
———. "The Ideology of the Abbey Theatre." In *The Cambridge Companion to Twentieth-Century Irish Drama*, edited by Shaun Richards, 33–60. Cambridge: Cambridge University Press, 2004.

Frost, Mark. *The Lost Companions and John Ruskin's Guild of St. George.* London: Anthem, 2014.
Garrigan Mattar, Sinéad. *Primitivism, Science, and the Irish Revival.* Oxford: Clarendon, 2004.
———. "'Wage for Each People Her Hand Has Destroyed': Lady Gregory's Colonial Nationalism." *Irish University Review* 34, no. 1 (Spring/Summer 2004): 49–66.
Geoghegan, Patrick M. *The Irish Act of Union: A Study in High Politics, 1798–1801.* Dublin: Gill and Macmillan, 1999.
———. "The Irish House of Commons, 1799–1800." In *The Irish Act of Union, 1800: Bicentennial Essays*, edited by Michael Brown, Patrick M. Geoghegan, and James Kelly, 129–43. Dublin: Irish Academic Press, 2003.
———. "The Making of the Union." In *Acts of Union: The Causes, Contexts and Consequences of the Act of Union*, edited by Dáire Keogh and Kevin Whelan, 34–45. Dublin: Four Courts Press, 2001.
Gilley, Sheridan. *Newman and His Age.* London: Darton, 1990.
Glynn, Joseph A. "Irish Convent Industries." *The New Ireland Review* 1 (June 1894): 236–44.
Graham, Colin. *Ideologies of Epic: Nation, Empire and Victorian Epic Poetry.* Manchester: Manchester University Press, 1998.
Gregory, James. *Reformers, Patrons and Philanthropists: The Cowper-Temples and High Politics in Victorian England.* London: Tauris, 2010.
Grene, Nicholas. *Synge: A Critical Study of the Plays.* London: Macmillan, 1985.
Grieve, Alastair. "Rossetti and the Scandal of Art for Art's Sake in the 1860s." In *After the Pre-Raphaelites*, edited by Elizabeth Prettejohn, 17–35. Manchester: Manchester University Press, 1999.
Guest, Montague J. "Introduction." In *Lady Charlotte Schreiber's Journals*, edited by Montague J. Guest, vii–xxx. London: John Lane, 1911.
Guild Howard, William, ed., trans., and com. *Laokoon: Lessing, Herder and Goethe.* New York: Henry Holt, 1910.
Halio, J. L. *A Midsummer Night's Dream.* Shakespeare in Production Series. Manchester: Manchester University Press, 2003.
Haskell, Francis. *Rediscoveries in Art.* London: Phaidon, 1980.
Heinrich, Anselm. "Ruskin and the National Theatre." In *Ruskin, the Theatre and Victorian Visual Culture*, edited by Anselm Heinrich, Katherine Newey, and Jeffrey Richards, 97–113. Basingstoke: Palgrave Macmillan, 2009.
Heinrich, Anselm, Katherine Newey, and Jeffrey Richards, eds., *Ruskin, the Theatre and Victorian Visual Culture.* Basingstoke: Palgrave Macmillan, 2009.
Helland, Janice. "Embroidered Spectacle: Celtic Revival as Aristocratic Display." In *The Irish Revival Reappraised*, edited by Betsey Taylor FitzSimon and James H. Murphy, 94–105. Dublin: Four Courts Press, 2004.

Hewison, Robert, Ian Warrell, and Stephen Wildman. *Ruskin, Turner and the Pre-Raphaelites.* London: Tate Gallery, 2000.
Hill, Donald L. "Critical and Explanatory Notes." In Walter Pater, *The Renaissance,* edited by Donald L. Hill, 277–464. Berkeley: University of California Press, 1980.
Hill, Judith. "Finding a Voice: Augusta Gregory, Raftery, and Cultural Nationalism, 1899–1900." *Irish University Review* 34, no. 1 (Spring/Summer 2004): 21–36.
———. *Lady Gregory, An Irish Life.* Stroud: Sutton, 2005.
Hilton, Tim. *John Ruskin: The Later Years.* New Haven: Yale University Press, 2000.
Hobson, J. A. *John Ruskin, Social Reformer.* London: Nisbet, 1899.
Hogan, Robert, and Michael O'Neill, eds. *Joseph Holloway's Abbey Theatre.* Carbondale: South Illinois University Press, 2009.
Hogan, Robert, Richard Burnham, and Daniel P. Poteet, eds. *The Abbey Theatre: The Rise of the Realists, 1910–1915.* Dublin: Dolmen, 1979.
Hough, Graham. *The Last Romantics.* London: Duckworth, 1983.
Holy Bible. New International Version. London: Hodder, 2001.
Hunt, William Holman. *Pre-Raphaelitism and the Pre-Raphaelite Brotherhood,* vol. 2. London, New York: Macmillan, 1905.
Innes, Christopher. *Edward Gordon Craig.* Cambridge: Cambridge University Press, 1983.
Innes, C. L. *Woman and Nation in Irish Literature and Society.* London: Harvester Wheatsheaf, 1993.
Irwin, Francina. "Amusement or Instruction? Watercolour Manuals and the Women Amateur." In *Women in the Victorian Art World,* ed. Clarissa Campbell Orr, 149–66. Manchester: Manchester University Press, 1995.
Jackson, Alvin. *Home Rule: An Irish History.* Oxford: Oxford University Press, 2003.
James, Henry., *Italian Hours.* London: Penguin, 1995.
Jenkins, Brian. *Sir William Gregory of Coole: The Biography of an Anglo-Irishman.* Gerrards Cross: Colin Smythe, 1986.
———. "The Marriage." In *Lady Gregory, Fifty Years After,* edited by Ann Saddlemyer and Colin Smythe, 70–84. Gerrards Cross: Colin Smythe, 1987.
Jenkyns, Richard. *The Victorians and Ancient Greece.* Cambridge, MA: Harvard University Press, 1981.
Katz Clarke, Brenna. *The Emergence of the Irish Peasant Play at the Abbey Theatre.* Ann Arbor: UMI Research Press, 1982.
Kelly, James. "The Act of Union: Its Origins and Background." In *Acts of Union: The Causes, Contexts and Consequences of the Act of Union,* edited by Dáire Keogh and Kevin Whelan, 46–66. Dublin: Four Courts Press, 2001.
Kennedy, Liam. *Colonialism, Religion and Nationalism in Ireland.* Belfast: Queen's University of Belfast, 1996.

Kiberd, Declan. *Inventing Ireland*. London: Vintage, 1996.
———. *Irish Classics*. Cambridge, MA: Harvard University Press, 2001.
King, Carla. "Co-operation and Rural Development: Plunkett's Approach." In *Rural Change in Ireland*, edited by John Davis, 45–57. Belfast: Institute of Irish Studies, QUB, 1999.
Kohfeldt, Mary Lou. *Lady Gregory, the Woman Behind the Irish Literary Renaissance*. London: Deutsch, 1984.
Kohfeldt Stevenson, Mary Lou. "The Cloud of Witnesses." In *Lady Gregory, Fifty Years After*, edited by Ann Saddlemyer and Colin Smythe, 56–69. Gerrards Cross: Colin Smythe, 1987.
Kopper, Edward A. *Lady Isabella Persse Gregory*. Boston: Twayne, 1976.
Kuch, Peter, ed. *G. W. Russell—A.E: Writings on Literature and Art*. In *Collected Works*, vol. 4. Gerrards Cross: Colin Smythe, 2011.
Landow, George P. *The Aesthetic and the Critical Theories of John Ruskin*. Princeton: Princeton University Press, 1971.
———. *William Holman Hunt and Typological Symbolism*. New Haven: Yale University Press, 1979.
Laurence, Dan H., and Nicholas Grene, eds. *Shaw, Lady Gregory and the Abbey*. Gerrards Cross: Colin Smythe, 1993.
Leeney, Cathy. *Irish Women Playwrights, 1900–1939: Gender and Violence on Stage*. New York: Peter Lang, 2010.
Leon, Derrick. *Ruskin, the Great Victorian*. London: Routledge, 1949.
Levitas, Ben. *The Theatre of Nation*. Oxford: Oxford University Press, 2002.
Lister, Raymond. *Victorian Narrative Painting*. London: Museum Press Ltd., 1966.
Longford, Elizabeth. *A Pilgrimage of Passion: The Life of Wilfrid Scawen Blunt*. London: Tauris Parke, 2007.
———. "Lady Gregory and Wilfrid Scawen Blunt." In *Lady Gregory, Fifty Years After*, edited by Ann Saddlemyer and Colin Smythe, 85–97. Gerrards Cross: Colin Smythe, 1987.
López-Rey, José. *Velazquez: The Artist as a Maker; with a Catalogue Raisonné of His Extant Works*. Lausanne-Paris: Bibliothéque des Arts, 1979.
Lyons, F. S. *Ireland Since the Famine*. London: Collins/Fontana, 1982.
Lysaght, Edward E. *Sir Horace Plunkett and His Place in the Irish Nation*. Dublin: Maunsel, 1916.
Macintosh, Fiona. "Viewing *Agamemnon* in Nineteenth-Century Britain." In Agamemnon *in Performance, 458 BC to 2004 AD*, edited by Edith Hall, Fiona Macintosh, Pantelis Michelakis, and Oliver Taplin, 139–62. Oxford: Oxford University Press, 2005.
Marsh, Jan. "Art, Ambition and Sisterhood in the 1850s." In *Women in the Victorian Art World*, edited by Clarissa Campbell Orr, 33–48. Manchester: Manchester University Press, 1995.

Martin, Brian. *John Henry Newman: His Life and Work*. London: Chatto and Windus, 1982.
Mathews, P. J. *Revival: The Abbey Theatre, Sinn Féin, the Gaelic League and the Co-operative Movement*. Cork: Cork University Press, 2003.
———. "The Irish Revival: A Reappraisal." In *New Voices in Irish Criticism*, edited by P. J. Mathews, 12–19. Dublin: Four Courts Press, 2000.
May, J. C. C. "Introduction." In *Diarmuid and Grania*. Manuscript Materials by W. B. Yeats and George Moore, edited by J. C. C. Mays, xxix–l. New York: Cornell University Press, 2005.
McAteer, Michael. "A Currency Crisis: Modernist Dialectics in *The Countess Cathleen*." In *The Irish Revival Reappraised*, edited by Betsey Taylor FitzSimon and James H. Murphy, 187–204. Dublin: Four Courts Press, 2004.
———. *Standish O'Grady, AE and Yeats: History, Politics, Culture*. Dublin: Irish Academic Press, 2002.
———. *Yeats and European Drama*. Cambridge: Cambridge University Press, 2010.
McCarthy, Bernadette. "W. B. Yeats, John Ruskin, and the 'Lidless Eye'." *Irish University Review* 41, no. 2 (Autumn/Winter 2011): 25–41.
McCartney, Donal. "From Parnell to Pearse." In *The Course of Irish History*, edited by T. W. Moody and F. X. Martin, 294–312. Dublin: Mercier, 1994.
McCormack, W. J. *Fool of the Family: A Life of J. M. Synge*. London: Weidenfeld & Nicolson, 2000.
———. *From Burke to Beckett: Ascendancy Tradition and Betrayal in Literary History*. Cork: Cork University Press, 1994.
McDiarmid, Lucy. "Lady Gregory, Wilfrid Blunt and London Table Talk." *Irish University Review* 34, no. 1 (Spring/Summer 2004): 67–80.
———. "Oscar Wilde, Lady Gregory, and Late Victorian Table-Talk." In *Oscar Wilde and Modern Culture: The Making of a Legend*, edited by Joseph Bristow, 46–62. Athens, OH: Ohio University Press, 2009.
———. *Poets and the Peacock Dinner: The Literary History of a Meal*. Oxford: Oxford University Press, 2014.
———. "The Demotic Lady Gregory." In *High and Low Moderns, Literature and Culture 1889–1939*, edited by Maria DiBattista and Lucy McDiarmid, 212–34. Oxford: Oxford University Press, 1996.
McGinley, Michael. *The La Touche Family in Ireland*. Greystones, Co. Wicklow: The La Touche Legacy Committee, 2004.
McMullan, Roy. *Victorian Outsider: A Biography of J. A. M. Whistler*. New York: Macmillan, 1973.
Meisel, Martin. *Realizations: Narrative, Pictorial, and Theatrical Arts in Nineteenth-Century England*. Princeton, NJ: Princeton University Press, 1983.

Moore, George. *Hail and Farewell!* London: Heinemann, 1947.
Moreno, Ana Martín. *Las Meninas.* Translated by Nigel Williams. Madrid: Aldeasa, Museo del Prado, 2003.
Morris, Catherine. *Alice Milligan and the Irish Cultural Revival.* Dublin: Four Courts Press, 2012.
Morris, William. *Factory Work, As It Is and Might Be.* New York: New York Labor News Co., 1922.
Morse, David. *High Victorian Culture.* London: Macmillan, 1993.
Murphy, Brian P. *Patrick Pearse and the Lost Republican Ideal.* Dublin: Duffy, 1991.
Murphy, Maureen. "Lady Gregory and the Gaelic League." In *Lady Gregory, Fifty Years After*, edited by Ann Saddlemyer and Colin Smythe, 143–62. Gerrards Cross: Colin Smythe, 1987.
Murphy, Paul. "Woman as Fantasy Object in Lady Gregory's Historical Tragedies." In *Women in Irish Drama: A Century of Authorship and Representation*, edited by Melissa Sihra, 28–41. Basingstoke: Palgrave Macmillan, 2007.
Murray, Christopher. *Twentieth-Century Irish Drama: Mirror up to Nation.* Manchester: Manchester University Press, 1997.
Newey, Katherine, and Jeffrey Richards. *John Ruskin and the Victorian Theatre.* Basingstoke: Palgrave Macmillan, 2010.
Nic Shiubhlaigh, Máire. *Splendid Years: Recollections of Maire Nic Shiubhlaigh as Told to Edward Kenny.* Dublin: Duffy, 1955.
Norman, Edward. *The Victorian Christian Socialists.* Cambridge: Cambridge University Press, 1987.
Norwood, Janice. "The Britannia Theatre: Visual Culture and the Repertoire of a Popular Theatre." In *Ruskin, the Theatre and Victorian Visual Culture*, edited by Anselm Heinrich, Katherine Newey, and Jeffrey Richards, 135–53. Basingstoke: Palgrave Macmillan, 2009.
Ó Buchalla, Séamas, coll. and ed. *Literary Writings of Patrick Pearse.* Dublin: Mercier, 1979.
O'Ceallaigh Ritschel, Nelson. *Productions of the Irish Theatre Movement 1899–1916, A Checklist.* Westport, CT: Greenwood, 2001.
O'Connell, Helen. *Ireland and the Fiction of Improvement.* Oxford: Oxford University Press, 2006.
O'Curry, Eugene. *Lectures on the Manuscript Material of Ancient Irish History.* Dublin: Duffy, 1861.
O'Day, Alan. *Irish Home Rule, 1867–1921.* Manchester: Manchester University Press, 1998.
O'Grady, Standish. *Selected Essays and Passages.* Dublin: Talbot; London: Unwin, 1918.

O'Leary, Philip. *The Prose Literature of the Celtic Revival, 1880–1921*. University Park, PA: Pennsylvania State University Press, 1994.
O'Riordan, Rev. M. *Catholicity and Progress in Ireland*. London: Kegan Paul, 1906.
Pater, Walter. *The Renaissance*. Edited by Donald L. Hill. Berkeley: University of California Press, 1980.
Paulin, Tom. *Minotaur: Poetry and the Nation State*. London: Faber and Faber, 1992.
Pearse, Pádraic H. *Political Writings and Speeches*. Dublin: Talbot, 1966.
———. *The Singer and Other Plays*. Dublin: Talbot, 1960.
Pethica, James. "A Young Man's Ghost: Lady Gregory and J. M. Synge." *Irish University Review* 34, no. 1 (Spring/Summer 2004): 1–20.
———. "Lady Gregory's Abbey Theatre Drama: Ireland Real and Ideal." In *The Cambridge Companion to Twentieth-Century Irish Drama*, edited by Shaun Richards, 62–78. Cambridge: Cambridge University Press, 2004.
———. "'Our Kathleen': Yeats's Collaboration with Lady Gregory in the Writing of *Cathleen ni Houlihan*." In *Yeats and Women*, edited by Deidre Toomey, 205–22. Basingstoke: Macmillan, 1997.
Pilkington, Lionel. *Theatre and the State in Twentieth-Century Ireland: Cultivating the People*. London: Routledge, 2001.
Pilz, Anna. "'A Bad Master:' Religion, Jacobitism, and the Politics of Representation in Lady Gregory's *The White Cockade*." In *Irish Women's Writing, 1878–1922*, edited by Anna Pilz and Whitney Standlee, 137–55. Manchester: Manchester University Press, 2016.
Pimley, Adrian. "The Working-Class Movement and the Irish Revolution, 1896–1923." In *The Revolution in Ireland, 1879–1923*, edited by D. G. Boyce, 193–216. Dublin: Gill and Macmillan, 1988.
Plunkett, Horace. "Co-operative Stores for Ireland." *The Nineteenth Century* 24 (September 1888): 410–8.
———. *Ireland in the New Century*. London: Murray, 1904.
———. *Noblesse Oblige, An Irish Rendering*. Dublin: Maunsel, 1908.
Prettejohn, Elizabeth. "Between Homer and Ovid: Metamorphoses of the 'Grand Style' in G. F. Watts." In *Representations of G. F. Watts: Art Making in Victorian Culture*, edited by Colin Trodd and Stephanie Brown, 49–64. Aldershot: Ashgate, 2004.
Prettejohn, Elizabeth. *The Art of the Pre-Raphaelites*. London: Tate Publishing, 2000.
Richards, Jeffrey. "John Ruskin, the Olympian Painters and the Amateur Stage." In *Ruskin, the Theatre and Visual Culture*, edited by Anselm Heinrich, Katherine Newey, and Jeffrey Richards, 19–41. Basingstoke: Palgrave Macmillan, 2009.

Roche, Anthony. *The Irish Dramatic Revival, 1899–1939*. London: Bloomsbury Methuen, 2015.
Rossetti, William Michael, ed. *Dante Gabriel Rossetti: His Family Letters*. London: Ellis and Elvey, 1895.
Rumpf, E., and A. C. Hepburn. *Nationalism and Socialism in Twentieth-Century Ireland*. Liverpool: Liverpool University Press, 1977.
Russell, George. *A Plea for Justice: Being a Demand for a Public Enquiry into the Attacks on Co-operative Societies in Ireland*. Dublin: Irish Homestead Ltd., 1921.
———. *Co-operation and Nationality*. Dublin: Irish Academic Press, 1982.
———. *The National Being*. Dublin: Maunsel, 1916.
Saddlemyer, Ann. "Augusta Gregory, Irish Nationalist: 'After All, What Is Wanted but a Hag and a Voice?'" In *Myth and Reality in Irish Literature*, edited by Joseph Ronsley, 29–40. Waterloo, ON: Wilfrid Laurier University Press, 1977.
———. *In Defence of Lady Gregory, Playwright*. Dublin: Dolmen, 1966.
Saddlemyer, Ann, sel. and ed. *Theatre Business: The Correspondence of the First Abbey Theatre Directors*. Gerrards Cross: Colin Smythe, 1982.
Sayce, A. H. "Preface." In *Troja: Results in the Latest Researches and Discoveries on the Site of Homer's Troy, and in the Heroic Tumuli and Other Sites, Made in the Year of 1882*, v–xxx. Henry Schliemann. London: Murray, 1884.
Schliemann, Henry [sic]. *Troja: Results in the Latest Researches and Discoveries on the Site of Homer's Troy, and in the Heroic Tumuli and Other Sites, Made in the Year of 1882*. London: Murray, 1884.
Schuchard, Ronald. *The Last Minstrels: Yeats and the Revival of the Bardic Arts*. Oxford: Oxford University Press, 2008.
———. "W. B. Yeats and the London Theatre Societies, 1901–1904." *The Review of English Studies* 29, no. 116 (November 1978): 415–46.
Sencourt, Robert. *The Life of Newman*. London: Dacre, 1948.
Shaw, George Bernard. *John Bull's Other Island*. London: Penguin, 1984.
———. *Our Theatre in the Nineties*, vol. 1. London: Constable, 1948.
Sisson, Elaine. *Pearse's Patriots*. Cork: Cork University Press, 2005.
Smith, Louis P. F. *The Evolution of Agricultural Co-operation*. Oxford: Blackwell, 1961.
Smith-Gordon, Lionel, and Cruise O'Brien. *Co-operation in Ireland*. Manchester: Co-operative Union Ltd., 1921.
Smythe, Colin. *A Guide to Coole Park, Co. Galway, Home of Lady Gregory*. Gerrards Cross: Colin Smythe, 1973.
———. "Foreword." In Lady Augusta Gregory, *Seventy Years, Being the Autobiography of Lady Gregory*, v–xi. Gerrards Cross: Colin Smythe, 1973.
Somerville, Edith, and Martin Ross, "The Whiteboys." In *The Irish R.M.*, 403–21. London: Sphere Books, 1970.

Spencer, Robin. "Whistler, Swinburne and Art for Art's Sake." In *After the Pre-Raphaelites*, edited by Elizabeth Prettejohn, 59–89. Manchester: Manchester University Press, 1999.
Stein, Richard L. *Victoria's Year: English Literature and Culture, 1837–38*. Oxford: Oxford University Press, 1987.
Stevens, Julie Anne. "Political Animals: Somerville and Ross and Percy French on Edwardian Ireland." In *Synge and Edwardian Ireland*, edited by Brian Cliff and Nicholas Grene, 102–18. Oxford: Oxford University Press, 2012.
Synge, John Millington. *Collected Works*, vol. 2. Edited by Alan Price. Gerrards Cross: Colin Smythe, 1982.
Tate, Andrew. "The First Theatrical Pre-Raphaelite? Ruskin's Molière." In *Ruskin, the Theatre and Victorian Visual Culture*, edited by Anselm Heinrich, Katherine Newey, and Jeffrey Richards, 114–31. Basingstoke: Palgrave Macmillan, 2009.
Tennyson, Alfred. *Poems*. London: Moxon, 1859.
"The Work of the Home Rule Union." *Journal of the Home Rule Union* 1, no. 1 (March 1888): 1–3.
Thomas, Julia. *Victorian Narrative Painting*. London: Tate Publishing, 2000.
Tolnay, Charles de. *Teremtő Géniuszok*. Budapest: Gondolat, 1987.
Upstone, Robert. *The Pre-Raphaelite Dream*. London: Tate Gallery, 2003.
von Holst, Niels. *Creators, Collectors and Connoisseurs*. London: Thames, 1967.
Walther, Ingo F., ed. *Masterpieces of Western Art*. Köln: Taschen, 2002.
Ward, Wilfrid. *The Life of John Henry Cardinal Newman*, vol. 1. London: Longmans, 1912.
Weber, Max. *The Protestant Ethic and the Spirit of Capitalism*. Translated by Talcott Parsons. London: Routledge, 2000.
Weintraub, Stanley. *Whistler: A Biography*. London: Collins, 1974.
Weitz, Eric. "Lady Gregory's 'Humour of Character': A *Commedia* Approach to *Spreading the News*." *Irish University Review* 34, no. 1 (Spring/Summer 2004): 144–56.
West, Trevor. *Horace Plunkett: Co-operation and Politics, An Irish Biography*. Gerrards Cross: Colin Smythe, 1986.
Whistler, James M. *The Gentle Art of Making Enemies*. London: Heinemann, 1919.
Winston, Greg. "Redefining Coole: Lady Gregory, Class Politics and the Land War." *Colby Quarterly* 37, no. 3 (2001): 205–22.
Yeats, William Butler. *Autobiographies*. Basingstoke: Macmillan, 1992.
———. *Collected Plays*. London: Macmillan, 1963.
———. *Essays and Introductions*. London: Macmillan, 1989.
———. *Green Helmet and Other Poems*. Churchtown, Dundrum: Cuala Press, 1910.
———. *Memoirs, Autobiography—First Draft, Journal*. Edited by Denis Donoghue. London: Macmillan, 1972.

———. "Preface." In *Cuchulain of Muirthemne*, edited by Lady Augusta Gregory, 11–7. Gerrards Cross: Colin Smythe, 1975.

———. *The Collected Letters of W. B. Yeats; Volume Two: 1896–1900*. Edited by Warwick Gould, John Kelly, and Deirdre Toomey. Oxford: Clarendon, 1997.

———. *The Collected Letters of W. B. Yeats; Volume Three: 1901–1904*. Edited by John Kelly and Ronald Schuchard. Oxford: Clarendon, 1994.

Zimmermann, Georges Denis. *Songs of Irish Rebellion: Irish Political Street Ballads and Rebel Songs, 1780–1900*. Dublin: Four Courts Press, 2002.

Index

A
Abbey Theatre, 1, 4, 10, 11, 14, 16, 20, 70, 92, 96, 100, 103, 106, 107, 109, 115, 116, 118, 121, 122, 128, 129, 131, 133, 139, 147, 148, 150, 151, 154, 156, 162, 163, 165–167, 173, 174, 188, 192, 194, 195, 198, 200, 209, 210, 213
  foundation, 10, 92, 97, 121
  staging, 121, 122, 131, 133, 163, 192
  tours, 92, 129, 164–167
Aberdeen, Lady, 89
Aberdeen, Lord, 89
Act of Union, The, 7, 118, 189, 190, 192, 202
Alexander, Sir George, 67
Alexandra, Empress Consort of Russia, 192
Alexandra, Queen Consort of the United Kingdom, 192
Alma-Tadema, Sir Lawrence, 12, 66–68, 71, 82, 124, 148

Anderson, Robert A., 85, 99, 115
Anglo-Irish Treaty, The, 14, 211
Anglo-Irish War, The, 14, 208, 211
Archer, William, 11, 95, 114
Arnold, Matthew, 17, 57, 65, 81, 115
Arundel Society, The, 3, 21, 22, 24, 33, 38
Asquith, Herbert Henry, 13, 179, 192
Atkinson, Robert, 55

B
Barrett, Wilson, 68, 94, 197
Barrington, Emilie Isabel Wilson, 35
Basterot, Count Florimond de, 92
Beardsley, Aubrey, 74
Beerbohm Tree, Sir Herbert, 12, 132
Bellini, Giovanni, 29, 32, 38, 46
Benson, Frank, 10, 12, 66, 75, 84, 132
Bernhardt, Sarah, 145
Bewley, Samuel, 7, 161
Binyon, Robert Laurence, 97

Blunt, Lady Anne Noel, 29
Blunt, Wilfrid Scawen, 29, 46, 181, 182, 186–187, 199, 201
Boehm, Sir Joseph Edgar, 22, 44
Bonar Law, Andrew, 201
Bonifazio, Veronese, 32
Botticelli, Sandro, 148
British Museum, The, 27, 33, 37, 45, 55, 67–69, 125
　Elgin Marbles, The, 27, 69, 125
Browning, Robert, 17, 92, 144
Browning, Sarianna, 144
Brugsch, Emil, 30, 52
Bulwer-Lytton, Edward, 71, 95, 113
Bulwer-Lytton, Robert, 113
Bulwer-Lytton, Victor, 113
Burke, Edmund, 43, 180
Burke, Florence, 90, 113
Burne-Jones, Edward, 2, 34, 41, 66
Burns, Robert, 17
Burton, Sir Frederic, 18, 22, 27, 32, 38, 42, 51
Byron, Lord, 6, 29, 95

C
Cadogan, Lady, 89
Canaletto, 19, 92
Carlyle, Thomas, 6, 128
Carpaccio, 29, 32, 46
Carracci, Annibale, 32
Carson, Lord Edward Henry, 201
Chapman, George, 64, 81
Charlesworth, Maria, 159
Chaucer, 63, 127
Christian Socialist Movement, The, 2, 196
Cimabue, 23, 32, 38, 44
Cole, Alan Summerly, 18
Coleridge, Samuel, 64
Colnaghi, Martin, 51
Colvin, Sir Sidney, 18, 55
Combe, Thomas, 144, 161

Commedia dell'arte, 108, 109, 119
Comyns Carr, Joseph William, 18, 94, 114
Congested Districts Board, The, 207
Connolly, James, 201
Connolly, Sean, 54
Constable, John, 37
Coole Park, 1, 8, 14, 17, 19, 24, 28, 36, 41, 43, 51, 53, 54, 61, 92, 93, 128, 135, 205, 207–209, 212, 213
Co-operative Movement, England, 11, 87
Co-operative Movement, Ireland, 1, 5, 10, 90, 141, 165
Co-operative Wholesale Society, 87, 116
Coquelin, Benoît-Constant, 131, 133, 151, 152
Coquelin, Ernest Alexander Honoré, 151
Correggio, Antonio Allegri da, 28, 32
Cowper-Temple, William, 161
Craig, Edith, 97, 121
Craig, Edward Gordon, 12, 72, 94, 125, 149
Craig, James (later Viscount Craigavon), 201
Crane, Walter, 67
Cullen, Cardinal Paul, 168–169
Cumming, Rev. John, 159

D
Dante Alighieri, 25, 44
d'Arbois de Jubainville, Marie Henri, 55
Degas, Edgar, 125
Department of Agriculture and Technical Instruction, 116
Dilke, Lady Emilia, 35
Disestablishment Act, The, 117
Disraeli, Benjamin, 38

INDEX 231

Doherty, John, 89
Dublin Lockout, The, 189, 201
Duffaud, Jean-Baptiste, 129
Dürer, Albrecht, 33
Dyck, Anthonis van, 28

E
Easter Rising, The, 12, 171, 188, 210, 211
Eastlake, Lady Elizabeth, 35
Eastlake, Sir Charles Lock, 21, 37
Edgeworth, Maria, 6–8
Edgeworth, Richard Lovell, 6
Edward, Prince of Wales, 27, 73
Egg, Leopold, 134
Eliot, George, 18, 42
Emmet, Robert, 172, 211
Ervine, John Greer, 188, 209
Eyck, Jan van, 12, 28, 137

F
Farr, Florence, 97, 121
Fay, Frank, 129, 131, 147
Fay, William, 83, 131, 191
Ferguson, Samuel, 63, 81, 182, 210
Fingall, Lady, 90, 91, 113
Finlay, Fr. Thomas, 85
Firth, William Powell, 37, 41, 148
Fra Angelico, 23, 32, 39
Froude, James Anthony, 86

G
Gaddi, Taddeo, 44
Gaelic League, The, 53, 54, 56, 60, 72, 75, 76, 79, 80, 115, 165, 195, 197, 201
Gautier, Théophile, 40, 48, 160
George, Henry, 115
Giorgione, 29, 38, 46

Giotto, 23, 24, 32, 39, 44
Gladstone, William Ewart, 13, 38, 73, 95, 162, 179, 192, 202
Godwin, Edward William, 67, 72
Goethe, Johann Wolfgang von, 63, 96, 165
Gonne, Maud, 4, 114, 118, 145
Government of Ireland Bills. *See* Home Rule Bills
Gozzoli, Benozzo, 23
Grand Tours, 8, 12, 18, 22–35, 92, 93, 129
Granville-Barker, Harley, 96, 114
Gray, John, 74, 83
Great War, The, 14, 205, 207, 210, 211
Gregory, Lady Augusta, 1, 15, 19, 42, 43, 46, 47, 79, 80, 83, 84, 111, 114, 115, 117, 118, 148, 150, 152–155, 179, 180, 192, 193, 195, 196, 198–200, 202, 206, 213
  and Blunt, 181, 182, 186, 187
  and Egypt, 29, 30, 181, 182, 186, 200
  essays and pamphlets; "Arabi and His Household", 181, 182; "The Felons of Our Land", 173, 181, 182, 200; "Ireland, Real and Ideal", 99; "An Italian Literary Drama", 118; Letter, *An Claidheamh Soluis*, 53, 79; *A Phantom's Pilgrimage, or Home Ruin*, 179; "The Poet Raftery", 79; "Raftery's Grave", 79
  and Greece, 9, 25, 26, 66, 69, 70
  and Gregory, Sir William, 1–4, 8, 9, 17–29, 31, 33–39, 41–44, 51, 53, 54, 57, 61, 69, 73, 92, 94, 105, 106, 136, 144, 162, 163, 167, 207
  and Hugh Lane pictures, 21, 206
  and Italy, 28, 33, 46, 108, 145, 205

and land reform, 10
and nationalism, 12, 79, 159, 178, 181, 182, 186, 199, 200
and Pearse, 13, 171, 173, 174, 210
and the *Playboy* riots, 102, 176–178
plays; *The Bogie Men*, 176, 191; *The Canavans*, 175, 176, 190, 191; *Coats*, 176, 191; *Damer's Gold*, 119, 121, 127, 150; *The Deliverer*, 146–148; *Dervorgilla*, 182–186; *The Doctor in Spite of Himself*, 110; *The Full Moon*, 139; *The Gaol Gate*, 140, 141, 183, 200; *Grania*, 75, 84, 182–184, 186, 200; *Hyacinth Halvey*, 1, 101, 116, 164; *The Image*, 138, 140, 191; *The Jackdaw*, 102, 103, 107, 128, 183; *Kincora*, 183, 184, 186, 200; *McDonough's Wife*, 190; *The Miser*, 127; *The Pot of Broth*, 129; *The Rising of the Moon*, 1, 164, 176–179; *The Rogueries of Scapin*, 110, 119; *Spreading the News*, 107, 118, 128, 140, 164, 183; *The Travelling Man*, 141, 143, 171, 179, 198; *Twenty-Five*, 98, 128, 129; *The White Cockade*, 174, 175, 178, 189–191, 198; *The Workhouse Ward*, 1; *The Would-Be Gentleman*, 119; *The Wrens*, 179, 188, 189
and religion, 158, 198
and stage pictures, 131, 146, 156
and Synge, 12, 76, 84, 96, 107, 129, 198
works; *Cuchulain of Muirthemne*, 10, 56, 59, 60, 70, 71, 73, 77, 78, 80, 83, 84, 139, 154, 206; *Gods and Fighting Men*, 10, 56, 76, 78, 84; *Mr. Gregory's Letter-Box*, 51, 61, 80, 191; *The Kiltartan History Book*, 202; *The Kiltartan Molière*, 110; *Sir William Gregory K.C.M.G., An Autobiography*, 51
and Yeats, William Butler, 1, 4, 5, 9, 113
Gregory, Margaret, 14, 207, 208
Gregory, Richard, 19, 208
Gregory, Robert, 14, 19, 28, 47, 54, 60, 79, 126, 145, 202, 205–209, 213
Gregory, Sir William Henry, 1–4, 8, 9, 17–29, 31, 33–39, 41–44, 51, 53, 54, 57, 61, 69, 73, 92, 94, 105, 106, 136, 144, 162, 163, 167, 207
Gregory, William, 2, 19, 61, 62
Griffith, Arthur, 61, 201
Guinness, Arthur, 7, 161

H
Haag, Peter de, 28
Hals, Frans, 28
Hauptman, Gerhart, 96
Heatherley's Art School, 51
Hegel, Georg Friedrich, 126
Hellenism, 39, 51, 54, 60–66, 73, 74, 77, 81, 83, 127
Henry, Grace, 130
Henry, Paul, 130, 151
Hermetic Order of the Golden Dawn, The, 121, 124, 149
Herodotus, 25
Hogarth, William, 12, 20, 135
Home Arts and Industries Association, The, 89
Homer, 25, 45, 52–54, 58, 63–65, 67, 69, 73, 78, 79, 81, 82
Home Rule Bills, 180, 187
Horace, 15, 20, 85, 97, 112, 113, 115, 116, 149, 182, 195, 212

Horniman, Annie, 4, 121, 163
Hull, Eleanor, 55, 80
Hunt, William Holman, 2, 45, 66, 119, 133, 148, 153, 155, 157, 177
Hyde, Douglas, 53–55, 80, 174, 178

I
Ibsen, Henrik, 11
Irish Agricultural Organisation, The, 85, 165
Irish Civil War, The, 173
Irish Literary Theatre, The, 75, 86, 92, 94, 96, 106, 107, 115, 118, 182
Irish War of Independence, The. *See* Anglo-Irish War, The
Irving, Sir Henry, 12, 66, 94, 125, 132, 147

J
Jameson, Anna, 35
Johnson, Benjamin, 96
Jordaens, Jacob, 137

K
Keats, John, 17, 81
Keble, John, 105
Keogh, J. Augustus, 209

L
Lane, Hugh, 14, 20, 21, 43, 167, 196, 199, 206, 213
La Touche, David Digues, 193
La Touche, John, 5
La Touche, John David, 7, 161
La Touche, Maria, 5
La Touche, Rose, 161, 194

Layard, Lady Enid, 4, 15, 26–28, 45, 52, 63, 93
Layard, Sir Austen Henry, 2, 3, 8, 18, 23, 26, 32, 44, 51, 52
Lee, Vernon, 35
Leighton, Sir Frederic, 18, 66
Leonardo da Vinci, 38
Lessing, Gotthold Ephraim, 36, 123
Lindsay, Sir Coutts, 18, 22
Logue, Cardinal Michael, 106
Londonderry, Lady, 90
Louvre, The, 27, 31, 129
Lugné-Poe, Aurélien, 131
Luini, Bernardino, 32
Lutyens, Sir Edwin Landseer, 167, 168
Lyall, Sir Alfred, 51

M
MacBride, John, 211
MacDonagh, Thomas, 4, 188
Mac Fhionnlaoich, Peadar, 80
Madox Brown, Ford, 128
Mahaffy, Rev. John Pentland, 56
Malory, Sir Thomas, 78
Manet, Édouard, 125
Mantegna, Andrea, 29
Marlowe, Christopher, 96
Marmontel, Jean-François, 119
Marsh, Catherine, 159
Martineau, Robert Braithwaite, 134, 148
Martyn, Edward, 75, 86, 90, 133
Marx, Karl, 105
Maxence, Edgar, 129
Mazo, Juan Bautista del, 137
Meer, Jan van der, 28
Melbourne, Lord, 43
Memling, Hans, 23, 45
Messina, Antonello da, 31
Meyer, Kuno, 55

Michelangelo, 24, 25, 38
Millais, Sir John Everett, 2, 148
Millet, Jean-François, 41, 60, 129
Milligan, Alice, 4, 75–77, 83, 84, 118, 188
Molière, 63, 95, 96, 109, 110, 119, 131, 152, 165
  and *commedia dell'arte*, 109
  and Lady Gregory, 109, 110, 131, 165
  and Pre-Raphaelitism, 95, 110
  and Ruskin, 95, 96, 109, 110
Monet, Claude, 125
Moore, Albert, 41
Moore, George, 75, 84, 90, 97, 106, 116, 174, 178, 212
Moran, David Patrick, 129
Morris, William, 2, 11, 16, 41, 178
Mulkere, Pat, 53, 54
Municipal Gallery of Modern Art, Dublin, 14, 20, 43, 167
Murillo, Bartolomé, 33, 38, 92

N
National Gallery of Dublin, The, 146, 206
National Gallery of London, The, 206
National University of Ireland, The, 194, 207
Newman, Cardinal John Henry, 13
Nisard, Désiré, 160
Nutt, Alfred, 76

O
Oakeley, Frederick, 106
O'Brien, Barry, 86
O'Casey, Sean, 1, 36
O'Connell, Daniel, 7, 182, 202
O'Curry, Eugene, 10, 55, 56, 80, 168
O'Donovan, Fred, 209

O'Grady, Standish, 5, 10, 57, 59, 80, 84, 163, 194, 210
O'Hagan, John, 168
Ovid, 82, 137
Owen, Robert, 88
Oxford Movement, The, 37, 105
Oxford murals, 160, 169
Oxford, University of, 2, 16, 19, 25, 162, 207

P
Palmerston, Lord, 92
Parmigianino, 32
Parnell, Charles Stewart, 13, 148, 179
Parry, John Orlando, 128
Parry, Tom, 135
Pater, Walter, 37, 38, 48, 126, 145, 149
Patmore, Coventry, 170, 192
Pearse, Patrick, 4, 12, 16, 171, 188, 196, 197, 213
  and education, 13, 174, 210
  plays; *Íosagán*, 171; *The Singer*, 171
Peel, Sir Robert, 61
Persse, Geoffrey, 205
Persse, Rudolph, 205
Pheidias, 69
Phidias, 25, 27, 37, 69, 70, 146. *See also* Pheidias
Phillips, Sir Claude, 18
Pigot, John Edward, 57
Pinturicchio, 23
Pistolesi, Erasmo, 20
Pitt, William, 92
Plunkett, Sir Horace, 5, 115, 165
Plutarch, 25
Pound, Ezra, 209, 210, 213
Poynter, Sir Edward John, 22, 34, 37
Prado Museum, The, 136
Pre-Raphaelite Brotherhood, 12, 23, 28, 37, 39, 66, 134, 135, 153, 160

Pre-Raphaelitism, 39, 48, 66, 93, 94, 144, 148, 153
Pugin, Augustus Welby, 37
Purcell, Lewis (David Parkhill), 188
Purser, Sarah, 13
Pusey, Edward Bouverie, 105

R
Raffalovich, Marc-André, 74
Raffeisen bank system, 86, 98
Raffeisen Credit Society, 99
Raftery, Anthony, 53
Raphael, 23, 24, 28, 38
Redmond, John Edward, 181
Rembrandt, Harmenszoon van Rijn, 28
Renan, Ernest, 13, 169
Reni, Guido, 32
Renoir, Pierre-Auguste, 129
Ricketts, Charles, 94, 97, 121, 124
Robinson, Lennox, 36
Robinson, Sir Charles, 18, 33, 51
Roosevelt, Theodore, 192
Rossetti, Dante Gabriel, 2, 34, 66, 125, 144, 153, 186
Rossetti, William Michael, 153
Rousseau, Jean-Jacques, 6
Rowland Hart, Alice, 89
Roxborough, 17, 18, 135
Royal Academy of Arts, The, 2, 18, 37
Royal Irish Academy, The, 38, 55, 60
Rubens, Peter Paul, 12, 137
Ruskin, John, 2, 3, 15, 16, 20, 37, 42, 43, 48, 81, 82, 112–114, 116, 128, 152, 153, 155, 186, 192–194
 on art and education, 8, 20
 on art and morality, 39, 186
 on art and society, 21, 22
 essays and lectures; "The Aesthetic and Mathematic School of Art in Florence", 44; "The Awakening Conscience", 156, 177; "Greek and Christian Art", 48; "The Light of the World", 157, 177; "Pre-Raphaelitism", 39, 48, 66, 94; "The Schools of Art in Florence; Lecture II: Cimabue", 44
 and Hellenism, 39
 and Medievalism, 62, 65, 78, 185
 and St. George's Guild, 10, 89, 162, 166
 and St. George's Museum, 21, 167;
 the Whistler-Ruskin trial, 9
 works; *Academy Notes*, 119; *Art of England*, 65, 82; *Bibliotheca Pastorum*, 45; *Fors Clavigera*, 3, 5, 40, 110, 162, 163, 169, 181; *Giotto and his Works in Padua*, 24; *A Joy Forever*, 44; *Modern Painters*, 3, 7, 22, 25, 64, 95, 146, 160; *The Museum and Guild of St. George*, 112; *Poems*, 23, 44, 57; *The Seven Lamps of Architecture*, 3, 68; *The Stones of Venice*, 3, 7, 22, 28, 54, 68, 145; *Time and Tide*, 21, 88, 162; *Unto This Last*, 3, 162
Russell, George, 5, 11, 13, 36, 61, 70, 77, 87, 111, 182, 211, 214
Rutherford Mayne (Samuel John Waddell), 188
Ruysdael, Jacob von, 28

S
Schiller, Johann Christoph Friedrich von, 63
Schliemann, Heinrich, 8, 25, 52
Scott, Sir Walter, 6, 17, 95

Shakespeare, William, 6, 11, 17, 76, 95
Shaw, George Bernard, 1, 15, 36, 41, 149, 191, 193, 209
Sheridan, Mary, 159
Sheridan, Richard Brinsley, 96
Sherwood, Mary Martha, 159
South Kensington Museum, The, 18, 27, 33
Stanfield, Clarkson, 135
Steen, Jan, 28, 31
Stokes, Whitley, 55, 57
Sturge Moore, Thomas, 126
Sullivan, William Kirby, 168
Swinburne, Algernon, 40
Symons, Arthur William, 152
Synge, John Millington, 1, 36, 129, 150–152, 154
  plays; *In the Shadow of the Glen*, 107, 132; *The Playboy of the Western World*, 103, 107, 132, 139; *Riders to the Sea*, 130; *The Well of the Saints*, 107

T
Tableau vivant, 107, 122–124, 127, 131
Talbot, Lord, 61
Taylor, Tom, 22, 41, 135
Tennyson, Lord, 17, 78, 92, 135, 144
Terry, Ellen, 66, 145
Tintoretto, 29, 38, 153
Titian, 38, 137, 161
Todhunter, John, 67, 94
Tone, Theobald Wolfe, 182, 211
Tractarian Movement. *See* Oxford Movement
Turner, Joseph Mallord William, 2, 93

U
Ua Laoghaire, Peadar, 75
United Irishman Rebellion, The, 86

V
Vandaleur, John, 89, 112
Vaughan, Henry, 146
Velázquez, Diego Rodríguez da Silva y, 12, 92, 136–138, 148, 154, 156
Velde, Willem van de, 31
Vere, Aubrey Thomas De, 168
Veronese, Paolo, 23, 29
Victoria, Princess, 192
Victoria, Queen and Empress, 2, 44, 63, 192

W
Ward, William, 106
Watteau, Jean-Antoine, 38
Watts, George Frederic, 2, 22, 51, 66
Weber, Max, 104, 116
Wellesley, Lord, 61, 62, 92
Wesley, Rev. John, 13, 158, 170
Weyden, Rogier van der, 33, 38
Whistler, James Abbott McNeill, 48, 125, 149
Wilde, Oscar, 35, 40, 47, 74, 125, 135, 149
Wilhelm II, German Emperor, 192
Winckelmann, Johann Joachim, 36
Windisch, Ernst Wilhelm Oskar, 55, 78
Wordsworth, William, 193
Wyndham Land Act, The, 97, 98, 194

Y
Yeats, Jack Butler, 13, 19, 91, 151
Yeats, John Butler, 34, 70
Yeats, William Butler, 1, 4, 5, 9, 83, 113, 114, 152, 154, 155
  and art, 5, 8
  and Coole Park, 19, 36, 92, 208
  pamphlet; *On the Boiler*, 194

plays; *The Black Horse*, 179; *Cathleen ni Houlihan*, 129, 131, 173, 178, 186, 198; *The Countess Cathleen*, 75, 91, 96, 114, 115, 124; *Deirdre*, 76, 84, 113, 127; *Diarmuid and Grania*, 75, 84, 184; *The Golden Helmet*, 127; *The Green Helmet*, 127; *The Hour-Glass*, 126, 146, 147; *On Baile's Strand*, 76, 139, 146; *Plays for an Irish Theatre*, 147; *The Shadowy Waters*, 127, 146, 164; *Where There is Nothing*, 178

poems; "Easter 1916", 211; "The Rose Tree", 211

and Ruskin, 5, 11, 72, 121, 145, 146; "Sixteen Dead Men", 211

and staging, 12, 94, 122, 123, 127

and Turner, 93, 146

The manufacturer's authorised representative in the EU is Springer Nature Customer Service Centre GmbH, Europaplatz 3, 69115 Heidelberg, Germany. If you have any concerns regarding our products, please contact ProductSafety@springernature.com

Printed and bound by CPI Group (UK) Ltd, Croydon, CR0 4YY
23/03/2026
02076672-0008